John Newenham Hoare

**Buddhism as known in China**

John Newenham Hoare
**Buddhism as known in China**
ISBN/EAN: 9783743315051
Manufactured in Europe, USA, Canada, Australia, Japa
Cover: Foto ©Lupo / pixelio.de

Manufactured and distributed by brebook publishing software (www.brebook.com)

John Newenham Hoare

**Buddhism as known in China**

# THE IROQUOIS;

OR,

The Bright Side of Indian Character.

BY

MINNIE MYRTLE.

NEW YORK:
D. APPLETON AND COMPANY,
346 AND 348 BROADWAY.
1855.

## Dedicatory Letter,

TO

COL. THOMAS McKENNEY, AND PHILLIP E. THOMAS.

WITHOUT their knowledge, I presume to dedicate my first volume of Indian History to those whose names I have heard most frequently, as friends of the red man. The title of the first indicates that he has been on the war-path, while the other belongs to the Society whose members are so eminently the missionaries of peace. The one was for many years conspicuous as a public man, and the other has been seen only in the most private walks, but they have been ever intimately associated in efforts for promoting the best interests of Indians of every name and race. The "good works" of the one, in his official capacity and as an author, are well known, while those of the other have been necessarily silent and unseen, except by his friends, and those who were the recipients of the blessings he has so munificently scattered ; but having wandered through the scenes of their labors, I have found them to have been fellow-laborers, the designs of each being cordially approved and forwarded by the other, and their sympathies always the same.

In behalf of the Indian, to whom each name is dear as father, protector and friend, and as a testimony of her own reverence and grateful affection, this slight tribute is offered by the

AUTHOR.

# TABLE OF CONTENTS.

|  | PAGE. |
|---|---|
| INTRODUCTION, | 11 |

### CHAPTER I.

| NATIONAL TRAITS OF CHARACTER, | 19 |
|---|---|
| Christian Atrocities, | 21 |
| Indian Homes, | 23 |
| Civilized Barbarism, | 25 |
| King Philip, | 27 |
| Hospitality, | 29 |
| The Christian and Indian contrasted, | 31 |

### CHAPTER II.

| NATIONAL GOVERNMENT; OR, LONG HOUSE OF THE IROQUOIS LEAGUE, | 32 |
|---|---|
| Origin of the League, | 33 |
| Design of the League, | 35 |
| Indian Traits, | 37 |
| Councils, | 39 |
| Wampum and Calumet, | 41 |
| Indian Women, | 42 |

### CHAPTER III.

| THE RELIGION OF THE IROQUOIS, | 44 |
|---|---|
| Anecdote, | 45 |
| Employment in Heaven, | 47 |
| Maple Festival, | 49 |
| Thanks to the Great Spirit, | 51 |

Address to Heno, . . . . . . . 53
Succotash, . . . . . . . . 55
Thanksgiving Address, . . . . . . 57
Guessing of Dreams, . . . . . . . 59
Indian Courtesy, . . . . . . . 61
The Council Fire, . . . . . . . 63
The Iroquois not Savages. . . . . . . 65

## CHAPTER IV.

CUSTOMS AND INDIVIDUAL TRAITS OF CHARACTER, . . 67
Indian Burials, . . . . . . . 69
Religious Duties, . . . . . . . 71
Indian Vengeance, . . . . . . . 73
Good for Evil, . . . . . . . 75
Cannassatego, . . . . . . . 76
Hans Hanson, . . . . . . . 77
Indian Honesty, . . . . . . . 79
Indian Beauty, . . . . . . . 81

## CHAPTER V.

LOVE, MUSIC, AND POETRY, . . . . . . 83
Matrimonial Negotiations, . . . . . . 85
Social Affections, . . . . . . . 87
Legend of Ampatd Sapa, . . . . . . 89
Poetic Sentiment of the Indians, . . . . 91
A Love Legend, . . . . . . . 93
Indian Nobleness, . . . . . . . 95
Instances of Civilization, . . . . . . 97
Characteristic Songs, . . . . . . 99
Transportation of Children, . . . . . 101
Honor to the Noble Dead, . . . . . 103

## CHAPTER VI

LEGENDARY LITERATURE, . . . . . . 105
Indian Legend, . . . . . . . 107
Medicinal Feast, . . . . . . . 109
A Hunting Legend, . . . . . . . 115
Adventures of the Hunter Ho-cha-gah, . . . 116
A Pigmy Legend, . . . . . . . 121
Legend of the Jo-go-o, or Pigmies destroying the Monster Buffaloes, . 121
A War Legend, . . . . . . . 123
War Dance, . . . . . . . 125
The Virgin of War, . . . . . . . 126
Indian Fireside, . . . . . . . 129
Mythological Legends, . . . . . . 131
The Legend of He-no, the Thunderer, . . . . 131

## CONTENTS.

|  | PAGE |
|---|---|
| Ga-oh, | 132 |
| The Seven Stars, | 133 |
| The Three Sisters, | 134 |
| The Spirit of Corn, | 135 |

### CHAPTER VII.

| A Captive's Life among Indians, Illustrated by the Life of "The White Woman," | 136 |
|---|---|
| Treatment of Prisoners, | 137 |
| Respect towards Women, | 139 |
| Story of Mary Jewison, | 141 |
| The Deserted Baby, | 153 |
| Mission Burial Ground, | 155 |

### CHAPTER VIII.

| Eloquence among the Iroquois—Red Jacket, or Sa-go-ye-wat-ha, | 158 |
|---|---|
| Red Jacket, | 159 |
| Plea of the Women, | 161 |
| Indian Superstitions, | 163 |
| Eloquence of Red Jacket, | 167 |
| The Missionaries, | 171 |
| Witchcraft, | 173 |

### CHAPTER IX.

| Sarcasm and Sagacity—Red Jacket, or Sa-go-ye-wat-ha, | 174 |
|---|---|
| Interview with Red Jacket, | 175 |
| Vanity of Red Jacket, | 185 |
| Last hours of Red Jacket, | 197 |
| Death of Red Jacket, | 199 |
| Red Jacket's Grave, | 201 |

### CHAPTER X.

| Dignity of Character among the Iroquois, Illustrated by the Life of Farmer's Brother and Young-King, | 202 |
|---|---|
| Farmer's Brother, | 203 |
| Generosity to Captives, | 205 |
| Ignorance of Money, | 209 |
| Indian Fund, | 211 |
| American Barbarism, | 215 |
| Young-King, | 217 |
| Death of Young-King, | 219 |

### CHAPTER XI.

| Indian Magnanimity Illustrated by the Life of Cornplanter, | 220 |
|---|---|
| Cornplanter, | 221 |
| Cornplanter's Generosity, | 223 |

Code of Morality, . . . . . . 225
Cornplanter's Appeal, . . . . . . 229
Cornplanter's Son, . . . . . . . 235

## CHAPTER XII.

REFINEMENT AND SENSIBILITY IN INDIAN CHARACTER, ILLUSTRATED IN THE
LIFE OF LOGAN, . . . . . . 237
Logan, . . . . . . . . 239
Logan's Wrongs, . . . . . . 241
Speech of Logan, . . . . . . 243

## CHAPTER XIII.

THE DARKEST PAGE OF INDIAN HISTORY, . . . 245
Report upon the Indians, . . . . . 247
Appeal of the Indians, . . . . . . 249
Society of Friends, . . . . . . 251
Big Kettle, . . . . . . . 252
Speech of Big Kettle, . . . . . . 253
Speech of Gayashuta, addressed to the Society of Friends, . 257
Speech of Black Hawk, . . . . . 259
Manners and Customs, . . . . . . 261
Red Jacket's Step-daughter, . . . . . 263

## CHAPTER XIV.

THE EDUCATED INDIAN, . . . . . 266
Indian Orations, . . . . . . 267
Injustice to the Indians, . . . . . 273
Indian Civilization, . . . . . . 275
Indian Oration, . . . . . . 279
Closing Remarks, . . . . . . 282

## CHAPTER XV.

THE FUTURE OF THE NORTH AMERICAN INDIAN, . . 264
Injustice to the Indians, . . . . . 265
Story of James Macdonald, . . . . . 287
Stigma attached to the Indians, . . . . 289
Inconsistency, . . . . . . . 291
Knsick, . . . . . . . . 293
Sabbath Morning among the Chippewas, . . . 295
Doom of the Indian, . . . . . . 297

APPENDIX, . . . . . . . 298

# INTRODUCTION.

"A book about INDIANS,—who cares any thing about them?"

This will probably be the exclamation of many who glance at my title-page, for to those who know nothing concerning them, a whole book about Indians will seem a very prosy affair. To these I can answer nothing, for they will not proceed as far as my preface to see what *reason I can render* for this seeming folly. But to those who are willing to listen, I will say, that the Indians are a very interesting people, whether I have made an interesting book about them or not.

The Antiquarian, the Historian, and the Scholar, have been a long time studying Indian character, and have given us plenty of information concerning Indians, but it is all in ponderous tomes for State and College libraries, and quite inaccessible to the multitudes. Those who only take up such books as may be held in the hand, sitting by the fire, still remain very ignorant of the inhabitants who peopled the forests, before the Saxon set his foot upon our shore.

There is also a great deal of prejudice, the consequence

of this ignorance, and the consequence of the representations of our forefathers, who were brought into contact with the Indians, under circumstances that made it impossible to judge impartially and correctly.

This ignorance and prejudice I have attempted to dispel. I thought at first of only giving a series of Indian Biographies, but without some knowledge of the Government and Religion of the Iriquois, the lives of their great men could not be understood or appreciated. The histories which are in our schools, and from which our first impressions are obtained, are still very deficient in what they relate of Indian history, and most of them are still filling the minds of children and youth with very false ideas.

I knew little of what I was undertaking when I began, or I might have shrunk from the task. In my ignorance I thought a very small book would cover all the ground I had marked out, but I soon found it would not cover half of it, and I am obliged to leave the lives of Brandt the great Mohawk Chief, of Sir William Johnson and several other interesting chiefs and personages connected with Indian history, for another volume. If the success of these should be sufficiently encouraging, they may be followed by others, concerning Southern Indians, in volumes to correspond in design and character.

Though a difficult task, I have found it a very pleasing one. The mists of prejudice and ignorance have been cleared from my own mind by the light of truth, and I have been happy indeed, when, either in imagination or in reality, I have been seated by Indian firesides. I have read every thing I could hear of connected with my subjects, but aside from books have enjoyed peculiar facilities for prosecuting my labors. A teacher whom I loved in childhood, became a missionary among the Senecas in Western New York. In compliance with her wishes we took a little Indian girl into our family, who was my pupil and companion two years, and whom we all learned to love. Her father was the step-son of Red Jacket, the most renowned chief of the Iriquois, and through our correspondence with the missionaries, we continued, and deepened our interest in her people. It was long a favorite idea with me to write a book concerning them, and when I had decided to do so, I went to Cattaraugus and spent several months in order to become better acquainted with the Indians myself, and to be in daily communion with those who had been among them more than twenty years, and also to gain access to books and documents to be found nowhere else.

On glancing at the table of contents the book may seem fragmentary, but instead of devoting a whole long chapter to the dry details of "manners and customs," I have woven these usually uninteresting materials into the Biographies, so that no one part can be at all understood or appreciated without reading the whole.

My title will not be so attractive to American ears as if it related to any other unknown people. A tour in Arabia, or Africa, or Kamschatka, with far less important and interesting material, would secure a greater number of readers, as we are always more curious about things afar off.

I might have covered as many pages with "Indian atrocities," but these have been detailed in other histories till they are familiar to every ear, and I had neither room nor inclination for even a glance at war and its dark records.

I have not written the *whole truth*, yet what I have written is truth, in the minutest details.

Mr. Clarke in the "Onondaga," has in two large volumes given, a mass of useful information concerning missions, and Indian life and character; and in the "History of Pontiac," by Parkman, we have a glowing picture of forest life, and life-breathing portraits of forest men.

Charlevoix, La Hontan, Colden, Smith, Macaulay, Morse, and Bancroft, are well known historians, and their books are the fountains to which all resort for historical knowledge.

Mr. William L. Stone has given us several Indian Biographies, which are most interesting and truthful, presenting Indian rights and wrongs in a new light, and doing justice to Indian character. To these I am indebted for some of the most valuable materials of my book.

Mr. Schoolcraft has given us a world of wondrous things in his numerous quartos and folios, which will prove a treasure-house in all future time for philologists, ethnologists, and antiquarians of all names; and Mr. Lewis H. Morgan has written one of the most curious books in his "League of the Iriquois," in which we have the Government, Religion, and Customs of the Six Nations portrayed truly, and yet so brightly, that one is almost tempted to say, "What need is there of a better way?" There are few, however learned, who would not be surprised on reading his account of Indian "Church and State." Knowing his devotion to truth and accuracy, and his opportunities for obtaining correct knowledge of what he wrote, I have, in all I have taken from books concerning the Iriquois Confederacy, relied upon him. To him I am also indebted for criticisms and suggestions which will save the critics much trouble, though they will probably have plenty to do as it is.

The works of Col. Thomas L. McKenney, the well-known administrator of Indian affairs, contain the most life-like and glowing pictures of Indian character, and the most truthful appreciation of Indian life, for he knew our forest forefathers longer, and saw them under a greater variety of circumstances, than it was possible for another to do; and he rightly understood both the Indian and the white man, and the means of adapting them to each other.

Alas, that his noble plans for civilizing and Christianizing the red races of America should have been frustrated, when there was not only the hope, but the most encouraging prospect, that the work might be accomplished. His was no Utopian scheme, but one which successful operation had proved practicable. But it was not so to be. He could not save them; but through his own personal efforts, and influence as head of department, we have the gallery of Indian portraits, invaluable as specimens of art, and invaluable as the only correct representatives of a people so soon to have passed away. I am not only indebted to the books of Mr. McKenney, but to him, for every facility which it has been in his power to afford for information, and promoting the success of my plan.

In the poem of Alfred B. Street, "Frontenac," we have the government, religion, and festivals of the Long House in one beautiful picture. As a poem, it is one of the most artistic in our language; but its Indian hue has prevented its being appreciated, and it concerns a people so little known and so entirely misunderstood in prose, that its descriptions are like a panorama without light. I have quoted from it several songs, to embellish my sombre pages.

Tecumseh, by Colton, has been longer published, and is better known; and the poems of Hosmer are familiar to the readers of Magazines, and do not need me to commend them.

I have not wished to encumber my book with *notes* and *authorities*, and therefore express my obligations, by naming the principal sources of my information from books, in this way, and add that I have gleaned "here a little and there a little," wherever I could find any thing to suit my purpose.

Mr. Wright, in whose family I remained whilst seeking new materials, understands the Seneca language, and also many others, and gave me freely the results of his long and intimate experience of Indian life; whilst his wife, who also speaks the language with fluency, was enabled, by the observation which is woman's peculiar province, and as a highly cultivated intellectual woman, to give me the aid which no man, however learned he might be, could render.

There are also many educated Indians on my list of friends and helpers. Dr. Peter Wilson is well known as a highly gifted and educated man. Mr. N. T. Strong and M. B. Pierce are intelligent and accomplished gentlemen. To Mr. N. W. and Ely S. Parker I am much indebted, as their time and knowledge have been ever cordially at my service. The one is engaged in translating the Bible into the Seneca language, having been educated at the Normal School, Albany; and the other is one of the most honored and valuable servants in the employment of the State, as Engineer. Their sister is a highly intelligent and cultivated young lady, as one often meets in any society. These that I have mentioned are young, and pertain to the new order of things; but there are aged men and aged women still living, who give us some idea of the Indian as he was. I have been in their houses, and become acquainted with their hearts, and not among any people have I seen firesides where love and friendship wore a brighter smile, or hearts throbbed with more genuine Christian sympathy.

I experienced to the full their cordial hospitality, and bring away the mark of respect which they only bestow upon *favored ones*. The manner in which names are bestowed is one of their peculiar customs, and is quite an imposing ceremony. The name of every child is publicly confirmed in Council, in order to be a legal name; and when he grows to *man's estate*, another is given him, which is confirmed in the same public way. At the present time, when they bestow a name upon a stranger, it is usually done at the New Year's Council, whether the person is present or absent.

Mine was conferred at a private social gathering, a speech being made on the occasion by Sha-dye-no-wah (John Hudson), one of their most distinguished men, who adopted me into the Bear tribe as his niece. This token of regard was afterwards confirmed by a Council of the Nation, and this name I shall be ever proud to subscribe. It signifies "one who has a new style," or "tells new things."

Gui-ee-wa-zay.

INDIAN WOMAN IN COSTUME.

# THE IROQUOIS.

## CHAPTER I.

#### NATIONAL TRAITS OF CHARACTER.

In all the early histories of the American colonies—in the stories of Indian life and delineations of Indian character—we have these children of the wilderness represented as savage and barbarous, with scarcely a redeeming trait of character. And in the minds of a large portion of the community the sentiment still prevails, that they were bloodthirsty, revengeful, and merciless—justly a terror to both friends and foes. Children are impressed with the idea that an Indian is scarcely human, and as much to be feared as the most ferocious animal of the forest.

Novelists have now and then clothed a few with a garb which excites our admiration; but seldom has one been invested with qualities which we could love, unless it were also said that through some captive, taken in distant wars, he inherited a whiter skin and a paler blood.

But I am inclined to think that Indians are not alone in being savage—not alone barbarous, and heartless, and merciless.

It is said they were exterminating each other by aggressive and devastating wars before the white people came among them. But wars—certainly, aggressive and exterminating wars—are not proofs of barbarity. The bravest warrior was the most honored; and this has been ever true of Christian nations; and those who call themselves Christian, have not ceased yet to look upon him who could plan most successfully the wholesale slaughter of human beings, as the most deserving his king's and his country's laurels. How long since the pæan died away in praise of the Duke of Wellington? What have been the wars in which all Europe has been engaged since there have been any records of her history? For what are civilized and Christian nations now drenching their fields with blood?

It is said the Indian was cruel to the captive, and inflicted unspeakable tortures upon his enemy taken in battle. But, from what we know of them, it is not to be inferred that Indian chiefs were ever guilty of filling dungeons with innocent victims, or slaughtering hundreds and thousands of their own people, whose only sin was a quiet dissent from some religious dogma. Towards their enemies they were often relentless, and they had good reason to look upon white men as their enemies. They slew them in battle, plotted against them secretly, and in a few instances—few comparatively—subjected individuals to torture, burnt them at the stake, and, perhaps, flayed them alive. But who knows any thing of the precepts and practice of Roman Catholic Christendom, and quotes these things as proofs of unmitigated barbarity? At the very time that Indians were using the tomahawk and scalping-knife to avenge their wrongs, peaceful citizens in every country in Europe, where the Pope was the man of authority, were incarcerated for no crime whatever, and such refinements of torture invented and practised as it never entered in the heart of the fiercest Indian warrior that roamed the wilderness, to inflict upon man or beast. We know very little of the secrets of the Inquisition, and this little chills our blood with horror; yet these things were done in the name of Christ, the Saviour of the world —the Prince of Peace; and not savage, but civilized, *Christian* men looked on, not coldly, but rejoicingly, while women and children writhed in flames and weltered in blood!

Were the atrocities, committed in the Vale of Wyoming and Cherry Valley unprecedented among the Waldensian fastnesses and the mountains of Auvergne? Who has read Fox's Book of Martyrs and found any thing to parallel it in all the records of Indian warfare? The slaughter of St. Bartholomew's-day, the destruction of the Jews in Spain, and the Scotch Covenanters, were in obedience to the mandates of Christian princes, aye, and some of them devised by Christian women, who professed to be serving God, and to make the Bible the man of their counsel.

It is said also the Indian was treacherous, and in compliance with the conditions of no treaty was ever to be trusted. But our Puritan fathers cannot be wholly exonerated from the charge of faithlessness; and who does not blush to talk of Indian traitors when he remembers the Spanish invasion and the fall of the princely and magnanimous Montezuma?

"Indians believed in witches and burned them too!" Did not the sainted Baxter, with the Bible in his hand, pronounce it right? and was not the Indian permitted to be present. when a quiet, unoffending woman was cast into the fire by the decree of a Puritan council?

To come down to more decidedly Christian times, we

are yet called upon to shudder at the revelations of Howard and Miss Dix. It is not so very long since, in Protestant England, hanging was the punishment of a petty theft, and long and hopeless imprisonment, of a slight misdemeanor. I think it is within the memory of those who are not the *oldest inhabitants*, when men were set up to be stoned and spit upon by those who claimed the exclusive right to be called humane and merciful.

Again, it is said, the Indian mode of warfare is, without exception, the most inhuman and revolting. But I do not know that those who die by the barbed and poisoned arrow, linger in more unendurable torments, than those who are mangled by powder and balls. The tomahawk makes quick work of dying, and the custom of scalping among *Christian murderers* would save thousands from groaning days, and perhaps weeks, among heaps that cover victorious fields and fill hospitals with the wounded and the dying! But scalping was not an invention exclusively Indian. "It claims," says Prescott, "high authority, or, at least, antiquity." The Father of history, Herodotus, gives an account of it among the Scythians, showing that they performed the operation, and wore the scalps of their enemies taken in battle, as trophies, in the same manner as our North American Indians. Traces of the same custom are also found in the laws of the Visigoths, among the Franks, and even the Anglo-Saxons." The Southern Indians did not scalp, but they had a system of slavery, no trace of which is to be found among the customs, laws, or legends of the Iriquois.

Again : " They carried away women and children captive, and in their long journeys through the wilderness, they were subjected to heart-rending trials."

The wars of Christian men throw hundreds and thousands of women and children helpless upon the cold world, to toil, to beg, to starve!

This is not so bright a picture as is usually given of people who have written laws and stores of learning; but I cannot see that in any place the coloring is too dark. There is no danger of painting Indians, so that they will become attractive to civilized people; and there is no need of painting them more hideously than they paint themselves.

There is a bright and pleasing side to Indian character; and thinking that there has been enough written of their wars and their cruelties, of the hunter's and the fisherman's life, I have sat down by their firesides, and listened to their legends, and tried to become acquainted with their domestic habits, and to understand their finer feelings, and the truly noble traits of their character.

It is so long now since they were the lords of our soil, and formidable as our enemies,—they are so utterly wasted away and helpless that we can afford to listen to the truth, and to believe that even our enemies had virtues. Man was created in the image of God, and it cannot be that any thing human is utterly vile and contemptible. To remain in ignorance and censure without knowledge is easier than to study and toil for the truth, but with the present facilities for digging, Christian people cannot be excused in remaining content with dross.

Those who have always thought of Indians as roaming about in the forests, hunting and fishing or at war, will laugh, perhaps, at the idea of Indian *homes* and *domestic happiness;* yet there is no people of which we have any knowledge, among whom, in their primitive state, family ties and relationships were more distinctly defined or more religiously respected.

The treatment which they received from the white

people, whom they always considered as intruders, aroused and kept in exercise all their ferocious passions, so that none except those who mingled with them as missionaries or as captives, saw them in their true character—as they were to each other.

Almost any portrait which we have of Indians, represents them with tomahawk and scalping knife in hand, as if they possessed no other but a barbarous nature. Christian nations might with equal justice be always represented with cannon and balls and swords and pistols, as the emblems of their employments and their prevailing tastes.

The details of wars form far too great a portion of every history of civilized and barbarous nations; to conquer and to slay has been too long the glory of Christian people; he who has been most successful in subjugating and oppressing, in mowing down human beings, has too long worn the laurel crown,—been too long an object for the admiration of men and the love of woman.

We are weary of the pomp and circumstance of war—of princely banquets and gay cavalcades. The time and space we bestow upon Kings and Courts, and the homage we pay to empty titles, are unworthy our professed Republican spirit and preferences. Let us turn aside from the war path and sit down by the hearth stone of peace.

In the pictures which I shall give I shall confine myself principally to the Iriquois or Six Nations, a people who no more deserve the term savage, than we do that of heathen, because we have still lingering among us heathen superstitions, and many opinions and practices which deserve no better name!

The cannibals of some of the West India Islands, and the islands of the Pacific, may with justice be termed savage, but a people like the Iriquois who had a government, established offices, a system of religion eminently pure and spiritual, a code of honor and laws of hospitality excelling those of all other nations, should be considered something better than savage, or utterly barbarous.

The terrible tortures they inflicted upon their enemies have made their name a terror, and yet there were not so many burnt and hung and starved by them as perish among Christian nations by these means. The miseries they inflicted were light in comparison with those they suffered, and when individuals from them have come among us to expose the barbarity of savage white men, the deeds they relate equal any thing we know of Indian cruelty. The picture an Indian will give of civilized barbarism, leaves the revolting customs of the wilderness quite in the background. We experienced their revenge when we had put their souls and bodies on the rack, and with our *fire-water* had maddened their brains. There was a pure and beautiful spirituality in their faith, and their conduct was as much influenced by it as are any people, Christian or pagan.

Is there any thing more barbaric in the annals of Indian warfare than the narrative of the destruction of the Pequod Indians? In one place we read of the surprise of an Indian fort by night, when the inmates were slumbering unconscious of danger. When they awoke they were wrapped in flames, and when they attempted to flee, were shot down like wild beasts. From village to village, and wigwam to wigwam, the murderers proceeded, " being resolved," as our historian piously remarks, " by God's assistance, to make a final destruction of them," till finally a small but gallant band took refuge in a swamp " Burning with indignation and made sullen by despair; with hearts bursting with grief at the destruction of their nation, and spirits galled and sore at the fancied ignominy of their defeat, they refused to ask their lives at the hand of an insulting foe, and preferred death to submission. As the night drew on they were surrounded in their dismal retreat, and volleys of musketry poured into their midst, till nearly all were killed or buried in the mire." In the darkness of a thick fog which preceded the dawn of day, a few broke through the ranks of the besiegers and escaped to the woods.

Again, the same historian tells us that the few who remained "stood like *sullen dogs* to be killed rather than implore mercy; and the soldiers, on entering the swamps, found many sitting together in groups, when they approached; and resting their guns on the boughs of trees within a few yards of them, literally filled their bodies with bullets."[*] But they were Indians, and it was pronounced a pious work. "When the Gauls invaded Italy, and the Roman senators, in their purple robes and chairs of state, sat unmoved in the presence of barbarian conquerors, disdaining to flee and equally disdaining to supplicate mercy, it is applauded as noble—as dying like statesmen and philosophers. But when the Indian, with far more to lose, and infinitely greater provocation, sits upon the green mound, beneath the canopy of heaven, and refuses to ask mercy of civilized fiends, he is stigmatized as dogged, spiritless, and sullen." "What a different name has greatness, clothed in the garb of Christian princes and sitting beneath spacious domes, gorgeous with man's devices; and greatness, in the simple garb of nature, destitute, and alone in the wilderness!"

There is nothing in the character of Alexander of Macedon—who "conquered the world, and wept that he

[*] Irving.

had no more to conquer"—to compare with the noble qualities of King Philip, of Mount Hope; and among his warriors is a long list of brave men unrivalled in deeds of heroism, by any in ancient or modern story. But in what country, and by whom were they hunted and tortured and slain? Who was it that met together to rejoice and give thanks at every species of cruelty inflicted upon those who were fighting for their wives and their children, their altars and their God? When it is recorded that "men, women, and children, indiscriminately, were hewn down and lay in heaps upon the snow," it is spoken of as doing God service, because they were nominally heathen. "Before the fight was finished, the wigwams were set on fire, and into these, hundreds of innocent women and children had crowded themselves and perished in the general conflagration," and for this, thanksgivings are sent up to heaven. The head of Philip is strung bleeding upon a pole, and exposed in the public streets; but it is not done by savage warriors, and the crowd that huzzas at the revolting spectacle assemble on the Sabbath in a Puritan church, to listen to the gospel that proclaims peace and love to all men. His body is literally cut in slices to be distributed among the conquerors, and a Christian city rings with acclamations.

In speaking of this bloody contest one who is most eminent among the "Fathers" says, "Nor could they cease praying unto the Lord against Philip till they had prayed the bullet through his heart." "Two and twenty Indian Captains were slain and brought down to hell in one day." "A bullet took him in the head, and sent his cursed soul in a moment amongst the devils and blasphemers in hell forever."

Massasoit, the father of Philip, was the true friend to the English, and when he was about to die, took his two sons Alexander and Philip, and fondly commended them to the kindness of the new settlers, praying that the same peace and good will might be between them, that had existed between him and his white friends. Upon mere suspicion, only a little while afterwards, the elder, who succeeded his father as ruler among his people, was hunted in his forest home, and dragged before a court, the nature and object of which he could not understand; but the indignity which was offered him and the treachery of those who thus insulted him, so chafed his proud spirit, that a fever was the consequence, of which he died. And this is not all. The son and wife of Philip were sold into slavery, as were also many others of the Indians taken captive during the colonial wars. "Yes," says a distinguished orator,* "they were sold into slavery,—West Indian slavery! an Indian princess and her child sold from the cool breezes of Mount Hope, from the wild freedom of a New England forest, to gasp under the lash, beneath the blazing sun of the tropics! 'Bitter as death,' aye, bitter as hell! Is there any thing, I do not say in the range of humanity,—is there any thing animated, that would not struggle against this?"

Nor is this indeed all. A kinswoman of theirs, a princess in her own right, Wet-a-more of Pocasset, was pursued and harassed till she fell exhausted in the wilderness, and died of cold and starvation. There she was found by men professing to be shocked at Indian barbarity, her head severed from her body, and carried bleeding upon a pole to be exposed in the public highways of a country, ruled by men who have been honored as saints and martyrs. "Let me die among my kindred." "Bury me with my fathers," is the prayer of every Indian heart; and the most delicate and reverential kindness in their

* Everett.

treatment of the bodies of the dead, was considered a religious duty. There was nothing in all their customs that indicated a barbarism so gross and revolting as these acts which are recorded by New England historians without a censure, while the lamentations which the Indian utters in his grief at seeing his kindred dishonored and his religion reviled, are stigmatized as savage and fiendish.

If all, or even a few who ministered among them in holy things, had been like Eliot, who is called "the apostle to the Indians," and deserves to be ranked with the apostles of old; or Kirkland, who is endeared to the memory of every Iriquois who heard his name, it could not have become a proverb or a truth that civilization and Christianity wasted them away.

Not by one, but many, they are unscrupulously called 'dogs, wolves, bloodhounds, demons, devils incarnate, hellhounds, fiends, monsters, beasts,"—always considering them inferior beings, and scarcely allowing them to be human. Yet one, who was at that time a captive among them, represents them as "kind, loving, and generous," and concerning this same monster Philip, records nothing that should have condemned him in the eyes of those who believed in wars aggressive and defensive, and awarded honors to heroes, and martyrs, and conquerors.

By the Governor of Jamestown, a hand was severed from the arm of a peaceful, unoffending Indian, that he might be sent back a terror to his people, and through the magnanimity of a daughter and King of that same people, that Colony was saved from destruction. It was through their love and trust alone that Powhatan and Pocahontas lost their forest dominions.

Hospitality was one of the Indians' distinguishing virtues, and there was no such thing among them as individual starvation or want. As long as there was a cup of soup, it was divided. If a friend or stranger called he was welcome to all their wigwams could furnish, and to offer him food was not a custom merely, for it was a breach of politeness for him to refuse to eat, however full he might be.

Because their system was not like ours, it does not follow that it was not a system. We might have looked into a wigwam or lodge, and thought every thing in confusion; while to the occupants, there was a place for every thing and every thing in its place. Each had his couch, which answered for bed by night and seat by day, and no other person would have thought of appropriating it, any more than a private apartment would be thus appropriated among us.

The ceremonies at their festivals were as regular as in our churches; their rules of war were as well defined as those of Christian nations, and in their games and athletic sports, there was a code of honor which it was disgraceful to violate; their marriage vows were as well understood, and courtesy as formally practised at their dances.

The nature of the Indian was in all respects like the nature of people of any other nation, and if placed in the same circumstances he exhibited the same passions and vices. But in his forest home there was not the same temptation to great crimes, or what are usually termed the lesser ones of slander, scandal, and gossip, as exists among civilized nations.

They knew nothing of the desire of gain, and therefore were not made selfish by the love of hoarding, and there was no temptation to steal where they had all things common; and their reverence for truth and fidelity to promises, may well put all the nations of Christendom to shame.

I have written in something of the spirit which would characterize the history written by an Indian, yet it does not deserve to be called Indian partiality, but only justice and the spirit of humanity, or, if I may be allowed to say it, the spirit with which any Christian should be able to consider the character and deeds of his foes. I would not derogate from the virtues of our forefathers. They were at that time unrivalled, but the bigotry and superstition of the dark ages still lingered among them, and their own perils blinded them to the wickedness and cruelty of the means they took for defence. Four, and perhaps two centuries hence, I doubt not, some of our dogmas will seem as unchristian, as theirs seem to us; and I truly hope ere then our wars will seem as barbarous, and the fantastic dress of our soldiers as ridiculous, as we have been in the habit of representing the wars and wild drapery of the Indian of the forest.

How long were the Saxon and Celt in becoming a civilized and Christian people? How long since the helmet, the coat of mail, and the battle-axe were laid aside? To make himself more terrific, the Briton of the days of Henry II. drew the skin of a wild beast over his armor, with the head and ears standing upright, and mounted his war-horse to go forth crying "to arms!" "death to the invader!" The paint and the eagle plume of the Indian warrior were scarcely a more barbarous invention, nor his war-cry more terrible.

It is not just to compare the Indian of the fifteenth with the Christian of the fifteenth century. Compare him with the barbarian of Britain, of Russia, of Lapland, Kamtschatka and Tartary, and represent him as truly as these nations have been represented, and he will not suffer by the comparison.

## CHAPTER II.

#### NATIONAL GOVERNMENT; OR, LONG HOUSE OF THE IROQUOIS LEAGUE.

LET us look for a moment into the LONG HOUSE of the Indian confederacy, and learn something of the government of a people, whom we have been in the habit of considering ungoverned, and utterly lawless and rude.

In the country which stretches from the Hudson to Lake Erie, and from the St. Lawrence to the Susquehanna, there dwelt five separate nations, concerning whose origin we have no knowledge, and with regard to whom all conjecture is vain.

Concerning themselves they can only say, they grew up out of the ground, or sprung up like the trees of the forest. They cannot remember when they were not as the sand on the sea-shore for multitude, and when their laws and manners and customs were not the same as when white people came among them.

They had no written language, and, of course, no written lore; and not a trace of any thing their fathers did, is upon leaf or parchment; but by studying their legends and fables, observing and understanding their customs, we can easily imagine what they were.

The Five Nations, called by the French, the Iroquois, date the formation of the league only a few years before the white man first landed upon their shores, and it seems to be Columbus to whom they refer as the first invader.

They called themselves the Ho-de-no-sau-ne, or People of the Long House; implying that they were one family, sheltered by the same roof.

Each nation was divided into eight tribes or clans, which bear the names of Wolf, Bear, Beaver, Turtle, Deer, Snipe, Heron, Hawk, and at the formation of the League these names were retained and all their laws and customs made with reference to this division into tribes.

One of the historical traditions concerning this union relates that just before its formation there appeared among them a most extraordinary and formidable warrior, To-do da-ho, whose hair was a mass of living snakes, and whose fingers and toes also terminated in living serpents, that kept continually hissing and darting their forked tongues. The snakes were combed out of his hair by a Mohawk Sachem, who was afterwards called Ha-yo-went-ha, the man who combs.

To-do-da-ho, was at first opposed to the league, because as the Sachems were all to be of equal power, he would be deprived of his importance. But to compensate him for giving up the absolute authority he had been accustomed to exercise, the first Sachemship was named for him, and the title would descend to all who afterwards should fill the same office. And though he who inherits it has really no more power than the others, the name signifies to them a combination of more noble qualities than any other, and is regarded with a little more reverence.

After the first formation of the league, there seems to have been little change in the government or any of the institutions connected with it, though it is evident that there was a gradual progression in their domestic habits, and great improvements in agriculture. The journal of

2*

De Nonville, who was sent by the French, as commander of an expedition against the Six Nations in 1607, speaks of large villages, especially among the Senecas. In four towns the whole number of houses was three hundred and twenty four, and in these four villages alone he destroyed one million two hundred thousand (1,200,000) bushels of corn, besides great quantities of beans, squashes and other vegetables. There was also a large fort about fifteen miles from the present town of Rochester, of eight hundred paces in circumference, situated on a commanding height overlooking an extensive valley.

Had the invasions of the Saxons been deferred a century longer, they might have found a state of civilization in New York, as advanced as the Spaniards formed among the Aztecs. Their name, as a *united people*, had spread far and wide, and awakened terror in many a bosom.

"By far Mississippi the Illini shrank,
When the trail of the tortoise was seen on the bank.
On the hills of New England, the Pequod turned pale,
When the howl of the wolf swelled at night on the gale;
And the Cherokee shook in his green smiling bowers,
When the foot of the bear stamped his carpet of flowers."

As the Tuscaroras had been driven away, there were only five nations when the league was formed, but the exiles returned, and were admitted as one of the families of the Long House, in 1715.

The first council fire was kindled on the north shore of the Onondaga lake; and, in the metaphorical language of the Indian, was spoken of as *always burning*, to indicate that the people were ever acting in concert. The Mohawks dwelt at the eastern door, and kept watch towards the rising sun. The Senecas were the western door, and were expected to defend the western lodge, that no enemy should enter towards the setting sun.

The Onondagas were in the centre, and to them was committed the council brand and the wampum, and they were expected to understand the keeping of records by the wampum belt.

There were created fifty Sachemships, all the Sachems being of equal authority—nine belonging to the Mohawk nation, nine to the Oneida, fourteen to the Onondaga, ten to the Cayuga, and eight to the Seneca nation. They had no separate territory over which each ruled, but, in general council, attended to the affairs of the whole.

Formerly, when their numbers increased so that their fields could not furnish corn, nor their forests venison for so great a number, a band would go forth in search of new hunting-grounds, and thus be lost to their people and kindred. But now they were to belong to the confederacy wherever they might roam, and continue their allegiance.

It was not for the purpose of conquering and subjugating that the new government was formed, though they hoped, by this means, better to defend themselves against their border enemies, yet they became very formidable in their consolidated strength, and carried a war of extermination among all the surrounding nations, who would not join the league, or leave them in peace.

> 'Nought in the woods now their might could oppose,
> Nought could withstand their confederate blows—
> Banded in strength, and united in soul,
> They moved on their course with the cataract's roll."

Their names were very significant, and whether belonging to persons or places, were descriptive of something in their lives or national history.

To the Onondagas belonged the privilege of naming

the Sachems, when the league was formed, and as these names were to descend to all the Sachems of posterity, it was a perpetual honor to the nation. In council they were addressed as Ho-de-sau-no-gata—name-bearers.

Onondaga signifies *on the hills*, as their principal village, at the time they became known, was upon an eminence overlooking a beautiful country.

The Oneidas were the *granite people*, sprung from a stone, and they, too, dwelt upon a hill, from which they could look far away through an extensive and fertile valley, on the borders of Oneida lake. The stone which was the rallying point of the people, is a great *boulder*, differing in geological formation from any within a hundred miles. In council, they came afterwards to be called the *great tree* people, from some occurrence in a treaty beneath a big tree. The original Oneida stone may be seen in the cemetery at Utica.

The first settlement of the Cayugas was at the foot of Cayuga lake, and they were called *the people at the mucky land*. In council they were called the *great-pipe people*. The tradition concerning them is explanatory of all Indian names. The *ideal* was seldom understood by those who interpreted them. When it is said, the man of this nation whose voice was first heard in council, was in the habit of smoking a great pipe, it is true, but conveys nothing to us, that it conveys to the Indians. When the chiefs and sachems were all seated in the council chamber, they commenced smoking, filling their pipes anew when a speech was about to be made, that they might listen without interruption. The Cayuga had a large pipe, so that his tobacco lasted longer than that of others, and he could, therefore, longer attend, and was better able to concentrate his thoughts; to say he was the great-pipe man, was the same as saying he was more thoughtful, and listening more attentively, he was better able to judge.

The device of the Mohawks was a *flint and steel*, because they first proposed the formation of the league, and struck the first council fire. In Council they were called Da-de-o-ga, the people of *the two policies*, because a portion were in favor of the league, and a portion were not.

The Senecas being at the door, were called the *first fire;* the Cayugas, the second ; and those next in order, the third and fourth, on to the Mohawks, who were the fifth. As they had no cisterns or wells, they built their habitations upon the borders of the rivers, near bubbling springs, and on the shores of lakes. The boundaries between the different nations were distinctly defined, and in their hunting excursions they confined themselves to their own territory, whilst within the limits under the jurisdiction of the league, but without their united borders, they roamed unrestrained, and all had equal liberty on the soil of their enemies.

It seems a curious problem now, how such a people were to be called together ; but their runners were almost as fleet of foot as the deer in the forest, and their trails were the connecting links, not only between village and village, clans and nations, but stretched far away to the Mississippi and the Gulf of Mexico, the Atlantic ocean and the northern lakes. They were a mere footpath, just wide enough for one to *walk therein*, but they were sometimes so deep by the myriad footsteps which traversed them for centuries, that the sides were several inches deep. And these trails have become the thoroughfare of our great nation. In them the Indians wound along beneath the mountains and through the valleys, carrying the light canoe upon their shoulders, in which they skimmed the broadest lakes and deepest rivers, and were so familiar with all the connecting links, that the darkest recesses of the forest were threaded as easily as the streets of a village, and almost as quickly as the fiery engine wheels its way over the smooth iron pathway. I have heard a young Indian say, that his father had often run from Lake Erie to the Gulf of Mexico, and for four or five days at a time, scarcely stopping to eat by the way. And I have heard an aged Indian say, that in the days of his youth, he would *run* the distance between certain boundaries, which must have included forty miles, returning the same day, and thought it no great feat. Only a few years ago there was a trial of speed between an Indian runner and several horsemen, or their caparisoned steeds, and the runner left the horsemen far in the rear. But it is not by these thoroughfares alone that the Indian is to be traced in all our borders. Their expressive and musical names are upon every hill-side, in every glen; in the foaming cataract and on the bosom of the broad lake,—from the mountain top to the green islet in the midst of the waves, we listen to their silvery voices.

"Ye say that all have passed away,
 The noble race and brave,
That their light canoes have vanished
 From off the crested wave;
That 'mid the forests where they roamed,
 There rings no hunters' shout;
But their name is on your waters,
 Ye may not wash it out.

Ye say their cone-like cabins,
 That clustered o'er the vale,
Have disappeared like withered leaves
 Before the autumn gale;

> But their memory liveth on your hills,
> Their baptism on your shore,
> Your ever living waters speak
> Their dialect of yore."

The several nations held nearly the same relationship to each other and the league, that the several States do to the Federal Government, and it has been said that they gave to our Fathers the idea of E PLURIBUS UNUM.

Their Councils were divided into three classes. The Civil Council for the purpose of considering their foreign relations, and transacting business upon foreign affairs; the Mourning Council, which was called upon the death of a Sachem, to fill a vacancy, if one had occurred, or confer upon a brave warrior the title and office of Chief; and the Religious Councils, convened, as the name implies, for religious observances.

The chiefs did not form any part of the original corps of officers, but were admitted afterwards, and in their figurative language were styled the *braces of the Long House*, because a chieftainship was the reward of merit, and conferred upon those who had " gained honor in war," or those who had in some other way earned distinction, and were ambitious of renown. And it is recorded as a curious fact in their history, that all their great orators were among the Chiefs. Except the three of the first fifty Sachems, there has never one attained to any distinction until Logan, who was the son of a Cayuga Chief, and himself a Sachem. The Sachems attended entirely to the affairs of peace, and had not so much to arouse their enthusiasm, as those who had mingled in the excitements of war. No Sachem could be at the same time a civil officer and a warrior; if he took the war-path, he laid aside for the time his governmental duties. That their League was not instituted for the purpose of making war, is evident from the fact, that there was no *war department* connected with the government. All war expeditions were private enterprises. The nations not belonging to the League were considered enemies, and any warrior was at liberty to form a party and constitute himself leader or captain, and go forth to conquer; if he was successful, he was honored with a chief-ship and seat in the Council, but no special military power was conferred on him, as the Indian Confederacy seemed to have as much fear of military supremacy as our own government.

But there was this difference between their government and ours—when the council was not sitting there was no administration of affairs. If any thing happened in any tribe or nation that required the advice or deliberation of the assembled Sachems, a runner was sent to the nation nearest, and they sent a messenger to the next, and so on, till all had been apprised.

If, for instance, the Senecas wished a council called, the Sachems of this nation convened and determined whether the matter was of sufficient importance to require a council of the Six Nations. If they concluded it was, they sent a *runner*, with a wampum belt, to the Cayugas. The Cayugas informed the Onondagas in the same manner, and they the Oneidas, and the Oneidas the Mohawks. If it was something which interested all, the effect was like an electric shock; and not the Sachems and chiefs and warriors alone, but women and little children gathered around the council fire, coming from the farthest limits of their territory, heeding no toil or danger in their zeal for the common welfare.

No message was of any weight unless it was accompanied by the wampum belt. This originally consisted of

BELT.

small shells, strung upon strings of deer-skin. After their acquaintance with the Dutch they used manufactured wampum, which resembled small pieces of broken pipe stem. The belts consisted of several strings, woven together, and were some of them black and some white. The process by which they treasured up speeches and events was a kind of mnemonics, and done entirely by association. "This belt preserves my words," was the common expression at the end of every speech or sentence, and each part was associated with a particular portion of the belt or string which was held in the hand. When messengers were sent from tribe to tribe, or nation to nation, the wampum belt was the proof of its genuineness, and without it no messenger was heeded. White was the emblem of peace, and black of war, or danger.

The calumet of peace is another mysterious symbol among the Indians, and not less respected than the sceptre of a king. It is a species of pipe of stone, with the head finely polished, and the *quill* two feet and a half long, made of a strong reed. The red calumets are most esteemed, and often trimmed with white, yellow, and green feathers.

"Whilst high he lifted in his hand
The sign of peace, the calumet;
So sacred to the Indian soul,
With its stem of reed, and its dark red bowl,
Flaunting with feathers—white, yellow, and green."

It is the *flag of truce* among Indian nations, and a violation of it as disgraceful among them as an insult to the waving stars and stripes of the United States, or the *Lion* and the *Unicorn*, when these national emblems are borne to the enemy's camp as a signal that strife may cease.

Smoking the calumet together was a pledge of amity,

and was often used as a figure of speech, in the expression of friendship. Their language is a language of metaphors, and very difficult to be translated or interpreted into any other, and is to them full of *classical allusions*, as every important event is transmitted by transferring it to some person as a name, or baptizing with it some mountain, lake, or stream.

No son or daughter of any tribe was allowed to marry a person belonging to a tribe of the same name in his own or any other nation. A Deer of the Seneca nation could marry a Turtle of his own, or of the Mohawk or Cayuga nation, and so of each of the others. But a Wolf could not marry a Wolf, or a Heron a Heron.

The children belonged to the tribe of the mother. If she was of the Deer tribe all her children were of the Deer tribe. They called her mother, and also called her sisters mother, and her sister's children, brothers and sisters; and hence arose the impossibility of marrying in their own clan. They looked upon all belonging to it as one family, and a marriage within those degrees of consanguinity was as disgraceful and revolting in their eyes as a marriage with us between real brothers and sisters.

The offices also, Sachems, etc., were inherited in the line of the mothers. So it will be seen that the women were treated with quite as much respect as among Christian governments, and though they cultivated the fields and were the servants of men in some respects, their toil was very light, and it is the testimony of captives who have resided a long time among them, that their lords were uniformly kind and considerate.

The emblem of power worn by the Sachem was a *deer's antlers*, and if in any instance the women disapproved of the election or acts of a Sachem, they had the power to *remove his horns* and return him to private life. Their officers or *runners* from council to council were chosen by themselves and denominated *women's men*, and by these their interests were always fully represented. If at any time they wished any subject considered, by means of their runners, they called a council in their clan; if it was a matter of more general interest there was a council of the nation, and if the opinions of the women or Sachems of other nations were necessary, a grand council was called as readily to attend to them as to the interests of men. Thus a way was provided for them to have *a voice* in the affairs of the nation, without endangering their *womanly reserve* or subjecting them to the masculine reproach of publicity, or a desire to assume the offices and powers of men!

It is not recorded that they were more unreasonable than men, or more disposed to disputations, or that they ever abused their privileges! Neither do we find that they ever encroached upon the powers granted them, or " meddled with that which did not belong to them." They never manifested any desire to become warriors, or Sachems, or chiefs; but, on the contrary, planted corn, dressed deer-skins, and worked wampum belts for centuries without a murmur, and their pale sisters might more contentedly follow their example if treated with the same deference and consideration!

The land, they said, belonged to the warriors who defended it, and to the women who tilled it, and who were also the mothers and wives of the warriors, and if the men had not degraded themselves by intemperance and left themselves to be bribed to act dishonestly, and make treaties contrary to the rules of their people, and the judgment of the *best* men and *all* the women, their glory would not have thus faded away!

## CHAPTER III.

#### THE RELIGION OF THE IROQUOIS.

The council fire was the watchword in Indian government, in Indian politics, and Indian life. Around it old and young rallied on all occasions of public interest, and connected with it were the most delightful associations, memories, and legends of Indian history.

Indian eloquence has been the theme of poet and historian, and it was at the council fire that the enthusiasm of the orator was kindled; here the war-song awoke its echoes; here was heard

"The sound of revelry by night,"

when victory filled their hearts with rejoicing; and here were celebrated their solemn feasts.

When they gathered together, they came over the mountain and through the valley; crossed the silvery lake and the flowing river; listened to the music of the winds among the forest boughs, the songs of the birds, and the rippling of the waters; and to their quick impulsive spirits, all the voices of nature were inspiration.

The kindling of the council fire was the signal for the display of their eloquence, when danger threatened from their enemies, and their young men panted for the warpath; and when they returned, around its glowing embers was chanted the mournful requiem for those who had fallen in battle. Here, too, were offered the prayers that they might be taken to the "happy home beyond the setting sun;" and here, at each returning festival, the song of thanksgiving went up to heaven, with the burning incense, for the good gifts which were showered upon the people.

There was little of what we term social life among the Indians. There were among them large villages, but there were no streets. They had houses and occupied them during some portion of the year, season after season, perhaps for centuries; but still they were considered, in a measure, temporary abodes. The hunters left them many months in the winter, for their excursions into distant forests, and the warriors were often absent weeks, and sometimes years. Often the women accompanied them on the war path and the hunting tour, and they returned to their homes, as to a resting-place, till they were ready again to go forth.

At the annual festivals they all gathered, and these were the seasons of sociality, of amusement, and religious instruction.

Not very long ago, a Romish priest visited a small Indian settlement, for the purpose of establishing a church. The people met together to listen to the expounding of the new doctrine and ceremonies; and after respectful attention to all the preacher had to say, an aged chief arose, and deliberately and coolly remarked that he could not see the necessity of a change from their Pagan customs and doctrines to these which had been presented, as they were so similar. So they went on in the old way, and the priest found no foothold for his worse than Pagan mummeries.

The Iroquois believed in a state of future rewards and

punishments, where the good would be separated from the bad; but they did not descend into the depths of the heart to find sin, or trouble themselves about the motives of action. Their code of morality, as well as religious creed, was very simple; but all that it required they performed.

They believed in one God—Ha-wen-ne yu—the Great ruler, and ascribed to Him all good. They also believed in the Evil One, who was similar to the Devil of the Bible, as they believed him ever going about doing evil, "seeking whom he might devour." But they also supposed him to possess creative powers, saying that as God created man and all useful animals, so the Evil-minded created all monsters, noxious reptiles, and poisonous plants. As one delighted in the virtue and happiness of his creatures, the other delighted in discord and unhappiness.

There have been found individuals who worshipped visible and tangible objects; but, as a people, theirs was an entirely spiritual religion, and in this respect, differed from that of all other heathen nations.

The author of "principalities and powers" could not more thoroughly believe in guardian angels, and "princes of the powers of the air," than these simple people, who never heard of Revelation; and whose Theology, though systematic and well defined, never caused them any wars of words or of more "carnal weapons." Not only they themselves, but every thing in nature, that was beautiful to the eye or good for food, had a protecting spirit. There was the spirit of fire, of medicine and of water; the spirit of every herb and fruit-bearing tree; the spirit of the oak, the hemlock and the maple; the spirit of the blackberry, the blueberry and the whortleberry; the spirit of spearmint, of peppermint and tobacco; there was a spirit at every fountain and by every running stream, and with all they held communion—personifying every mountain and river and lake. The poet has done them no more than justice in the following lines: *

> "Gwe-u-gwe the lovely! Gwe-u-gwe the bright!
> Our bosoms rejoice in thy beautiful sight:
> Thou hearest our kah-we-yahs, we bathe in thy flow,
> And when we are hungered thy bounties we know.
>
> "In peace now is spread the pure plain of thy waves,
> Like the maidens that cast their kind looks on their Braves;
> But when the black tempest comes o'er with its sweep,
> Like the Braves on their war-path fierce rages thy deep.
>
> "Thou art lovely, when morning breaks forth from the sky,
> Thou art lovely when noon hurls his darts from on high,
> Thou art lovely, when sunset paints brightly thy brow,
> And in moonlight and starlight still lovely art thou.
>
> "Gwe-u-gwe, Gwe-u-gwe, how sad would we be
> Were the gloom of our forests not brightened by thee;
> Ha-wen-ne-yu would seem from his sons turned away,
> Gwe-u-gwe, Gwe-u-gwe, then list to our lay."

To any person who has taken pains to understand their character or their faith it must be strikingly evident that they were a peculiarly confiding and loving people. Their God was emphatically a God of love. They could not easily comprehend how the Good Spirit could meditate evil to any of his children. They looked up to him with confidence, and not only said and believed, but felt that he heard them and granted their prayers.

Some of the Indian nations expected to hunt and fish in the other world, and engage in all the occupations which employ them in this. But the Iroquois divested it more entirely of its sensual nature. All that was

---

* Street.

beautiful in this world their imaginations transferred to the next; and though they believed they took their bodies, and retained all their faculties, it was for pleasure and never for toil. There was "no marriage or giving in marriage," but families would recognize each other, and all live in one universal brotherhood, where neither dissension nor sorrow could enter, and where there was no more death. No people of whom we have any knowledge are so thoroughly imbued with religious sentiment, though it seldom became exalted into enthusiasm. It is simple trust and love, and pervaded all their thoughts and actions.

They had no governmental officers whose sole duty it was to regulate public affairs, and no religious teachers who devoted all their time to the "spiritual concerns" of the people. But there were some who had special duties to perform when they assembled for their festivals, who were called "keepers of the faith," and, in accordance with their universal custom, in promoting women, they, as well as men, were honored with this office.

They opened the ceremonies by some appropriate address, exercised a general suspervision during the celebrations and presided at the feasts. Neither Sachems, chiefs, warriors, or keepers of the faith received any compensation for the duties they performed, or wore any distinguishing costume.

During the year there were six national festivals, at which the ceremonies and observances were nearly the same; and all were of a decidedly religious character, and so conducted that they were looked forward to as seasons of enjoyment, in which all had an equal interest. There was not a class of religious and a class of irreligious people—a portion who lifted their hearts to God in gratitude and sung thanksgivings, and another portion who "cared for none of these things;" they were one nation, one church and one people, with the same government, the same temple and the same faith. Yet there were no penalties for disobedience, no excommunications, no anathemas and no proselyting. They were indeed a strange people, and one is sometimes tempted to doubt whether they were entirely human, but I think it would certainly be above, rather than below, the human family that they would occupy a place! It seems marvellous to those who have been all their lives attempting to unravel and perfect the complicated machinery of *society*, that whole nations could exist for centuries exemplifying to perfection the command of Paul, "to learn in whatever state they are in to be content."

There are many customs among them now that seem to have been obtained from the Jesuit missionaries who with their characteristic zeal were so early among them. Their strings of wampum by which they confess their sins bear a great resemblance to the beads of the Catholics, yet they seem to have no idea of atonement for sin.

The first festival was held in the spring when the sap began to flow, to return thanks to the maple for its sweet juices, and also to God for having given it to his red children. Dancing constituted a part of their religious worship, and they believed was particularly pleasing to Ha-wen-ne-yu. They had thirty-two distinct dances, and some of them were exceedingly graceful and beautiful. They danced all the way through this world and expected to dance in Heaven. They were not so much given to praying as to giving thanks, and only one festival was appointed for the purpose of asking a blessing. This was at the planting season, to implore that the "seed time and harvest" be one of prosperity, and that the earth might yield abundantly for their food.

The strawberry was one of their delicacies, and one which they believed they were to enjoy in another world. Some of them indeed expected the felicity of Heaven to consist in one continual strawberry feast, and this is something from which the most cultivated palate will not revolt, and is a proof that there was a great degree of refinement in their taste! So they had a special festival to give thanks for the Strawberry; another called the Green Corn festival, when the corn, and beans, and squashes ripened; another after the harvest, and a New Year's festival, which was the great jubilee of the Six Nations.

The ceremonies at each festival were nearly the same. They gathered in summer under the green boughs, and first made preparations for a great feast, which consisted of all the good things an Indian wife's storehouse could furnish, and which was conducted with the utmost order and solemnity.

After the feast, the men indulged in various sports and games, which were trials of strength and skill, and then was called the Council, at the opening of which, a speech was made, of which the following is a specimen.

"Friends and relatives:—The sun, the ruler of the day, is high in his path, and we must hasten to do our duty. We are assembled to observe an ancient custom. It is an institution handed down by our forefathers. It was given to them by the Great Spirit. He has ever required them to return thanks for all the blessings they receive. We have always endeavored to live faithful to this wise command.

"Friends and relatives:—It is to perform this duty that we are this day gathered together. The season when the maple tree yields its sweet waters has again returned. We are all thankful that it is so. We therefore expect all to join in one general thanksgiving to the Maple. We also expect you to join in a thanksgiving to the Great Spirit who has wisely made this tree for the good of man. We hope and expect order and harmony will prevail.

"Friends and relatives :—We are gratified to see so many here, and we thank you that you have all thought well of this matter. We thank the Great Spirit that he has been so kind to many of us in sparing our lives to participate in the festivities of the season."

During the session of the council, several similar addresses were made, accompanied by advice, intended to inspire them with a desire to live as they knew would be pleasing to the Great Spirit; when the services of the day were closed with a dance, called the Great Father dance "which was very spirited and beautiful:" for this there was a peculiar costume prescribed, and in it all joined. After this followed other dances, and then a thanksgiving address to the Great Spirit, during which, they continually threw tobacco upon the fire, that their words might ascend to Heaven upon the incense. It was only when addressing the Great Spirit directly that they used ncense.

"Great Spirit, who dwellest above, listen now to the words of thy people here assembled. The smoke of our offering arises. Give kind attention to our words as they arise to Thee in the smoke. We thank Thee for this return of the planting season. Give to us a good season that our crops may be plentiful.

"Continue to listen, for the smoke yet arises (throwing on Tobacco). Preserve us from all pestilential diseases. Give strength to us that we may not fall. Preserve our old men among us, and protect the young. Help us to celebrate with feeling the ceremonies of the season. Guide the minds of thy people that they may remember Thee in all their actions."

The poet has rendered this prayer in the following words: *

"Mighty, mighty, Ha-wen-ne-yu, Spirit, pure and mighty! hear us,
We thine own Ho-de-no-sonne, wilt thou be for ever near us!
Keep the sacred flame still burning! guide our chase, our planting cherish.
Make our warrior hearts yet taller! let our foes before us perish!
Kindly watch our waving harvests! make each Sachem's wisdom deeper!
Of our old men! of our women, of our children be the keeper!
Mighty Ha-wen-ne-yu, Spirit pure and mighty hear us!
We thine own Ho-de-no-sonne, wilt thou be for ever near us!

"Mighty, mighty, Ha-wen-ne-yu, thou dost, Spirit, purest, greatest,
Love thine own Ho-de-no-sonne, thou as well their foemen hatest.
Panther's heart and eye of eagle, moose's foot and fox's cunning,
Thou dost give our valiant people when the war path's blood is running!
But the eye of owl in daylight, foot of turtle, heart of woman,
Stupid brain of bear in winter, to our valiant people's foemen;
Mighty, holy, Hah-wen-ne-yu! Spirit pure and mighty! hear us.
We thine own Ho-de-no-sonne, wilt thou be for ever near us!
Yah-hah for ever near us! wilt thou be for ever near us!"

If there was not an abundance of rain, so that the corn did not flourish after it was planted, they often called another council, and held another festival, to pray for rain. At this time they addressed *Heno*, the Thunderer, in whose power it was to form clouds, and give water to refresh the earth. He was to the Indian what Jupiter was to the Roman, and inspired him with the same terror. He could inflict great evil, and calamities were ascribed to his vengeance. He was subject, as were all the lesser spirits, to Ha-wen-ne-yu, but was yet very powerful. He is represented in the form of a man, in the costume of a warrior, with a feather upon his head, which, like the wand

* Street.

of the fairy, preserved him from the influence of the EVIL-MINDED, and procured him whatever he desired. On his back he carried a basket filled with stones, which he threw at witches and evil spirits, as he rode hrough the clouds. The Great Spirit was implored to take care of him, and at every festival thanks were rendered to *Heno*, and supplications made for his watchful goodness. They called themselves his Grandchildren; and if the earth was parched, and the plants were withering, they met and laid before him their distresses.

"HENO, our Grandfather, now listen to the words of thy Grandchildren. We feel grieved. Our minds are sorely troubled. We fear our supporters will fail, and bring famine upon us. We ask our Grandfather to come and give us rain, that the earth may not dry up, and refuse to produce us support. Thy Grandchildren all send their salutations to their Grandfather."

Fearing that some of the people had done wrong, and it was for their sins that the "early and latter rains" were withheld, they, at the same time, prayed to the Great Spirit, throwing tobacco upon the fire, that their words might reach his ear and prove acceptable.

"Great Spirit, listen to the words of thy suffering children. They come to thee with pure minds. If they have done wrong, they have confessed and turned their minds. Be kind to us. Hear our grievances and supply our wants. Direct that *Heno* may come and give us rain, that our supporters may not fail, and famine come to our homes."

Those who have been in the habit of thinking the Indians a godless, prayerless, and perfectly heathen race, will read, with surprise, those outpourings of their hearts in perfect love and trust, and their simple dependence upon the Great Giver for all they enjoyed. If they did wrong, they *believed* He would forgive them; if they did right, they believed He approved and loved them. They had no Sabbaths, ⁺ they instituted regular periods of worship and formal ceremonies. These periods were indicated to them by natural events, and they heeded the voice of the spring-time and harvest, and " looked through nature up to Nature's God."

At the strawberry festival, the feast consisted entirely of strawberries, eaten with maple sugar, in bark trays; and it was at these feasts alone that they all ate together, and before partaking, they were accustomed to *say grace*, as devoutly and reverentially as Christian people.

A popular poet has thus rendered the thanksgiving prayer at the strawberry festival, which was repeated at every returning season, when they met to express their gratitude for this delicious fruit : *

"Earth, we thank thee! thy great frame
Bears the stone from whence we came;
And the boundless sweeping gloom,
Of our glorious league the Home.
Thou the strawberry's seed dost fold,
Thou its little roots dost hold,
First of all the fruits that raise
Gifts for us in summer days.
 Thanks, too, thanks we give thee, lowly
 Ha-wen-ne-yu, great and holy!
 Maker wise! of all the sire—
 Earth and water, air and fire.

Water, thanks! we safely glide,
On thy bosom long and wide;
Thou dost give the strawberry vine
Drink when hot the sunbeams shine,
Till its leaves spread fresh and bright,
And its buds burst forth in white.

* Street.

> Thanks, too, thanks we give thee, lowly,
> Ha-wen-ne-yu, great and holy!
> Maker wise! of all the sire—
> Earth and water, air and fire.
>
> Air, we thank thee for the breeze,
> Sweeping off the dire disease :
> Thou dost bring the gentle rains;
> Thou dost cool our feverish veins;
> Thou dost kiss the strawberry flower,
> Till its little wreath of snow
> Swings its fragrance to and fro.
>> Thanks, too, thanks we give thee, lowly
>> Ha-wen-ne-yu, great and holy!
>> Maker wise! of all the sire—
>> Earth and water, air and fire!
>
> Fire, we thank thee for thy ball,
> With its glory brightening all;
> And the blaze which warms our blood,
> Lights our weed, and cooks our food.
> To thy glance the strawberry swells,
> With its ripening particles,
> Till the fruit is at our tread,
> In its beauty, rich and red.
>> Thanks, too, thanks we give thee, lowly,
>> Ha-wen-ne-yu, great and holy :
>> Maker wise! of all the sire—
>> Earth and water, air and fire!"

At the green corn festival, the feast consisted principally of succotash, which is supposed by many to be a *Yankee dish*, but which dates farther back than centuries, and is purely Indian, being a soup of corn, and beans, boiled together. Any thing in the way of soup can scarcely be more delicious.

But the grand Indian jubilee was the New Year's festival, held in the month of February.

This festival lasted nine days, and the ceremonies commenced by two persons, generally of those called Keepers of the Faith, making a call at every house morning and evening, dressed so as to disguise the real personages.

They would envelope themselves in buffalo or bearskins, fastened about their heads with wreaths of cornhusks, and falling loosely over the body or girdled about the loins. Their arms and wrists, too, were ornamented with wreaths of husks, and in their hands they took corn pounders. On entering a house they knocked upon the floor to command silence, and then made a speech.

"Listen, listen, listen. The ceremonies which the Great Spirit commanded us to perform, are about to commence. Prepare your houses. Clear away the rubbish, drive out all evil animals; we wish nothing to obstruct the coming observances. We enjoin every one to obey our requirements. Should any of your friends be taken sick and die, we command you not to mourn for them, nor allow any of your friends to mourn. But lay the body aside and enjoy the coming ceremonies with us; when they are over we will mourn with you."

When the address was finished they sang a thanksgiving song and departed, to repeat the ceremony in every house.

And so scrupulous were they in performing these ceremonies, that if a person did die during this festival, the body was put aside, and no evidence of sorrow was visible till the end of the nine days, when the usual funeral rites were performed, and the mourning hymns were chanted as if the calamity had just occurred.

In all their religious festivals they had only one sacrifice, and this was at the beginning of the year.

All white animals were considered consecrated to the Great Spirit, as white was the emblem of purity and faith.

But dogs alone were sacrificed. On the first day of the festival one was chosen, and sometimes two, " without spot or blemish," and strangled, carefully avoiding shedding of blood or breaking the bones. He was then painted with red spots and decorated with feathers, and around his neck hung a string of wampum. He was then suspended in the air about twenty feet from the ground, where he remained till the fifth day, when he was taken down and burned on an altar of wood. As they did not recognize any species of atonement, believing that good deeds balanced the evil, this could not have been a sacrifice for sin, as superficial observers supposed, neither was it a *scape-goat* to carry away the sins of the people. Their sins had nothing to do with it. The dog was a favorite animal, and they believed a favorite with the Great Spirit, and therefore burned him, that his spirit might ascend to heaven with their petitions, that they might find favor in the eyes of God.

As they laid him upon the altar, the great thanksgiving address was made, whilst tobacco was continually thrown upon the fire that their prayers might ascend upon the clouds of smoke, and is curious as a specimen of a heathen prayer.

"Hail! hail! hail! Listen now with an open ear to the words of thy people, as they ascend to thy dwelling in the smoke of thy offering. Look down upon us beneficently.

" Continue to listen : The united voice of thy people continues to ascend to thee. Give us power to celebrate at all times with zeal and fidelity the sacred ceremonies which thou hast given us. Continue to listen: We thank thee that the lives of so many of thy children are spared, to participate in these ceremonies. Give to our warriors and mothers strength to perform thy sacred ceremonies.

We thank thee that thou hast preserved them pure unto this day.

"We thank thee that the lives of so many of thy children are spared to participate in the ceremonies of this occasion.

"We give thanks to our mother the earth which sustains us. We thank thee that thou hast caused her to yield so plentifully of her fruits. Cause that in the coming season, she may not withhold of her fulness, and leave any to suffer want.

"We return thanks to the rivers and streams, and thank thee that thou hast supplied them with life, for our comfort and happiness. Grant that this blessing may continue.

"We return thanks to all the herbs and plants of the earth. We return thanks to the three sisters. We return thanks to the bushes and trees which provide us with fruit. We thank theo that thou hast blest them and made them produce for the good of thy creatures. We return thanks to the winds, which moving have banished all diseases. We thank thee that thou hast thus ordered.

"We return thanks to our grandfather Heno. We thank thee that thou hast provided the rain, to give us water, and to cause all plants to grow. We ask thee to continue these great blessings.

"We return thanks to the moon and stars which give us light when the sun has gone to rest. Continue to us this goodness. We return thanks to the sun, that he has looked upon us with a beneficent eye. We thank thee, that thou hast in thy unbounded wisdom commanded the sun to regulate the seasons, to dispense heat and cold, and to watch over the comfort of thy people. Give unto us wisdom that will guide us in the path of truth. Keep us from all evil ways, that the sun may never hide his face from us for shame, and leave us in darkness. Lastly, we return thanks to thee, our Creator and Ruler. In thee are embodied all things. We believe that thou canst do no evil; that thou doest all things for our good and happiness. Be kind to us, as thou hast been to our fathers, in times long gone by. Hearken unto our words as they have ascended; and may they be pleasing to thee, our Creator, the preserver and ruler of all things, visible and invisible."

All the ceremonies upon these festival days were not strictly religious, but consisted of various sports and pastimes for amusement. On one day all the people went about making calls, in little parties. One of each group carried a wooden shovel, and immediately after entering the house, began to stir the ashes, and then to scatter a little upon the hearth, invoking the blessing of the Great Spirit upon the household.

Another amusement was to form little parties to go about and collect materials for a feast. Each family was expected to contribute something. If the messengers entered a house and nothing was bestowed, they were justified in taking whatever they could, without, at the time, being discovered. If undetected, they were allowed to bear away their treasures; but if detected, they were obliged immediately to give them up and try again. A feast was made with the avails of their begging and purloining, and a dance followed.

Another diversion was the guessing of dreams. Some person went about from house to house telling a wonderful dream he had had, and requesting any one who pleased to relate it. Whether those who attempted, guessed rightly or not, the dreamer after a while acknowledged that the true interpretation had been given, and then he was obliged to *pay a forfeit*, and whatever was required, he cheerfully performed, however great the sacrifice.

There was a great variety of games, and the design and effect of all their festivities was, in addition to their spiritual improvement, to promote friendly feeling and healthy exhilaration; and, in this, the children of darkness were certainly wiser in their generation than *some* of the children of light! Those who thought it necessary to the honor of religion that all merriment should be banished from the domestic and social circle, might have learned something from the forest heathen, whom they were in the habit of pronouncing utterly benighted. The Catholics adopted the policy of baptizing paganism, wherever they went. Instead of requiring the heathen to give up their national or religious ceremonies, they engrafted them upon their own, and thus removed all obstacles to their becoming, or being called Christians. The Puritans went to the other extreme, and would allow little that bore the name of pleasure. The pagan must renounce not only his religion but his health, in order to became a faithful servant of the Lord. Every thing that was natural was "carnal," and thus religion became repulsive, and, in the eyes of many, synonymous with every thing disagreeable. In a system which differed from this they could see no good thing, and were sadly deficient in a knowledge of human nature, and the facility of becoming all things to all men, thereby to save some. In throwing off the fetters of superstition they were scarcely in advance of the red men of the wilderness. The beliefs of the Christian and pagan in witches almost entirely coincided, and the manner of punishing them was nearly the same. The stories of ghosts and hobgoblins to which I listened in childhood, and which were related in perfect good faith are not less ridiculous or more indicative of heathen blindness than those which I hear in the wigwam.

The fables, fairy tales, and rural sports of our Saxon ancestors have never been recorded as evidence of their inferiority, or as very heinous misdemeanors. Their descendants have felt it to be a duty to honor them, and have clothed their customs in the garb of fascination; neither their ferocity, their barbarism, nor their superstitions have been held up to scorn. The dark side of the picture has been kept entirely out of view. Pages and volumes have been devoted also by historians to the Olympic and Pythian games, and the "crowns of the victors;" yet they involved no more light, or knowledge, or skill, and far less moral purity than the national games of the sons of the forest. The Indian had no laurel wreaths, believing that to excel was sufficient; but his code of honor was as nice as that of feudal lords in the days of chivalry, and no Indian ventured to incur censure by transgressing the rules of courtesy. In their dances it was the custom for women to choose their partners, and no warrior thought of offering his hand to a maiden till she had signified that it would be agreeable to her!

The Aztecs were more advanced in many respects than the Iroquois; but their worship was a continued series of bloody sacrifices, without any of that beautiful spirituality which we see in those who drew near to the Great Spirit, not only with their lips but with their hearts, and recognized his fostering care in all the events of their lives.

The sacrifice of dogs was universal among all the North American Indians; but for a long time it was alluded to as a heathenish custom, without any attempt to understand its import. Cotton Mather speaks of it by saying, "That the Indians, in their wars with us, finding a sore inconvenience by our *dogs*, sacrificed a *dog* to the *devil*, after which no *English* dog would bark at an *Indian* for divers months ensuing." This would imply that the devil had an interpreter, in order to understand the nature of the sacrifice, and the manner of influencing the dog; for the author does not give him the credit of being so thorough a linguist as to understand himself, as appears by the following affirmation.—" Once finding that the dæmons in a possessed young woman understood the *Latin, Greek*, and *Hebrew* tongues, my curiosity induced me to make trial of this *Indian* language, and the *dæmons* did seem as if they did not understand it."\* And as the Indians were considered little less than demons themselves, a learned divine was excusable for not attempting to acquaint himself with their language or their character.

But there are those rising up among themselves who will wipe out this stain upon their national honor, and vindicate the faith and the customs of their fathers.

Since wars and rumors of wars have ceased, there has been some attempt to understand Indian character and habits, and they have been found to be no worse, at least, than those of other heathen nations, who were the inhabitants of classic Greece and Rome.

The Jews held three yearly festivals, and several monthly festivals; and one was in commemoration of the *first fruits*, and another at the *in-gathering of harvest*, and another at the commencement of the year.

Among the Iroquois there were no particular ceremonies of purification; but among some of the Western tribes, there was a custom which resembled that of the Jews, when they used scarlet, and cedar, and hyssop.

Dogs were not sacrificed by the Jews; but these were the only domestic animals the Indians had. At the death

\* Stone.

of his friend, Patroclus sacrificed two dogs of purest
white, saying, " To the gods the purest things must be offered." The Greeks and Romans each had a festival,
which lasted nine days, the ceremonies of which were
strikingly similar to those which attended the annual
thank offerings which went up in the forest and on the
prairie, by the lake and the streamlet in the American
wilderness. But when we read that the Indian ornamented himself with the husks of his favorite zea-maize,
and went from house to house with a basket to gather offerings from the people, we call it heathenish and barbarous, while the story of Ceres, the goddess of corn, whose
head was ornamented with sheafs, and who held in her
hand a hoe and basket, is picturesque and beautiful!

To make dancing a part of a religious festival, is, among
Indians, irreverent and grovelling. While we are taught
to read, with pious emotion, how Miriam and her maidens
went out with timbrels and dances to celebrate the over-
throw of the Egyptians, and the women of all the cities
of Israel came forth singing and dancing, and exclaimed,
" Saul hath slain his thousands, and David his tens of
thousands," and David, the man after God's own heart,
" danced before the Lord."

The sacred fire in the temple of Vesta was kept ever
burning, and the Romans looked upon the extinguishing
of the vestal flame as a prognostication of the destruction
of their city. In all this there is not so much of poetry
or beauty or purity as dwelt in the bosom of those who
kindled the mysterious council fire in the heart of the
forest, to burn for ever as a symbol of the love and patriotism which glowed in the bosoms of those who rallied
around it, and called themselves the UNITED PEOPLE.

The nymphs and naiads of the woods of Greece and
Italy are the embellishments of every classic song, but

they are no more beautiful than the guardian-spirits of every tree and leaf and flower with which the imagination of the Indian peopled our own forest wilds.

The Christian orator goes back to those dark days of ignorance and superstition for the *allusions* which are to give point and brilliancy to his metaphors, and the poems which have for their framework the grossest of all heathen mythology are still the text-books, for years, of Christian students, whose mission is to preach the Gospel to all the nations of the earth.

We read of Indian women who were *Keepers of the Faith*, and revolt at their incantations and unintelligible mummeries, but our delicacy is thought in no danger from being initiated into the mysteries of the Priestess of Appollo, the oracles of Delhi and the feasts of Eleusinia.

The wealthy virgins of Greece and Rome were present with fruits in golden baskets at Bacchanalian revels, but they have never been held up as monsters, while our school-books have teemed with amours of gods and goddesses, such as find no place on the darkest pages of Indian lore.

We listen to the story of the woman in the moon, who is constantly employed in weaving a net, which a cat ravels whenever she sleeps, and that the world is to come to an end when the net is finished, and call it ridiculous. While the story of Penelope weaving her purple web by day to be unraveled by night, and thus prolong the absence of her husband Ulysses, who went to the siege of Troy, is a conception worthy of being expanded into a poem of a thousand lines, and translated into all languages.

The Indian had no Cupids, or their representatives, to attend the affairs of the heart, but he had *charms* which obtained the love of any fair maiden whom he desired, and *charms* which secured him the love of his wife during his long absence on the war-path and hunting excursions, and made every thing that he could do bright and beautiful in her eyes. And they had no Bacchus to preside at drunken revels, for they "did not tarry long at the wine, or look upon it when it was red." But they had spirits to preside at the pure fountain, where alone they went to slake their thirst.

Human sacrifices were offered annually among the Aztecs, but never among the Iroquois. But even these were not entirely the result of Indian barbarity. "Human sacrifices have been practised by many nations, not excepting the most polished nations of antiquity." "They were of frequent occurrence among the Greeks, as every school-boy knows, and in Egypt. In Rome they were so common as to require to be interdicted by an express law, less than a hundred years before the Christian Era,—a law recorded in a very honest strain of exultation by Pliny, notwithstanding which, traces of the existence of the practice may be discerned to a much later period." *

Zurita was an eminent jurist from Spain, who resided nineteen years among the Aztecs, and is indignant that they should be called *barbarians,* saying, "It is an epithet which could come from no one who had personal knowledge of the capacity of the people or their institutions, and which in some respects is quite as well merited by Europeans."

If the Aztecs did not deserve the term *barbarians,* surely I shall be thought just in denying the term *savage* to belong to the Iroquois; and from their mythology, if nothing else, it is evident that they were destitute neither of genius nor of poetry. They were heathen and Pagans, but not savages, and before we boast that we have attained

* Prescott.

unto perfection, let us remember that Spiritualists and Mormons have arisen in the nineteenth century, and multitudes have wended their way to Salt Lake City, who were trained in the churches of New England!

# CHAPTER IV.

#### CUSTOMS AND INDIVIDUAL TRAITS OF CHARACTER.

THE more I read, and the better I understand Indian history, the more am I impressed with the injustice which has been done the Iroquois, not only in dispossessing them of their inheritance, but in the estimation which has been made of their character. They have been represented, as seen in the transition state, the most unfavorable possible for judging them correctly.

In the chapter upon National Traits of Character, I have, in two or three instances, quoted Washington Irving, and might again allow his opinions to relieve my own from the charge of partiality.

He says, in speaking of this same subject, that " the current opinion of Indian character is too apt to be formed from the miserable hordes which infest the frontiers, and hang on the skirts of settlements. These are too commonly composed of degenerate beings, corrupted and enfeebled by the vices of society, without being benefited by its civilization. The proud independence which formed the main pillar of native virtue, has been shaken down, and the whole moral fabric lies in ruins. Their spirits are humiliated and debased by a sense of inferiority, and their native courage cowed and daunted by the superior knowledge and power of their enlightened neighbors. Society has advanced upon them like one of those withering airs that will sometimes breed desolation over a whole region of fertility. It has enervated their strength, multiplied their diseases, and superinduced upon their original barbarity the low vices of artificial life. It has given them a thousand superfluous wants, while it has diminished their means of mere existence. It has driven before it the animals of the chase, who fly from the sound of the axe and the smoke of the settlement, and seek refuge in the depths of remote forests and yet untrodden wilds. Thus do we often find the Indians on our frontiers to be mere wrecks and remnants of once powerful tribes, who have lingered in the vicinity of settlements, and sunk into precarious and vagabond existence. Poverty, repining and hopeless poverty, a canker of the mind before unknown to them, corrodes their spirits, and blights every free and noble quality of their natures. They loiter like vagrants about the settlements, among spacious dwellings replete with elaborate comforts, which only render them sensible of the comparative wretchedness of their own condition. Luxury spreads its ample board before their eyes; but they are excluded from the banquet. Plenty revels over the fields; but they are starving in the midst of its abundance. The whole wilderness has blossomed into a garden; but they feel as reptiles that infest it. How different was their state while undisputed lords of the soil! Their wants were few, and the means of gratification within their reach. They saw every one around them sharing the same lot, enduring the same hardships, feeding on the same aliments, arrayed in the same rude garments.

"No roof then rose that was not open to the homeless stranger; no smoke curled among the trees, but he was welcome to sit down by its fire, and join the hunter in his repast.

"In discussing Indian character, writers have been too prone to indulge in vulgar prejudice and passionate exaggeration, instead of the candid temper of true philosophy. They have not sufficiently considered the peculiar circumstances in which the Indians have been placed, and the peculiar principles under which they have been educated. No being acts more rigidly from rule than the Indian. His whole conduct is regulated according to some general maxims early implanted in his mind. The moral laws which govern him are few; but he conforms to them all; the white man abounds in laws of religion, morals, and manners, but how many does he violate?

"In their intercourse with the Indians, the white people were continually trampling upon their religion, and their sacred rights. They were expected to look meekly on while the grave was robbed of its treasures, and the bones of their fathers were left to bleach upon the field. And when exasperated by the brutality of their conquerors, and driven to deeds of vengeance, there was very little appreciation of the motives which influenced them, and no attempt to palliate their cruelties."

It was their custom to bury with the dead their best clothing, and the various implements they had been in the habit of using whilst living. If it was a warrior they were preparing for burial, they placed his tomahawk by his side, and his knife in his shield; with the hunter, his bow and arrow, and implements for cooking his food; with the women, their kettles, and cooking apparatus, and also food for all. Tobacco was deposited in every grave, for to smoke was an Indian's idea of felicity in the body and out of it, and in this there was not so much difference as one might wish, between them and gentlemen of paler hue.

Among the Iroquois, and many other Indian nations,

it was the custom to place the dead upon scaffolds built for this purpose, from tree to tree, or within a temporary inclosure, and underneath a fire was kept burning for several days.

They had probably known instances of persons reviving after they were supposed to be dead; a ndthis led to the conclusion, that the spirit sometimes returned to animate the body, after it had once fled. If there were no signs of life for ten days, the fire was extinguished, and the body left unmolested, till decomposition had begun to take place, when the remains were buried, or as was often the case, kept in the lodge for years. If they were obliged to desert a settlement where they had long resided, these skeletons were collected from all the families, and buried in one common grave, with the same ceremonies as when a single individual was interred.

They did not suppose the spirit was instantaneously transferred from earth to heaven, but that it wandered in aerial regions for many moons. In later days they allow only ten days for its flight. Their period of mourning continues only whilst the spirit is wandering; as soon as they believe it has entered heaven, they commence rejoicing, saying, there is no longer cause for sorrow, because it is now where happiness dwells for ever. Sometimes a piteous wailing was kept up every night for a long time, but it was only their own bereavement that they bewailed, as they had no fear about the fate of those who died. Not till they had heard of *Purgatory* from the Jesuits, or of *endless woe* from Protestants, did they look upon death with terror, or life as any thing but a blessing.

They were sometimes in the habit of addressing the dead, as if they could hear. The following are the words of a mother, as she bent over her son, to look for the last time upon his beloved face.

" My son, listen once more to the words of thy mother. Thou wast brought into life with her pains; thou wast nourished with her life. She has attempted to be faithful in raising thee up. When thou wert young she loved thee as her life. Thy presence has been a source of great joy to her. Upon thee she depended for support and comfort in her declining days. But thou hast outstripped her and gone before. Our great and wise Creator has ordered it thus. By His will I am left to taste more of the miseries of this world. Thy friends and relations have gathered about thy body, to look upon thee for the last time. They mourn as with one mind thy departure from among us. We too have but a few days more and our journey will be ended. We part now, and you are conveyed from our sight. But we shall soon meet again, and shall look upon each other. Then we shall part no more. Our Maker has called thee to his home. Thither will we follow."

It has been said and written that the Indians were in the habit of murdering the aged to get them out of the way. There might have occurred, once in a century, an instance when, to relieve great suffering, an aged person was put to death. If they were on a long journey, or there was great scarcity, they might do this from pure kindness and benevolence, but not to save themselves trouble.

After the adoption of the League of the Iroquois, and they dwelt together in villages, this was one of the duties enjoined by their religious teachers at their festivals—" It is the will of the Great Spirit that you reverence the aged, even though they be helpless as infants." And also " kindness to the orphan, and hospitality to all."

" If you tie up the clothes of an orphan child, the Great Spirit will notice it and reward you for it."

" To adopt orphans, and bring them up in virtuous ways, is pleasing to the Great Spirit."

"If a stranger wanders about your abode, welcome him to your home, be hospitable towards him, speak to him with kind words, and forget not always to mention the Great Spirit."

Upon the opening of their morning councils, a ceremony of condolence was performed, and an appropriate speech delivered in memory of those who had died or been slain in battle since their last meeting. The ceremonies on these occasions were very solemn, and their speeches full of pathos and tenderness. The funerals of chiefs, warriors, and distinguished women were attended by the heads of tribes, and all their people; and the respect in which they held their women is evinced by the honors they paid them when dead, being the same as those they bestowed upon chiefs and warriors.

Their lamentations on being driven far away from the graves of their fathers have been the theme of all historians and travellers.

Said an Indian chief, in his remonstrance against the treaty that was to remove the remnant of the Six Nations beyond the Mississippi, "We cannot go to the west, and leave the graves of our fathers to the care of strangers. The unhallowed clods would lie heavily upon our bosoms in that distant land if we should do this."

"Bury me by my grandmother," said a little boy of seven years of age, a few moments before his death. "She used to be kind to me."

"Lay me in the churchyard by my mother," said a little orphan girl, who had been under the care of the missionaries, when she learned she could not recover.

"I shall be sorry if we must go far away to the west," said an aged woman, who had seen *eighty winters*, "for I had hoped to be laid by my mother in yonder churchyard."

"In ancient times they had a beautiful custom of capturing a bird, and freeing it over the grave on the evening of burial, to bear away the spirit to its heavenly rest." And their anxiety to obtain the bodies of their warriors slain in battle, and the impossibility of leaving the aged and helpless to die alone in the wilderness, was the result of a belief that the souls of those who received not the burial rites wandered about restless and unhappy.

It may be easily imagined that a people who so loved their homes and revered their fathers' graves, would become fierce with indignation and rage, on seeing themselves treated as without human feeling and the sacred relics of the dead ploughed up and scattered as indifferently as the stones, or the bones of the moose and the deer of the forest. It was this feeling which often prompted them to acts of hostility, which those who experienced them ascribed to wanton cruelty and barbarity. An instance occurred in New England, where the grave of a Sachem's mother was robbed of the skins which had been placed there for her use, and the chieftain gathered his people together and exhorted them to revenge. In him it was the promptings of filial piety, and the dictates of his religion. He thus speaks:

"When last the glorious light of all the sky was underneath this globe, and birds grew silent, I began, as my custom is, to take repose. Before mine eyes were fast closed, methought I saw a vision, at which my spirit was much troubled, and trembling at that doleful sight the spirit cried aloud—'Behold, my son, whom I have cherished, see the breasts that gave thee suck, the hands that lapped thee warm, and fed thee oft. Canst thou forget to take revenge of those wild people who have defaced my monuments, disdaining our antiquities and honorable customs? See now the Sachem's grave lies like the common people, defaced by an ignoble race. Thy mother doth complain, and implores thy aid against those thievish people, who have newly intruded upon our land. If this be suffered I shall not rest quiet in my everlasting habitation.'"

A tribe has been known to visit the spot which had been, in former times, the burial place of their people, though long deserted, and spend hours in silent meditation; and not till every hope had died in their bosoms, or the last drop of blood was shed, did they leave the sod which covered the dust of any of their kindred to the footsteps of the stranger.

To their hospitality I have often alluded, and there are many anecdotes to illustrate this trait in their character. The selfishness which they continually saw in those who were greedy of gain, was something which they could not comprehend.

In many of their villages there was a Stranger's Home —a house for strangers, where they were placed, while the old men went about collecting skins for them to sleep upon, and food for them to eat, expecting no reward.

They called it very rude for people to stare at them, as they passed in the streets, and said that they had as much curiosity as white people, but they did not gratify it by intruding upon them and examining them. They would sometimes hide behind trees, in order to look at strangers, but never stood openly and gazed at them. Their respectful attention to missionaries was often the result of their rules of politeness, as it is a part of the Indian's code, that every person should have a *respectful hearing*. Their councils are eminent for decorum, and no person is interrupted during a speech. Some Indians, after respectfully listening to a missionary, thought they would relate to him some of their legends. But the good man could

WIGWAM.

BARK CANOE.

not restrain his indignation, and pronounced them foolish fables, while what he told them was sacred truth. The Indian was, in his turn, offended, and said, " We listen to your stories. Why do you not listen to ours? You are not instructed in the common rules of civility!"

A hunter, in his wanderings for game, fell among the back settlements of Virginia, and on account of the inclemency of the weather, sought refuge at the house of a planter, whom he met at his door. He was refused admission. Being both hungry and thirsty, he asked for a bit of bread and a cup of cold water. But the answer to every appeal was, " No, you shall have nothing here. *Get you gone, you Indian dog.*"

Some months afterwards this same planter lost himself in the woods, and after a weary day of wandering, came to an Indian cabin, into which he was welcomed. On inquiring the way and distance to a settlement, and finding it was too far for him to think of going that night, he asked if he could remain. Very cordially the inmates replied that he was at liberty to stay, and all they had was at his service. They gave him food, they made a bright fire to cheer and warm him, and supplied him with clean deerskins for his couch, and promised to conduct him the next day on his journey. In the morning the Indian hunter and the planter set out together through the forest. When they came in sight of the white man's dwelling, the hunter, about to leave, turned to his companion, and said, " Do you not know me?" The white man was struck with horror that he had been so long in the power of one whom he had so inhumanly treated, and expected now to experience his revenge. But, on beginning to make excuses, the Indian interrupted him, saying, " When you see poor Indians fainting for a cup of cold water, don't say again, ' Get you gone, you Indian dog,' " and turned back to his hunting grounds. Which best deserved the appellation, Christian? and to which will it be most likely to be said, "Inasmuch as ye have done it unto the least of these, ye have done it unto me?"

## CANNASATEGO

Was a chief of the Onondaga nation. Of him Dr. Franklin tells the following story:—Conrad Meyses, an interpreter, who had been naturalized among the Indians, and could speak several of their dialects, was passing through the country on a governmental mission, and stopped at the house of Cannasatego, by whom he was warmly welcomed. Clean furs were spread for him to sit upon, and venison and succotash placed before him to eat. When he was refreshed, and had lighted his pipe, the chief conversed with him cheerfully, asking him concerning his health and prosperity since they had met, and expressing undiminished friendship for his old acquaintances, who were known to both, till the ordinary topics were exhausted, when he revived conversation by asking concerning the customs of white people, which he could not understand.

"Conrad," said he "you have lived long among our white neighbors, and know their customs. I have been sometimes at Albany, and have observed that, once in seven days they shut up their shops, and assemble in the *great house;* tell me what it is for?—what do they do there?"

"They meet there," said Conrad, "to hear and learn good things."

"I do not doubt they tell you so," said the Indian. "They have often told me the same; but I doubt the truth of it; and I will tell you the reason. I went the other day to Albany to sell my skins, and buy powder, knives, blankets, &c. I usually trade with Hans Hanson, but I thought this time I would try some other merchant. I went first to Hans, however, and asked him how much he would give for beaver. He said he could not give more than four shillings a pound, but that he could not talk about it then, as it was the day they shut their shops, and went to meeting to hear about *good things.* I thought, as I could not do any business, I might as well go to the meeting too. So we went together. There stood up a man in black, who began talking very angrily. I could not understand what he said; but as he looked very much at me and Hans, I thought he was angry at seeing me there. So I went out and sat by the door till the meeting broke up. I thought, too, he said something about beaver, and that this might be the subject of their meeting. When they came out, I asked Hans if he had not concluded to give more than four shillings a pound? "No," said he, "I cannot give so much; I cannot give more than three shillings and sixpence." I then spoke to several other dealers, and they all sang the same song—*three and sixpence—three and sixpence!* This made it clear to me that the purpose of the meeting was not to learn good things, but to consult how to cheat Indians, in the price of beaver. Consider but a little Conrad, and you will see that if they met so often to learn good things, they would certainly have learned some before this time. But they are still ignorant. If a white man, in travelling through our country, enters one of our cabins, we all treat him as I do you; we dry him if he is wet; we warm him if he is cold, and give him meat and drink if he is hungry and thirsty; we spread soft furs for him to sleep upon, and ask nothing in return. But if I go into a white man's house at Albany, and ask for food and drink, they say, "Get out, you Indian dog." You see they have not yet learned those *little* good things which we need no meetings to be instructed in, because our mothers taught them to us when we were children; and therefore it is impossible their meetings should be for any such purpose, as they say, or have any such effect; they are only to contrive the cheating of Indians in the price of beaver!

In shrewdness and quickness of perception, the Indian was not at all deficient, and there was a great deal of quiet humor lurking in their natures.

An officer presented a Chief with a medal, on one side of which President Washington was represented as *armed with a sword*, and on the other, the Indian was *burying the hatchet*. The Chief saw at once the idea conveyed, and sarcastically asked, " Why does not the President also *bury his sword?*"

A Swedish minister having assembled several Chiefs, related to them the principal facts on which the Christian religion is founded—the eating of the apple—the coming of Christ to make an atonement—his miracles and sufferings. When he had finished, an Indian orator stood up to thank him : " What you have told us," said he, " is all very good. It is indeed bad to eat apples. It is better to make them all into cider. We are much obliged by your kindness in coming so far to tell us these things you have heard from your mothers."

Whatever may be said of other nations, the Iroquois certainly considered it a great stain upon their national escutcheon, to violate a treaty, and if any nation belonging to their confederacy was guilty of this breach of honor, it was severely punished. The Delawares were a subjugated nation, and not at liberty to make war without the knowledge and approbation of the confederacy. A treaty had been made with a western nation, and the Delawares invaded their territory, with a full knowledge that they were at peace with, and under the protection of the Iroquois. For this they were reprimanded, and forbidden in future to go to war at all, and deprived of all civil authority,—in their phraseology, *they made them women!* This was a great degradation, as war alone could furnish them an opportunity to gain distinction, and distinction alone could gain them a position of honor in the administration of the government. They had been a very brave and warlike nation, but never afterwards recovered from this humiliation.

There is no instance of the Six Nations having violated a treaty that was legally made, and which they perfectly understood. They were faithful to their British allies, and "poured out their blood like waters," and in return were deserted and left to the mercy of their enemies. Not till they saw the faithlessness of those whom they had trusted and relied upon, did they turn against them.

Falsehood and evasion were no part of the original character of Indians of any name, and an instance of theft was seldom known among them. Bars and bolts are still strangers in their settlements, and among the unchristianized; the custom still prevails of placing the mortar pestle upon the threshold when the family are all absent, and the famous locks that received the prize at the World's Fair could not more effectually *keep all intruders away*, than this simple signal. No Indian thought of entering a cabin where the mortar pestle stood sentinel!

The food of the Indian consisted in the flesh of animals which were killed in the chase, and the few vegetables they cultivated, with corn or maize, which was their staple article; and of this they have three kinds. The white, red, and white-flint. If you ride through an Indian settlement, you will see hundreds of bushels of corn hanging by the braided husks upon poles to dry. When fit for use it is pounded in large stone or wooden mortars, and usually by two women at a time. The operation is very similar in appearance to the churning in the old-fashioned dash-churn in New England. When the meal is sufficiently fine to pass through a coarse sieve, it is made into small loaves of *unleavened bread*, and boiled in large kettles, containing a dozen loaves at a time. It is very palatable and healthy. Hominy was also a favorite dish with the Indians, and is now so common every where that it needs no description.

From the Indian, too, are obtained the knowledge of tobacco, and in the use of this, "all nations of every kindred, tongue, and people," have shown their appreciation of Indian taste and refinement. It is strange that civilized people should have so generally adopted their most filthy and uncivilized habit!

Maple sugar must have been in use among them for centuries, "as is proved by their festival to give thanks to the maple." Beans and squashes grew wild all over America, and were rendered fruitful by cultivation among the Iroquois. In the valley of the Genesee, the first white people who came, of whom we have any definite knowledge, found large orchards, and in some places peach trees, which were of Indian cultivation.

They made a tea of the fine green boughs of the hemlock steeped in water, which I have drank when among them in preference to any other.

Their cooking utensils were very few, and housewifery occupied very little of the Indian matron's time. She tilled the soil, and from the simple manner of tilling it, her labor was very light.

The cradle or baby-frame, the birch canoe, and the moccasin were the prettiest articles of Indian manufacture, though since their intercourse with white people they have

MOCASIN.

added an infinite variety of boxes, bags, and baskets, which they embroider both richly and tastefully. Indeed I know not if the women of any people can excel them in fancy work. Where any part of their costume is wrought, the devices are always neat, and exhibit great skill in the blending of colors. A full Indian dress is very rich and costly, being mostly of the finest broadcloth, embroidered with beads around the borders, and with ornaments of silver around the neck and down the front. Originally they were clothed entirely in the skins of animals, but the new materials are made exactly in the old fashion. The *kilt* was very much like that worn by the Highlander, and is richly embroidered. The *leggin* was fastened above the knee, and fell loosely to the top of the moccasin, being also deeply embroidered.

There were six dances, at which it was necessary to wear a peculiar costume. The head-dress of the warriors was adorned with plumes, and his girdle, gay with many colors, was thrown gracefully over the left shoulder, tied under the right arm at the waist, and hung in fringes to the knee.

The style of beauty of the Indian women is so different from that of the Roman and Grecian, Circassian and Saxon, that at first one would scarcely pronounce any of them beautiful. But, as a people, I am inclined to think them better looking than the Saxon, though there are none among them so beautiful as some among us.

Miss Bremer describes one whom she met on the banks of the Mississippi, who might be the type of as large a class among Indian women, as a city belle is, in the throng in which she moves. She says of her—" She was so brilliant, and of such unusual beauty, that she literally seemed to light up the whole room as she entered. Her shoulders were broad and round, and her carriage drooping, as is usual with Indian women, who are early accustomed to carry burdens on their backs; but the beauty of the countenance was so extraordinary, that I cannot but think that if such a face were to be seen in one of the drawing-rooms of the fashionable world, it would there be regarded as the type of a beauty hitherto unknown. It was the wild beauty of the forest, at the same time melancholy and splendid. The bashful glow in those large, magnificent eyes, shaded by unusually long, dark eye-lashes, cannot be described, nor yet the glance, nor the splendid light of the smile, which at times lit up the countenance like a flash, showing the loveliest white teeth. She was quite young, and had been married two years to a brave young warrior, who, I was told, was so fond of her, that he would not allow her to carry burdens, but always got a horse for her when she went to the town. Her name was Feather Cloud."

There is not the variety among Indian beauties that exists among white people. We have all shades, from the lightest blonde to the darkest brunette; but the shade is nearly the same upon every forest maiden's face. The hair is raven black, the cheeks are full, and the eye like jet. But there is still opportunity for Nature to show her skill; though there may be few so splendidly beautiful as Feather Cloud, there are few who may not be called comely; and I have seen many who might vie with the blondes and brunettes of any drawing-room.

# CHAPTER V.

### LOVE, MUSIC, AND POETRY.

It has been the conclusion of historians generally, and of travellers and students almost universally, that the North American Indians were entirely destitute of *la belle passion* —that "of the marvellous passion which originates in a higher development of the powers of the human heart, and is founded upon a cultivation of the affections between the sexes, they were entirely ignorant." I shall not attempt to refute learned historians or philosophers, neither will I assert a different opinion. Yet there are many among the wise and thinking who say this cannot be.

In reading very extensively, and conversing with those who have lived many years a forest life, I have learned many things which might be cited to prove a more pleasant theory, but they may possibly be only *exceptions to the rule*, and I shall therefore merely relate the facts, leaving my readers to theorize for themselves.

In the contents of this chapter I have not confined myself to the Iroquois, but roamed among all the northern nations, and have by no means appropriated all that has been written and said on the subject.

It is the impression among all people this side of the Mediterranean, that the women of Turkey all live in harems; but our Minister, who has just returned from a four years' sojourn in Constantinople, says he has never found in that city a *respectable Turk who had more than one wife!* This is the law of God, and to disobey it wars against nature. Among the Indians, polygamy was sometimes practised, but was by no means common, and was ever disgraceful. It is insisted, too, by their aged people, that before they were corrupted by their conquerors, there was scarcely any thing among them which Christian principle would condemn as vice.

To excel in oratory certainly requires a very superior development, and in this no people excelled the Iroquois. Love, in all its purity, dwells very little among even Christian people, and something far worse than polygamy prevails in the most cultivated circles among civilized nations.

There is not so much of nature's nobility among the peasantry of Europe as among the forest Indians; yet their capability of love and the domestic affections is not disputed, and it is this alone which renders life endurable; were it not for this they would be desperadoes whom all the fetters of despotism could not trammel or subdue. But they are dwellers in one place, whilst the Indian is a rover, quite independent of home and domestic comfort.

The manner in which marriages were contracted, made it impossible that there should be courtships or long romantic love affairs among the children of the wilderness, and their habits of life made social intercourse almost impossible. Young men and maidens, had very little opportunity to become acquainted, and if there sprang up in their bosoms a mutual attachment, it could not be cultivated without the consent of the friends of both parties, and so accustomed were they to obedience, that the thought of defying those who had authority over them was seldom or never indulged. I have smiled, as I have heard an Indian youth speak of the opportunities he had enjoyed for being married, in the same way as young women make this boast among us. And this may be done without compromising the delicacy of those alluded to, as it is not supposed that the parties most concerned know any thing of the matter.

The grandmothers, if living, if not the mothers, and when there are no mothers, the aunts, or nearest relatives, make the propositions. If it is considered desirable that a son, or daughter, marry the son or daughter in a neighboring lodge, a present of some kind is left at the door in a basket. This signifies to all within that a marriage negotiation is contemplated. If it is agreeable, the basket is brought in, and its contents being accepted, it is returned with a present which indicates that *the way is open* to further negotiation. If the proposal is rejected, the basket is left standing without the door, and she who brought it comes after there has been time for deliberation and takes it home. This is a decided refusal. If it is returned replenished, she sends another present of a different kind, and soon afterwards enters herself and consults with the matrons of the family with whom she seeks an alliance, and if all are pleased that it should take place, each family informs the son and daughter, for the first time, of the pending negotiation. Then, if there is no objection, presents are again exchanged, and there is another meeting of the matrons at which the children are present. Very serious advice is given them concerning their deportment, and the duties of husbands and wives, and then the seat is prepared in the home of the bride and bridegroom, which is in future to be exclusively theirs, and in the presence of all they repair to it, and are henceforth husband and wife. Their wedding tour is a hunting excursion, or rather this was the custom of the olden time; now there is usually a feast, and there is also an acre of land set apart by the bride's friends as her marriage portion. The father takes no interest in the matter, and is merely imformed of the marriage when it is consummated. The children are of the tribe of the mother, as are the children's children to the latest generation, and they are also of the same nation. If the mother is a Cayuga, the children are Cayugas; and if a Mohawk, the children are Mohawks. If the marriage proves unhappy, the parties are allowed to separate, and each is at liberty to marry again. But the mother has the sole right to the disposal of the children. She keeps them all if she chooses, and to their father they are ever mere strangers.

In regard to property, too, the wife retains whatever belonged to her before marriage, distinct from her husband, and can dispose of it as she pleases without his consent, and if she separates from him, takes it with her, and at her death, either before or after separation, her children inherit all she possessed.

A white man was once remonstrating with an Indian upon allowing the matrimonial bond to be so lightly broken, when the Indian replied: "You marry squaw, she know you always keep her, so she scold, scold, scold, and not cook your venison. I marry squaw, and she know I leave her if she not good. So she not scold, but cook my venison, and always pleasant, we live long together."

There were few penalties for any species of crime. To call a thing *bad* was usually sufficient in Indian communities to deter from all that they considered evil. That which we denounce as criminal, was not called so by them.

The staid and burly Englishman, never mingled with

the Indians in a way to gain their confidence or learn their true character. Their way of life was repulsive to him, but the Frenchman could become a hunter and roam for years in the forests, or live in a wigwam, and conform in all things to Indian customs with the same *nonchalance* as he could walk upon tapestry and recline upon divans. This is the reason we usually have so much more pleasing pictures of Indian life from French than English traders. Englishmen would not be very likely to become the *confidants* of hunters or warriors, or to have an opportunity to listen to the love songs of Indian maidens.

It is certainly wonderful that a people who knew nothing of physiology, and had no learned treatises upon physical degeneracy, should have so thoroughly provided against deterioration by laws concerning intermarriage. Their wigwams were built for the convenience of several families. A lodge was constructed, and when it became necessary, additions were made till it became one or two hundred feet in length, and the abode of a little multitude, but all who occupied it were within the degrees of consanguinity which forbade marriage—they were brothers and sisters, and treated each other as such. But disputing and wrangling form no part of the nurseries of an Indian cabin. It is quite amazing how many will live together in harmony and love.

But I have heard of several instances of suicide for disappointed affection which would compare well in recklessness and desperation with any recorded in French or Italian novels. It sometimes happened that the husband or wife whom the friends chose, proved so unsuitable that the nuptial tie was broken almost as soon as formed. And when this happened I believe the parties were left the second time to select for themselves. It sometimes, too, became impossible for the friends to force upon young people a yoke which they felt they could never bear. And often, as among the aristocratic circles of court society, it was worn a little while and then thrown off by one, leaving the other disconsolate and wretched. It, of course, most frequently happens that the wife is the deserted one.

Mrs. Hemans has immortalized the heart-broken one who perished in the Falls of St. Anthony some years ago, as related by a missionary. Her name was Ampatd Sapa.

"The husband was a successful hunter, and they lived happily together many years, and had two children, who played around their fire, and whom they were glad to call their children. Many families by degrees settled around them, and built wigwams near theirs. Wishing to become more closely connected with them, they represented to the hunter that he ought to have several wives, as by that means he would become of more importance, and might before long be elected chief of the tribe."

He was well pleased with this counsel, and privately took a new wife; but, in order to bring her into his wigwam without displeasing his first wife, the mother of his children, he said to her:

"Thou knowest that I can never love any other woman as tenderly as I love thee; but I have seen that the labor of taking care of me and the children is too great for thee, and I have therefore determined to take another wife, who shall be thy servant; but thou shalt be the principal one in the dwelling."

The wife was very much distressed when she heard these words. She prayed him to reflect on their former affection—their happiness during many years—their children. She besought him not to bring this second wife into their dwelling.

In vain. The next evening the husband brought the new wife into his wigwam.

"In the early dawn of the following morning a death song was heard on the Mississippi. A young Indian woman sat in a little canoe with her two small children, and rowed it out into the river in the direction of the falls. It was Ampatd Sapa. She sang in lamenting tones the sorrow of her heart, of her husband's infidelity, and her determination to die. Her friends heard the song, and saw her intention, but too late to prevent it.

"Her voice was soon silenced in the roar of the fall. The boat paused for a moment on the brink of the precipice, and the next was carried over it, and vanished in the foaming deep."

The Indians still believe that in the early dawn may be heard the lamenting song, deploring the infidelity of the husband; and they fancy that at times may be seen the mother, with the children clasped to her breast, in the misty shapes which arise from the fall around the Spirit Island.

"Roll on; my warrior's eye hath looked upon another's face,
And mine hath faded from his soul, as fades a moonbeam's trace;
My shadow comes not o'er his path, my whisper to his dream,
He flings away the broken reed; roll swifter yet, thou stream!
The voice that spoke of other days is hushed within *his* breast;
But mine its lonely music haunts, and will not let me rest.
It sings a low and mournful song of gladness that is gone;
I cannot live without that light—Father of Waves, roll on!
Will he not miss the bounding step, that met him from the chase!
The heart of love that made his home an ever sunny place!
The hand that spread the hunter's board, and decked his couch of yore!
He will not!—roll, dark, foaming stream, on to the better shore!
And there, my babe! though born, like me, for woman's weary lot;
Smile! to that wasting of the heart; my own I leave thee not.
Some gentle wind must whisper there, whose breath must waft away,
The burden of the heavy night, the sadness of the day."

The words are another's, but the sentiment is the same as uttered by the deserted one, and the same as uttered by a deserted one on the banks of Lake Erie. "I cannot live longer," said she, and swallowed the poisoned draught her own hands had mixed.

Not many specimens of Indian poetry have been preserved, yet they were ever singing.

They had a great variety of tunes, and are said to have had a good perception of time. They had not the regular intervals of tones and semitones, but a thousand different sounds recurring at as many irregular intervals. The music and the words of their songs were often *impromptu*, but the war-songs were in regular verses, and sung as they danced.

The voice of the Indian is very rich and capable of high cultivation; and as they become Christianized, this part of public worship is their great delight. During the August of 1790 an Italian nobleman, Count Adriana, visited Mr. Kirkland, at his mission station in Oneida, and was particularly charmed with the musical powers of the Indians, saying—" The melody of their music, and the softness and richness of their voices, he thought were equal to any he ever heard in Italy!"

During the French war a party of Indians came from the far north-west to visit Quebec. On their way they stopped at the Moravian Mission, on the banks of Lake Superior, and there a young Algonquin fell in love with a Chippewa maiden, who as ardently returned his passion. As she sailed away in her light canoe she uttered her love and sadness in the following wild strain :—

"I shall go with you my sweet heart, my Algonquin."
"Alas," I replied, "my native country is far, far away—my sweet heart, my Algonquin.

When I looked back again, where we parted, he was still looking after me, my sweet heart, my Algonquin,
He was still standing on a fallen tree, that had fallen in the water, my sweet heart, my Algonquin.
Alas, when I think of him, when I think of him, it is when I think of him—my Algonquin.

The following is another strain almost as simple, but less wild and sad:—

"I looked across the water,
    I bent o'er it and listened,
    I thought it was my lover,
    My true love's paddle glistened.
Joyous thus his light canoe, would the silver ripples wake,
But no, it is the loon alone, the loon upon the lake;
Ah me! it is the loon alone, the loon upon the lake.

"I see the fallen maple,
    Where he stood his red scarf waving,
    Though waters nearly bury
    Boughs they then were merely laving,
I heard his last farewell, as it echoed from the lake,
But no, it is the loon alone, the loon upon the lake;
Ah me! it is the loon alone, the loon upon the lake."

This is a literal translation, but there is the true spirit of the *love-lorn maiden*, and a high development of the poetic sentiment. There has been only now and then a wanderer among the forests, who could appreciate or discern the beautiful, though there have been poems, and novels in abundance concerning wild forest life, by those who wrote the wanderings of their imagination and their fancy. The bright picture has been too bright, and the dark picture too dark.

In the war songs of the Indian, there is never allusion to blood and carnage; and revenge is not made prominent among the natives for pursuing the enemy. Bold and daring deeds are incited as worthy of imitation, and fortitude and heroism are exalted as the loftiest virtues. They had characteristics, generated by their peculiar life, but there is nothing about them to prevent their becoming *like unto others*. White men have lived among them and learned to prefer the hunter's life. Indians have learned to prefer the habits of civilization, and shown themselves capable of education and refinement equal to any attained by any nation.

When children, they have the same joyous nature, the same quick perceptions, and exhibit the same varieties of character.

"As the twig is bent, the tree is inclined,"

is as true of them as of pale-faced children.

The following lines are a translation of a song heard among a troop of Chippewa children as they were playing at twilight around their dwellings, and the air was filled with myriads of fire-flies, which they were trying to catch. I have seen few prettier things among the children's songs of any people.

"Fire-fly, fire-fly, bright little thing,
Light me to bed, and my song I will sing;
Give me your light, as you fly o'er my head,
That I may merrily go to my bed;
Give me your light o'er the grass as you creep,
That I may joyfully go to my sleep;
Come little fire-fly—Come little beast—
Come! and I'll make you to-morrow a feast.
Come, little candle, that flies as I sing,
Bright little fairy bug,—night's little king;
Come, and I'll dance as you guide me along,
Come, and I'll pay you my bug with a song."

In their legends there is often allusion to *falling in*

*love*, in the way the same event takes place among other people. The following is obtained from a very authentic source, and certainly appears very natural:—

## A LOVE LEGEND.

*Iroquois.*

Over a deep gulf, not far from Canandaigua Lake, hangs a wild and fearful precipice, which has been known to the Indian as far back as tradition goes, by the name of "Lover's Leap," for here two lovers preferred to die together rather than live apart.

When the Senecas and Algonquins were at war, a young Algonquin Chief was taken prisoner, and condemned to die. While in the "cabin of death," to wait his doom, the youthful and beautiful daughter of the Sachem brought him food. He too was rich in all those manly gifts which an Indian maiden is taught to admire in warrior and in chieftain, and though her father's enemy, she loved him, and resolved to save his life.

Ere the morning watch, when the gray dawn was just stealing from behind the hill-tops, she stole with stealthy tread to the side of the noble captive, and cutting the thongs which bound him, bade him in breathless accents to follow her.

The sentinel, weary with his night-watchings, had fallen asleep, but ere they had descended the winding pathway which led to the lake on whose gentle bosom they had hoped to rest, the shrill war-whoop fell on their ears and they knew they were pursued. Like the fawn or the squirrel they bounded through the thick woods and down the steeps to the border of the lake, where the light canoe awaited them, and plied the dashing paddles with the desperate energy of those who row for life. But it was in vain; nearer came the terrific yell and then the splashing of a dozen oars, and as many savage warriors swiftly gliding over the waters in full view of the fugitives.

They reached the shore and fled through a woody pathway over the hills; but, seeing the brave youth by her side was fainting from his still bleeding wounds, the maiden turned quickly and came to a table-crested rock that overlooked the gulf. There, hand in hand, they paused, and calmly gazed on the group below, who instantly filled the air with shrieks, as they perceived the pair, and knew them to be within their reach. The damsel knew her father by his eagle plume, and when he saw his victim he bent his bow and pointed the poisoned arrow at his heart; but ere the string was snapped, Wun-nut-hay, the beautiful, stood between her lover and the stern old man, and falling at the feet of the warrior begged him to spare the youth; "nay," said she, "we will plunge together over the precipice rather than that one shall die and the other live."

But rage now blinded him to her tears and shut his ears to her entreaties; he commanded his followers to seize the lad, and warrior after warrior bounded up the cliffs in obedience to his command, but at the moment they put forth their hands to grasp the foe, the lovers, locked in firm embrace, flung themselves

"From the steep rock and perished!"

Then the father's breast was rent, but too late to save his child. At the bottom of the gulf, one hundred and fifty feet from where he stood, lay the mangled bodies of the two, and there he commanded that they should be buried. Two hollows like sunken graves are to this day pointed out as the "burial place of the lovers." It is a wild, romantic haunt, but quiet now, save where a brook slowly murmurs along as if to chant a requiem for the dead.

Col. McKenney, who was for seventeen years at the head of the Indian department at Washington, and who has mingled with Indians of every nation and tribe, in the wildest and the most civilized state, does not hesitate to confirm them in the assertion always to be heard among themselves, that they are *the people*. He is as genuine a Saxon as myself, but is willing to allow the red children the preference in all that is truly noble and good. Not among any people whose history I have read, have I found instances of stronger attachment, whether of love, of conjugal or parental affection, than he relates; and the most strong heart would melt in listening to the touching incidents of which his memory is so full; and that they are full of pathos and awake to the tenderest sympathy, cannot now be ascribed to the youthful enthusiasm of the narrator, or his unripe judgment.

His head is now hoary with the frosts of many winters, and he must be considered good authority; and he says no people on the wide earth have hearts so warm and true as the genuine forest Indian.

In Jefferson's answers to the theories of Count de Buffon, concerning the deteriorating influence of American climate and soil upon animals and vegetables, he says there is no difference between the Indian and European, except what is produced by customs and modes of living. The Indian was taught to consider war as the noblest of pursuits. "Every thing he sees and hears tends to inspire him with an ardent desire for military fame. If a young man were to discover a fondness for women before he has been to war, he would become the contempt of the men, and the scorn and ridicule of the women. Or if he were to offer violence to a captive for selfish gratification, he would incur indelible disgrace. Their frigidity is the effect of manners, and not a defect of nature. Besides, a celebrated warrior is oftener courted by the females, than he has the occasion to court; and this is a point of honor which the men aim at. Instances similar to that of Ruth and Boaz are not uncommon among them. For though the women are modest and diffident, and so bashful that they seldom lift up their eyes, and scarce ever look a man full in the face, yet customs and manners reconcile them to modes of acting which, judged of by Europeans, would be deemed inconsistent with the rules of female decorum and propriety."

" When Boaz had eaten and drank, and his heart was merry, he went to lie down at the end of a heap of corn, and Ruth came softly, and uncovered his feet, and laid her down."

"Instances like this," continues the same author, "are not uncommon among them. I once saw a young widow, whose husband, a warrior, had died about eight days before, hastening to finish her grief, tearing her hair and beating her breast, drinking spirits to make the tears flow, that she might grieve much in a short space of time, and be married that evening to another young warrior. Old men, whose wives are also advanced in years, often marry young women, though polygamy is not common among them. Neither do they seem to be deficient in natural affection. I have seen both fathers and mothers in the deepest affliction when their children have been dangerously ill. It is also said they are averse to society and social life. Can any thing be more inapplicable than this to a people who always live in towns or clans? Or can they be said to have no 'republic,' who conduct all their affairs in national councils, who pride themselves in national character, who consider an insult or injury done to an individual, as done to the whole, and resent it accordingly?"

I have quoted this author at some length, as he must be considered good authority, and says he writes what he knows. And as this is one of the great points of dispute concerning Indians, between philosophers and historians of the old world and the new, and is also a very interesting one, I have thought it worthy much pains in adducing opinions. The Iroquois were not justly called a wild or barbarous people at all. They were not all alike. Among their lodges there were degrees of order and neatness, the same as among us. Those who visit the rude log cabins of white settlers in the wilderness far away from the comforts and luxuries of cultivated circles, may have all their sensibilities shocked quite as much as our forefathers had in the wigwam. They had rules of etiquette, and were truly formalists in the management of public and social matters. Not to say I thank you, after partaking of a meal in a friend's or stranger's house, was considered quite an insult, and they did not consider it polite to enter a village without uttering some note of announcement. "Much less ought they to be characterized as a people of no vivacity, and who are excited to action or motion only by the call of hunger and thirst. Their dances, in which they so much delight, and which to an European would be the severest exercise, fully contradict this.

All the Indians of North America were in the habit of using various symbols to represent ideas, and by some this was carried so far as to deserve the name of picture writing. If a hunter was alone in the forest, wherever he encamped he would mark upon the smooth bark of a tree the device of his tribe, a bear, or heron, or deer, whichever it might be; the shape of the moon at the time, to indicate the day of the month; and so nice were their observations,

5

that they drew the quarters, half and full moon with wonderful exactness; an arrow pointing in the direction he was going; straight lines to denote the number of days he had been from home, and the forms of the various animals he had killed in the chase.

If there was a large party, the number of persons was shown by the faces or figures being drawn; if it was a war party, a knife drawn across the throat designated how many had been killed.

They were in the habit of marking their tribal device, very generally denominated *totem*, over the doors of their cabins, and sometimes upon their bodies. Among the western nations and the Indians of New England, scrolls of bark were used, and their symbols were very much like those in use among eastern nations before the invention of letters. The events of a war expedition have been found so definitely pictured that they could be easily understood by those who originally knew nothing of the matter; and parties of travellers have found descriptions of their movements, upon pieces of bark fastened to a pole and set up in the forest, so that it was easily recognized when read by one acquainted with their signs.

The following is a love song written in this way, and curious only as showing the amount they could communicate and the sentiments they could express by picture writing:

> "It is my form and person that makes me great.
> Hear the voice of my song—it is my voice;
> I shield myself with secret coverings.
> All your thoughts are known to me; blush!
> I could draw you hence were you on a distant island;
> Though you were in another hemisphere;
> I speak to your naked heart!"

The following seems to be an imaginary address of the frogs to the snow flakes and ice in spring, when they are weary of being imprisoned, and long to burst their bonds, and commence their rejoicings, for the return of the warm sun and the sweet breath of spring.

They are interesting only as specimens of Indian imagination and poetry:

### SONG OF THE OKOGISS, OR FROGS, IN SPRING.

See how the white spirit presses—
Presses us—presses us, heavy and long;
Presses us down to the frost-bitten earth;
Alas! ye are heavy, ye spirits so white;
Alas! you are cold—you are cold, you are cold.
Ah! cease shining spirits that fell from the skies;
Ah! cease to crush us and keep us in dread;
Ah! when will ye vanish and Seegwin return!

### HAWK CHANT OF THE SAGINAWS.

The hawks turn their heads nimbly around;
They turn to look back on their flight;
The spirits of sunplace have whispered the words.
They fly with their messages swift;
They look as they fearfully go;
They look to the farthermost end of the world,
Their eyes glancing bright and their beaks boding harm.

Their war songs, as translated, do not convey to us any just idea of what they were to the Indian. It is true of every thing national of whatever people, that those alone can understand its true import who have the same associations; who have been subject to the same influences, and whose enthusiasm is awakened by the same suggestions.

To the Indian in his wild home, with his national costume, surrounded by warriors ready to go forth to battle, and young men panting for fame, their war songs were soul-inspiring, and kindled an enthusiasm which can scarcely be imagined by those who have not witnessed a war-dance and listened to a war song.

The following is a specimen, but tame indeed compared with the original:

> But who are my foes? they shall die.
> They shall fly o'er the plains like a fox;
> They shall shake like a leaf in the storm,
> Perfidious dogs—they roast our sons with fire.
>
> Five winters in hunting we'll spend,
> While mourning our warriors slain,
>   Till our youth grown to men
>   For the battle path trained,
> Our days like our father's we'll end.
>
> Ye are dead noble men! ye are gone
> My brother—my fellow—my friend!——
> On the death path where brave men must go;
> But we live to revenge you! we haste
> To die as our forefathers died.
>
> The eagles scream on high;
> They whet their forked beaks,
> Raise, raise the battle cry,
> 'Tis fame our leader seeks.
>
> The battle birds swoop from the sky,
> They thirst for the warrior's heart;
> They look from their circles on high,
> And scorn every flesh but the brave.
>
> I fall, but my body shall lie,
> A name for the gallant to tell;
> The gods shall repeat it on high,
> And young men grow brave at the sound.
>
>   Hear my voice ye heroes!
> On that day when our warriors sprang
> With shouts on the dastardly foe,

BABY FRAME.

>  Just vengeance my heart burned to take
>  On the cruel and treacherous breed,
>    The Bwoin—the Fox—the Sauk.
>
>  And here, on my breast, have I bled;
>  See—see! my battle scars!
>  Ye mountains tremble at my yell!
>    I strike for life.

The Indian mother has certainly invented the most convenient method of carrying and lullabying her baby. All babies are nearly of the same size, and nobody need to be told how long or wide a baby frame is made. It is a straight board, sometimes with side pieces, and always with a hoop over the head from which to suspend a curtain for the protection of the little eyes from the sun, and thus enveloped in a blanket and laced to the frame, they were carried upon the back of the mother by a stay which came over her forehead, and with much less fatigue than in the arms. The baby is kept in the frame a great portion of the time when it is an infant, and it is astonishing how contented it remains in its little prison. When the mother is at work in the field she hangs her baby on a low limb of a tree, where it is rocked by the wind. When she is busy in the house, she suspends it on a nail or seats it in the corner, and sometimes hangs it where she can swing it to and fro as she passes, "singing as she goes."

The following is a baby song, which will compare well with the songs of a similar sentiment among any people; and as in other cases, the translation is not so good as the original:

### CRADLE SONG.

>  Swinging, swinging, lullaby,
>    Sleep, little daughter sleep,
>  'Tis your mother watching by;
>    Swinging, swinging she will keep
>  Little daughter lullaby.

'Tis your mother loves you dearest,
  Sleep, sleep, daughter sleep;
Swinging, swinging, ever nearest,
  Baby, baby do not weep,
Little daughter lullaby.

Swinging, swinging, lullaby,
  Sleep, sleep little one,
And thy mother will be nigh;
  Swing, swing, not alone,
Little baby lullaby.

As an instance of the appreciation in which the Iroquois held the noble qualities of the heart, their enthusiasm, and the honors they thought it not wrong to bestow upon woman, may be related the story of the daughter of Black Chief, who was a Seneca Sachem residing at Squawky Hill, in the valley of the Genesee:

Black Chief was one of their brave men in time of war, and also endowed with all the noble, generous qualities which win love and honor in time of peace. He had an only daughter, who was greatly endeared to her people, because, like her father, she had a soul ever prompting her to generous deeds. She was also very beautiful, and possessed a mind of superior order, and was in every way gifted, worthy to be the Chieftain's daughter. When her father died they honored her above all other women, and gave to her the title and authority of Princess.

They had a superstition, that during her life, the Iroquois would again be restored to their ancient power, and take a place among the nations of the earth. So, many were the prayers which ascended to the Great Spirit for the long life of their young queen. They gathered flowers and strewed in her path when she went forth, and brought to her the finest venison and the rarest fruits for her table. She was not made haughty and imperious by her honors, but continued gentle and affectionate, though it was but a little while that she remained to receive these tokens of unaffected homage. The Great Spirit did not see fit to answer their prayers. In an evil hour the pestilence swept the land, and whole villages were desolated in a night. In the midst of their calamities, they thought less of themselves than of the daughter of their beloved Chief. Whilst the hand of the destroyer left her unharmed, they were not made utterly wretched. But when their lamentations were dying away, and health again brought cheerfulness to their dwellings, she was stricken, and the light which had been so beautiful in their eyes went out in utter darkness. Now the wail of the mourners around the couch of the dead was sincere and heart-rending. They did not build for her the "Cabin of Death," but constructed a scaffold among the trees of a neighboring grove, and adorning her with all that their skill or taste could devise, placed her upon it in a sitting posture, and from far and near all the people gathered together to join in the solemn rites, which were to testify their love for the living and their grief for the dead. Her lifeless form was embowered with roses and running vines, and garlands of flowers were wreathed at her feet. All that the Indian considered most valuable—golden ears of his beloved maize, and the most costly furs, were scattered in profusion around her.

Every night fires were lighted and watchmen stationed to guard her body from danger, and every morning they again assembled to renew the utterance of their grief.

The mourning continued many days, and when it was no longer possible to preserve her in their sight, she was buried, while at her grave was chanted a solemn dirge by the mingled voices of a great multitude, whe filled the air with such plaintive wailings as can come only from broken hearts.

I cannot help pausing here to ask, if such a people deserve no better doom than annihilation? if those who call themselves Christians "have done what they could," to tune these harps of the wilderness to accord with those of the cherubim and seraphim in the choirs above?

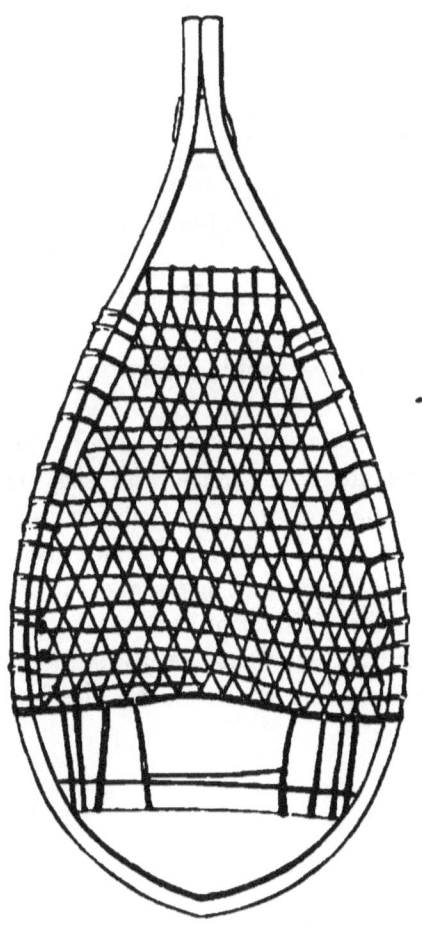

# CHAPTER VI.
### LEGENDARY LITERATURE.

IF, centuries ago, some amateur chronicler had wandered peacefully among the North American Indians, making himself familiar with their language and welcome at their firesides, that he might listen to their legends and record them as they were related in their family circles, in the same way as bands of Eastern wanderers were accustomed to revel in Arabian tales, we might have had some idea of the poetry and enthusiasm and glowing images of a people whose thoughts and fancies soared so freely and wildly, and gave to their compositions a richness and beauty, only rivalled on Grecian plains and among Celtic bards.

Tradition tells us that Homer was a blind ballad singer, and that his immortal lines were gathered here and there among the people long after he slept with his fathers.

The poems of Ossian were collected among the Highlands of Scotland, from those who sang them as their fathers sang them, and were as ignorant as the Indian of our forests of metrical rules and written lore, yet they are the admiration of poets and sages, and considered unparalleled by any thing civilization can boast.

On long winter evenings the Indian hunters gathered around their firesides, to listen to the historical traditions, legends of war and hunting, and their fairy tales, which had been handed down through their fathers and fathers' fathers with scarcely any variation for centuries, kindling the enthusiasm of the warriors and inspiring the little child with the desire some day to realize similar dreams, and hand his name down to posterity as the author of similar exploits.

They have a superstitious fear of relating fables in summer; not till after the snow comes will they talk of snakes, lest they should creep into their beds, or of evil genii lest they in some way be revenged.

It is very difficult for a stranger to rightly understand the *morale* of their stories, though it is said by those who know them best, that to them the story was always an illustration of some important event or principle.

To strangers they offer all the rites of hospitality, but do not open their hearts. If you ask them they will tell you a story, but it will not be such a story as they tell when alone. They will fear your ridicule, and suppress their humor and their pathos; and so thoroughly have they learned to distrust pale faces, that when they know that he who is present is a friend, they will still shrink from admitting him within the secret portals of their souls.

And when you have learned all that language can convey, there are still a thousand images, suggestions and associations recurring to the Indian, which can strike no chord in your heart. The myriad voices of nature are dumb to you, but to him they are full of life and power.

LEGEND OF THE SENECAS CONCERNING THEIR ORIGIN.

All the legends when related by different people, have slight variations, but the general features are the same, and are preserved with remarkable exactness, considering that they have beeen handed down for centuries in this oral way. The following is all the account the Senecas can give concerning their origin.

They grew out of the crest of a mountain, at the head of Canandaigua lake. The mountain which gave them birth is Ge-nun-de-wah-gauh, or the Great Hill. Hence they are called the Great Hill People.

A little boy during his rambles in the woods, found a pretty serpent, which he carried home for a plaything. In the course of time the serpent grew to be very large, and so voracious that he devoured all who came within the reach of his monstrous jaws. At length he coiled himself around the base of the mountain, so that none could pass to and fro, without falling victims to his ravenous appetite, and besides, the atmosphere was poisoned by his fetid breath. But starvation stared them in the face, and the people determined upon a sally, hoping to destroy the monster and escape unharmed. The serpent was so large that there was no hope of leaping over his body, and there was no way but to attempt a passage where the head and tail met. In a body all the people rushed down, determined on victory or death, and were all destroyed, except a little boy and his sister, who were left alone to defy the monster. Then came a pleasant dream to the boy, which directed him to string his bow with the silken tresses of his sister, and shoot the serpent in the eye, or underneath a scale. The child obeyed, and the arrow performed the work of death. In the convulsive throes of the serpent, the heads of the multitudes which he had devoured, were thrown upon the earth, and when he uncoiled, they rolled with him into the lake, where being petrified by the water, they still remain in the form of round stones, which cover the bed of the lake to this day!

This is about as marvellous as the preservation of Romulus and Remus, and exhibits the same kind of propensity to account for what is unaccountable, and give themselves " a local habitation and a name." It is also quite as credible as many of the stories concerning the early history of the heroes of ancient history and fable, which are thought worth recording by every author who writes of Greece and Rome, and are read by every child with wonder.

### MEDICINE LEGENDS.

The two following, are the legends concerning the principal medicines used among the Iroquois. The ancient manner of administering them, was to take a small wooden goblet, and go to a running stream, and dipping towards the way which the stream ran, fill the goblet and return to set it by the fire, with some tobacco near it. A prayer is offered, while tobacco is thrown upon the fire, that the words may ascend upon the smoke.

The medicine is placed upon a piece of skin near the goblet, and being very finely pounded, is taken up with a wooden spoon and dusted upon the water in three places, in spots in the form of a triangle, thus—*.* The medicine man then looks at it critically, and if it spreads itself over the surface of the water and whirls about, it is a sign that the invalid will be healed. If it sinks directly in the places where it is placed—there is no hope—the sick person will die, and they throw the whole away.

Once in six months there is a great feast made, at the hunting season in the fall and spring. On the night of the feast, as soon as it is dark, all who are present assemble in one room, where no light or fire is allowed to burn, and placing the medicine near the covered embers, and the tobacco by its side, they commence singing something which proclaims that the crow is coming to their feast, and also many other birds, and various animals, the brains of whose species form part of the medicine. At the end of the song, some one imitates the *caw* of the crow, and the songs of the birds, and howl of the wolf, &c., as if the animals were present.

Three times in the course of the night they offer a prayer, while throwing tobacco upon the smothered flames, asking that the people may be protected from all harm, and if they receive wounds that the medicine may be effectual in healing them.

At the commencement of the ceremonies the doors are locked, and no one is allowed to enter or leave the house while they continue. Neither is any one allowed to sleep, as this would spoil the medicine. The feast begins just before dawn of day. The master of ceremonies first takes a deer's head, and biting off a piece, imitates the cry of the crow, and passes the head of the animal to another, who does the same, till all have tasted, and imitated the peculiar note of some bird or animal.

As soon as it begins to be light, the presiding officer takes a duck's bill, and dipping it full of the medicine, gives it to each one present, who puts it in a bit of skin, and wrapping it in several coverings, keeps it carefully till the next semi-annual feast. The skin of a panther is preferred for the first envelope, if it can be obtained.

Those who take a part in the ceremonies are MEDICINE MEN; Chiefs are allowed to be present, and any others who have been cured of any disease by the medicine.

Without the building, the young people gather for merriment, and the fragments of the feast are given to them when it is finished.

When the medicine is used which is described in the second legend, the tune is sung which was heard at its discovery, both at the ceremonies of the feast and the time of administering it.

They seem to think the ceremonies effectual in making the medicinal qualities of the compound imperishable. Each medicine man has a large quantity which he keeps in a bag, and in order not to exhaust the whole, now and then adds pulverized corn roots, squash vines, &c., and whenever it is administered, several persons assemble and sing. Both kinds are considered especially useful in healing wounds received in war.

In reading the first legend, there will be seen very humorous allusions to the habits of the pigeon, the heron, and crow, and the whole is a curious invention, inspiring faith in the means used for healing, and I have seen many who affirmed that they had tested the wonderful powers of each!

## No. 1.

There once lived a man who was a great hunter. His generosity was the theme of praise in all the country, for he not only supplied his own family with food, but distributed game among his friends and neighbors, and even called the birds and the animals of the forest to partake of his abundance. For this reason he received the appellation of "Protector of birds and animals."

He lived a hunter's life till war broke out between his own and some distant nation, and then he took the war-path. He was as brave a warrior as skilful hunter, and slew a great multitude of the enemy, till all were lying dead around him, except one, who was a *mighty man of valor*, and in an unguarded moment the hunter received a blow from his tomahawk, in the head, which felled him to the earth. His enemy then took his scalp and fled.

Some of his own party had seen what befell him, and,

supposing him dead, had left him on the field of battle; but a Fox who wandered this way immediately recognized his old benefactor. Sorrowful indeed was he to find him slain, and began to revolve in his mind some means of restoring him to life. "Perhaps," said he, "some of my friends may know of a medicine by which his wounds may be healed, and he may live again." So saying, he ran into the forest and uttered the *death lament*, which was the signal for all the animals to congregate. From far and near they came, till hundreds and thousands of every name had assembled around the body of the hunter, eagerly inquiring what had happened. The Fox explains how he had accidentally come that way and found their friend stretched lifeless upon the earth. The animals draw near and examine him more closely, to be sure that life is extinct. They roll him over and over upon the ground and are satisfied that he is dead—there is not a single sign of life.

"Then they hold a GRAND COUNCIL, of which the Bear is speaker. When all are ready to listen, he asks if any one present is acquainted with any medicine which would restore the dead man to life. With great alacrity each one examines his *medicine-box*, but finds nothing adapted to this purpose. Being defeated in their noble object of restoring their friend, all join in a mournful howl—a requiem for the dead. This attracted a singing bird—the Oriole, who came quickly to learn the cause of the assembling of this great concourse, and their great lamentation. The Bear made known the calamity which had befallen them, and, as the birds would feel themselves equally afflicted, he requested the Oriole to flee away and invite all the feathered tribes to come to the council, and see if their united wisdom cannot devise a remedy that will restore their friend to life.

Soon are assembled all the birds of the air, even the

Great Eagle of the Iroquois, who is seldom induced to appear upon the earth, hastens to pay her respects to the remains of the renowned and benevolent hunter. All being satisfied that he was really dead, the united council of birds and animals, which remained convened, decided that his scalp must be recovered, saying, any bird or animal who pleased might volunteer to go upon this holy mission. The Fox was the first to offer his services, and departed full of hope that his zeal would be crowned with success. But after many days he returned, saying, he could find no traces of man's footsteps—not a *chick* or *child* belonged to any settlement. The great love which they bore their friend prompted several others to go upon the same mission; and to the animals belonged the first right, as they had first found him. But at length the birds were anxious to show their devotion, and the Pigeon Hawk begged leave to make the first flight, as she was more swift of wing than any other, and could visit the whole world in the shortest space of time. They had scarcely missed him when he returned. He said he had been over the entire earth and found it not; but they did not consider his voyage satisfactory, as he had flown so swiftly that it was impossible for him to see any thing distinctly by the way!

Next the White Heron proposed that she be sent, because she was so slow of wing that she could see every object as she passed! On her aerial voyage she discovered a plain covered with the vines of the wild bean, laden with the delicious fruit. It was too great a temptation for the Heron to resist, and she descended to enjoy a feast. So gluttonously did she partake that she could not rise again from the earth, and the council, after many days of anxious waiting, called for a substitute. Here the Crow came forward and acknowledged his fitness for such an office, as he also was slow of wing and was *accustomed to hover over settlements*, and to discern them afar off! and he would not be suspected of any particular design if he should linger near the one that contained the scalp!

The warrior who possessed the coveted treasure, knew the birds and animals were holding a council on the field of battle to devise means to recover it; but when the crow drew near he was not alarmed. The smoke of the wigwams indicated a settlement, and as the crow sailed lazily through the air at a great height above the roofs of the cabins, he espied a scalp which he knew must be the one he sought, stretched out to dry.

After various unsuccessful stratagems, he was able to seize it, and flew away to exhibit his trophy to the council.

Now they attempt to fit it to the head; but, being dry, it is impossible, and search is made to find something with which to moisten it; but it is in vain. Then slowly moves forward the Great Eagle, and bids them listen to her words:

"My wings are never furled; night and day, for years and hundreds of years, the dews of heaven have been collecting upon my back, as I sat in my nest, above the clouds, and perhaps these waters may have a virtue no earthly fountain can possess; we will see."

Then she plucked a feather from her wing and dipped it in the dewy elixir, which was applied to the shrivelled scalp, and lo! it became pliable and fresh as if just removed. Now it would fit, but there must be a healing power to cause the flesh to unite, and again to awaken life.

All are anxious to do something in this great work, and therefore all go forth to bring rare leaves and flowers and seeds and bark, the flesh of animals and the brains of birds, to form a healing mixture. When they return it is prepared, and being moistened with the dew is applied to the scalp, and instantly it adheres and becomes firm. They cause the hunter to sit up, and he looks around in astonishment upon his numerous friends, unable to divine the meaning of so strange an assemblage.

Then they bid him stand upon his feet, and tell him how he was found dead upon the plain, and how great was the lamentation of all those who had so long experienced his kindness, and the efforts they had made to restore him. They then give him the compound which had been the means of bringing him again to life, saying "it was the gift of the Great Spirit to man. He alone had directed them in the affairs of the council; had brought the eagle to furnish the heavenly moisture, and give them wisdom in making the preparation, that they might furnish to man a medicine which should be effectual for every wound."

When they had finished, the animals departed to their forest haunts, the eagle soared again to her eyry, and the birds of the air flew away to their nests in the tall trees, all happy and rejoicing that they had accomplished this great good.

The hunter returned to his home and spread abroad the news of the miracle, and the knowledge of the wonderful medicine, which is used to this day among the Iroquois, who are the favorites of the Great Spirit.

### No. 2.

An Indian hunter went forth to hunt, and as he wandered in the forest he heard a strain of beautiful music far off among the trees. He listened but could not tell whence it came, and knew it could not be by any human voice, or from any instrument he had ever heard. As he came near it ceased. The next evening he went forth again, but he heard not the music, and again, but in vain.

Then came the Great Spirit to him in a dream and told him he must fast, and wash himself till he was purified, and then he might go forth, and he would hear again the music. So he purified himself and went again among the darkest trees of the forest, and soon his ear caught the sweet strains, and as he drew near they became more beautiful, and he listened till he had learned them, and could make the same sweet sounds. Then he saw that it was a plant, with a tall green stem and long tapering leaves. He took his knife and cut the stalk, but ere he had scarcely finished, it healed and was the same as before. He cut it again, and again it healed, and then he knew that it would heal diseases, and he took it home and dried it by the fire, and pulverized it; and applying a few particles of it to a dangerous wound, no sooner had it touched the flesh than it was whole. Thus the Great Spirit taught the Indian the nature of medicinal plants, and directed him where they were to be found.

## A HUNTING LEGEND.

One of the ancient Grecian philosophers, whose life and sayings are deemed worthy of recording, once astonished the people by relating the adventures he had experienced on a long journey through many countries, where he met "speaking trees, pigmies, phœnixes, satyrs and dragons," and many other things equally marvellous, of which I could not help being reminded when I heard the hunter's legend.

Of Anaxagoras, another Grecian philosopher, it is related as one of his predictions, that on a certain day a stone would fall from the sun, and on the appointed day, a stone did fall from the sun in a part of Thrace, near the river Ægos. And Plutarch states that this stone was not only shown, but in his time greatly reverenced by the Peloponnesians. At another time it was asserted that a large stone fell from heaven, and Anaxagoras said that the whole heavens was composed of stones, and that by its rapid revolutions they were all held together, and when those revolutions get slower, they fall down.

At another time he said, when the weather was very fair, that there would be a heavy rain and storm, and went to the Olympic games in a shaggy skin or leathern dress, prepared for such a change; and as it did rain according to his predictions, the people honored him as though he possessed supernatural knowledge.

But the Indian philosophers tell the wonderful experience of the hunter to make exaggeration and falsehood contemptible and ridiculous.

### ADVENTURES OF THE HUNTER HO-CHA-GAH.

Ho-cha-gah was a hunter of great renown. His wife had plenty of venison. In his tent were many furs and nice skins, and the story of his adventures has come down through many generations.

He built him a little hut beside a lake, where the dark forest came down to its silvery border, and stretched far away over the mountain. Every day he took his bow and quiver of arrows, and went forth to find the deer or the wolf, and trap the beaver or the otter, but this time he was not successful. Many months he lingered in hopes to find something to reward his labors, but in vain. The spring came and he must return home. But he thought at least he would have something new to relate, so he resolved to launch upon the water a new-fashioned boat, and see whither it would conduct him. The food which he had not consumed he encased in bags of slippery elm and sank them in the water, that they might be preserved should he return again to hunt beside the lake. Himself he inclosed in a bottle of the same material and set out on his floating expedition.

For a long time he glided smoothly over the surface, but at length he experienced a strange sensation as if he were sailing through the air. Then he struck a rock, and then another, bounding along like a billow, till he was again upon the placid stream. The noise was like thunder, and he knew he must have descended from a great height with the foam of waters.

Soon he was cast upon the beach, and now wished to come out of his hiding place, for he was faint for want of food. But he could not open his prison, and feared he must die without relating his adventures. But he was awakened one morning by a noise like the beak of a bird, against the side of the bottle which was now dry and hard, and soon the light entered, and he saw a crow picking its way to him in hopes of finding food.

Now he was able to extricate himself and came forth, and saw that he had came safely over the cataract of Niagara!

With this he went home and astonished his friends, who looked upon him as almost a superior being, and believed he was miraculously preserved by the Great Spirit.

His love of adventures was not satisfied, and in a little time he went again to the forest and made his camp by the lake, where he had been before so unsuccessful in hunting. Now he found plenty of game, and when spring came, he thought he would try still another mode of voyaging—he would like to fly through the air. Seeing a flock of geese upon the waters, he thought if he were secured to their feet he might rise with them and be carried along through the aerial regions, and look down upon the valleys beneath. So he took strips of bark and stealthily crept into the water, and swimming along, suddenly encircled them with his string, and tied himself to their feet, when with a great screaming they rose and he was borne along over mountains, and rivers, and valleys, where he saw strange people, and plains, and heard strange and beautiful music. After awhile he was borne so far aloft, that he could scarcely breathe; then he severed the string and descended again to earth. On alighting, he found himself snugly settled in a hollow tree. He received no harm, but could see no way of escape. For several days he was a prisoner, and again in danger of starving, when he heard voices and endeavored to speak. The noise he made attracted the attention of those who passed by, and thinking it some animal, they felled the tree, and lo! to their astonishment, it was a man.

As soon as he was set free, he proceeded on his way and came to a large stream, the color of which was bright crimson. Never before had he seen any thing so beautiful. He drank of it and the taste was like a ripe strawberry. He followed it to its source, and found it issued from one of these berries, the size of which was marvellous, and gave rise to a never failing rivulet, to refresh the hunter when he was weary and found no food.

Again he pursued his way, and whilst wandering in the forest he saw something that looked like a great cloud. Slowly it sailed to and fro, and when it descended he saw that it was an army of grasshoppers each as large as a canoe. They were frightful to behold.

Again he thought he would spend the winter in hunting, and plunged into the thick forest where the bear and buffalo made their haunts. But in vain he bent his bow and set his trap. They all eluded his vigilance. Then in a dream was suggested to him the *hunter's charm.*

He used it, and there came flocking to him from all the country every animal of the forest, so near that he could touch them, and so tame that he could sleep in the midst of them unharmed. Then he built him a hut to dry his venison, and though he had enough, he was still surrounded. Every four-footed and creeping thing infested his dwelling till he was obliged to flee.

Again he returned hence and related his marvellous adventures, which now none believed, yet he was not satisfied. His thirst for fame was insatiable, and his egotism inexhaustible. Absenting himself another long period, he returned with still greater beasts.

He crossed a stream of a rich golden hue, and being thirsty drank of its waters, and was astonished at the delicious flavor. On tracing it, he found it to issue from a mandrake which was an inexhaustible fountain, and sent forth its juices to refresh the wayfarer, lest he faint in the wilderness.

Pursuing his way he saw a duck sailing upon a dimpling pool, and bent his bow for its destruction; the arrow passed through the duck, and glancing upon the waters, pierced a deer that was slaking her thirst at the fountain; not having spent its force, the arrow glided on and entered a tree, making an opening from which issued a stream of richest honey. Here he rested and enjoyed a feast. Again when sitting beneath a spreading walnut-tree, he saw a nut rolling over and over upon the ground; on striking it with his tomahawk, a seam was made in the shell, through which came forth a bear; and then another and another, till six monsters of the forest were reclining around him, whose home was the walnut-shell!

The bears in the walnut-shell remind us of the fairies in a hazel-nut shell, as sung by Drayton, our old

English poet, in the " Court of Fairy." In fear of falling into the hands of a hobgoblin the fairies,

> " Hop, and Mop, and Drop, so clear,
> Pip, and Trip, and Skip, that were
> To Mab, their sovereign dear,
>    Her special maids of honor;
> Fib, and Tib, and Prick, and Pin,
> Tick, and Quick, and Jill, and Jin,
> Sit, and Nit, and Wap, and Win,
>    The train that wait upon her.
>
> " Upon a Grasshopper they got,
> And what with awhile and with trot,
> For hedge nor ditch they spared not;
>    But after her they hie them.
> A Cob-web over them they throw
> To shield the wind if it should blow,
> Themselves they wisely could bestow,
>    Lest any should espy them.
>
> " At length one chanced to find a nut,
> *In the end of which a hole was cut,*
> Which lay upon a hazel-root,
>    There scattered by a Squirrel,
> Which out the kernel gotten had;
> When quoth this fay, 'Dear queen, be glad,
> Let Oberon be ne'er so mad,
>    I'll set you safe from peril.
>
> "' *Come all into this nut,*' quoth she,
> 'Come *closely in,* be ruled by me,
> Each one may here a *chooser* be,
>    *For room ye need not wrestle,*
> Nor need ye be together heapt,'
> So one by one therein they crept,
> And lying down they soundly slept
>    As safe as in a Castle!"

## A PIGMY LEGEND.

The memory of every son and daughter of the Saxons will furnish abundance of fairy tales to correspond with the most incredible of those related around Indian firesides. I heard, not long since, a little girl reading "Household Stories," translated from the German, and on reading her an Indian legend, she exclaimed, "Why, they are like my The stories," and I was myself struck with the resemblance. stories of "Little Red Ridinghood," "The Frog Prince," "The Three Little Men in the Wood," and a thousand others, have been the delight of Christian children for centuries, and nothing a heathen can relate is more ridiculous than "Mother Goose's Melodies." Yet they are a part of our national literature. No man, however wise, would consider himself educated who could not say—

"There was an old woman, and she, and she,
And out of her elbow grew an apple tree."

"Old mother Hubbard
Went to the cupboard, &c."

' "The Midsummer Night's Dream" of Shakspeare, or Spenser's "Fairy Queen," have not been the less admired because they were utterly improbable. I cannot relate any thing so beautiful in the way of Indian fairy stories, but those which I relate, and hundreds which have never been related, are exceedingly beautiful in their own metaphorical language; and I almost falter in attempting to convey any idea of their imaginative creations, in English. The following are faint transcripts of the original:

LEGEND OF THE JO-GO-O, OR PIGMIES DESTROYING THE MONSTER BUFFALOES.

The Pigmies were *little folk*, who lived far away to the

north among the clefts of the rocks. Ote-ho-we-geh, "The cold regions," designated the place of their abode, because it was so cold they could not grow. So they were not more than two feet in height, but they were very powerful, and ever on the alert doing good. Especially were they the friends of the red man, and knew if dangers threatened him in any part of the country.

The Do-ge-ya-go-wa, or Great Buffaloes, had their dwellings in the earth, and went from place to place in subterranean walks.

Three of these monsters were on their way to the Salt Lakes of the south, when three of the Pigmies, who always warred with giants and monsters, snakes, lizards and every thing prejudicial to man, set forth to destroy them. To be one day at the north, and the next far away thousands of miles to the south, was a trifling feat for them to perform, so swiftly did they go in their fairy canoes.

One day an Indian maiden was dipping water from a little brook that flowed into the O-hee-yo, and as she bent over the stream, the water reflected a strange appearance. On looking up she beheld the three Pigmies just alighting near where she stood. She knew immediately that there was danger, for they never at any other time made themselves visible to mortal eyes.

These monster buffaloes fed only on human flesh, and were therefore a great terror, as they could suddenly rise up out of the ground and destroy whole settlements, before there was time for any to flee. The Pigmies knew where they had gone, and that they would soon return, and bade the maiden flee to inform her people, that they might be ready for flight if they should not succeed in their mission; but told her they would meet her again at the stream and inform her if they were able to destroy them.

When they had finished their message, with one stroke of their paddles the canoe soared into the air and sailed along over the tree tops a great distance, and then descended again to the water, when another stroke bore it again aloft.

When they reached the place where the buffaloes appeared, they cut down the largest hickory trees and split them in two parts for their bows, and made them arrows of the tallest pines of the forest. With these they pierced them and sent the arrows with such force that they passed through the monsters, who fell, crushing whole forests beneath them. From their blood arose the small buffaloes, Do-ge-ya-go, while their bones have remained undecayed for untold centuries.

The Pigmies having accomplished their purpose, returned to inform the maiden at the stream, who listened to their story with delight, and ran to announce the glad tidings to her people, and then departed to their northern home.

All the little buffaloes from far and near came regularly to dance on the spot where their progenitors were slain, and the Indian, as he passes the place, shows a particle from some mammoth bone, to wear as a charm to procure him whatever he desires—the love of a beautiful maiden—success on the war path, or plenty of game in his hunting excursions.

## A WAR LEGEND.

In this story is developed the principle upon which war was waged among the Iroquois. Revenge for a great injury was the cause of the beginnings of strife. Then subjugation for the sake of peace, like the Romans of old, and the Iroquois have been justly called the " Romans of

America." There was something in their proud and dignified bearing, in their national policy, and their warlike exploits, like the people who extended their arms into every civilized and uncivilized land.

In the words of the poet, who has given metrical beauty to their legends, and added his own to their lofty enthusiasm:

"Roman remains in Britain, with their double lines of circumvallation, and the Druidic circles of moss-covered stones, are objects, not more interesting to the antiquary than the mighty tumuli of the west; and the ruins of walled towns in the wilds of Wisconsin. What are a few mouldering abbeys and falling turrets, compared with the colossal remains of empires in Central America? Poet and historian have lavished their descriptive skill on the burial rites of Alaric, whose bones repose in the sandy bed of the Busentinus, but not less imposing was the funeral of Blackbird, the Ohama Chief, who was inhumed bestriding his war-horse in a hill sepulchre that overlooks the Missouri.

"Red Jacket sitting in tears on a fallen oak, viewing the cleared fields of the white man, after a fruitless hunt for game in and around the haunts of his youth, was a nobler spectacle of sorrow than even Marius reclining amid the ruins of Carthage."

And Jefferson says: "Before we condemn the Indian of this continent as wanting genius, we must consider that letters had not yet been introduced among them. If the Indian at this time is compared with Europeans north of the Alps, when the Roman arms and arts first crossed the mountains, the comparison would be very unequal, because Europe at that time was swarming with numbers; because numbers produce emulation and multiply chances of improvement, and one improvement begets another. Yet I may safely ask, how many great poets—how many able mathematicians—how many great inventors in arts and sciences had Europe north of the Alps then produced? And it was sixteen centuries after this before a Newton could be found."

The manner in which the legend represents the Indian warrior meeting death at the stake is the manner in which every Indian warrior died. No refinement or duration of torture could extort from him a groan. The faith of the Christian martyr supports him in the hour of trial; but the Indian excels him in defying his tormenters, with only his own dauntless spirit to sustain him; he will die, too, rather than surrender, though he knows he will fall into the hands of those who, looking upon him as a fallen foe, will be merciful.

The war-dance, so often alluded to in Indian story, is said to be beyond description the most exciting and inspiring of all theatrical scenes. It is the acting of war. The song, which kindles enthusiasm, is first sung, with the same motive and the same effect as the martial music awakes it echoes on *Christian plains*, and then follows all the pomp and circumstance of war: arrows fly thick and fast, the tomahawk is wielded, the dead and dying strew the battle-field, and by various devices of paint and false scalps, hundreds are bleeding, when follows the shout of victory and the dirge for the slain. Those who have witnessed it say it is impossible for one who is not an actor to realize that it can be any thing less than a real battle. Those who pass through the initiatory process of being trained for warriors at a military school, can imagine the influence of the war-dance upon those to whom war is the only field of glory. I wish I could transfer to my paper something of the enthusiasm with which an Indian relates the legend.

## THE VIRGIN OF WAR.

There lived an aged Indian almost alone in the forest, with his wife and two sons. They had never heard of war or dissension; then the woods echoed only the hunter's happy song, and the sweet melodies of the birds. But there came a vision to the father concerning the future, when nations would hate one another, and the wilderness would resound to the shrill war-whoop, and the tomahawk and scalping-knife would be used among his people.

So he called his sons and bade them listen to his instructions. He made a bow and a quiver of arrows, and taught them skill in the use of them. He made a war club, and told them if they should be assailed they could with this slay their enemies. He gave them a scalping-knife and said, "with this you can secure the trophies of your victories." Then came the war-song and the dance in exultation of their triumphs. The children listened eagerly to their father's words, though they understood little of the tendency of his teachings; they became expert in the use of all the instruments their father had made, and indulged daily in the amusements which this practice afforded them, while their mother looked on in wonder at all these new things which had never before been seen by human eyes.

One day there came a stranger to their lodge when the old man and his sons were in the forest. He said to the wife he wished to meet her husband in order to take counsel with him, and if he would come to the little brook which ran through a distant field, he would see a large tree in the water; he must come and place his right foot upon the tree, and he himself would place his left foot upon the tree, and thus they would talk of the things which he had come to say. But before her husband left his lodge she must take the bow which he had been making, and cut the string nearly off, but say nothing to him about it, for a great evil would come upon her if she did not in all things obey his directions; and here the stranger looked very fiercely upon her, so that she trembled and did not dare to disobey.

When her husband returned she gave him the message, and before he set out to meet the messenger she secretly cut his bow-string and did not dream of evil.

The old man departed, and all day and night they waited, but he did not return. The children said, "what has become of our father? Let us go and seek him." So they took their bows and quivers and went to the little brook, and there saw their father's body lying in the water full of arrows. Then they knew that he had been killed, and that the stranger was their enemy. When they met upon the fallen tree the stranger pushed him into the water, and when he attempted to use his bow, the string snapped, and his enemy overcame him. He also took from him his bow and quiver and now had gone far away. "We must be revenged!" exclaimed the eldest of the boys; "this is what our father taught us. We must seek him who has slain our father, and take his scalp."

They took the body home and mourned and wept many days. Then they commenced with greater interest to sing the war-song and perform the dance, and wield the tomahawk, and their mother reproved them. But they said, this is what our father taught us we must do; and now we must go and seek him who has slain our father. We must be revenged.

Then they sharpened their arrows, and strung their bows, and departed on the war-path—not to gain fame or glory—not to conquer for the sake of extending their dominions—not to slay to gratify a thirst for blood; but to be avenged for a family wrong. They took the way their father went, and after many days found the people of the stranger, towards whom their hatred had been excited, and shot the first man that came within the flight of an arrow. In taking the scalp they were not expert, but succeeded in obtaining the trophy which was to tell of their success, and holding it up in sight of their enemies, exclaimed, " Follow us, but ye will not overtake us; thus shall it be done unto those who destroy life!"

This the multitude understood not, and looked in astonishment at the bleeding symbol of their vengeance. They returned and laid the scalp at the feet of their grandmother, for it was her son who had been killed, and to her they brought the compensation—blood for blood, had been shed. They then prepared it as their father had directed, and hung it upon the roof of their dwelling, as the testimony of their valor.

But they were not content. They had tasted of excitement, and panted again for the war-path. But now their enemies were prepared, and one was taken prisoner, yet they knew not what to do, for they had never before had conflicts with enemies. But the youthful warrior remembered his father's instructions concerning the treatment of prisoners, and told them he would die by fire— he would be burned at the stake. So with his own hands he piled the fagots and wound the withes about his body, and bade them apply the torch. They looked with horror upon the scene, and pity upon his sufferings, and would gladly have released him from such torture. But he defied them, saying it was not in their power to make him cry out for pain. He was dying a warrior's death, and scorned to receive compassion. Then he threw his hands in the air, and sung the war-song till his breath died away, thus setting an example to all who would win honor.

Now the remaining brother must again seek revenge. He induced a young companion to join him, and filling the air with their wild chorus, they went forth to slay many in return for him who had fallen into their hands. Their arrows flew thick and fast, while they concealed themselves from the sight of those whom they pursued, till many had fallen; then they took a prisoner, and returned home.

He too must die at the stake, and though not a warrior, he imitated the example set him by the youth who thirsted for glory, and exulted in his sufferings, singing the war-song as long as life remained.

His people were now enraged, and plotted the destruction of their enemies. A runner was sent to invite the chiefs of this war-seeking nation to meet them at an appointed place for the purpose of adjusting their difficulties. But the young warrior whose brother gloried in torture, said he feared their treachery, and would not allow the chiefs of his people to fall into their hands. No, the warriors should go forth prepared for battle. He had trained them in expectation of this day, and they were ready for war and ready for victory. Then echoed the war-whoop through all the forest, and they marched in battle array to lie in wait for their enemies.

They encamped on the brow of a hill, arriving at the designated time, but the little band which was to meet them to hold a council for peace was nowhere to be seen. They threw up a palisade for their defence, and commenced the festivities which were the warrior's pastime. What a scene for their enemies who now first looked from their concealment upon the war dance. In the midst of the forest was a great fire, around it here and there sat the old men in groups, while the young men with their painted cheeks gleaming in the red torch-light, and the

6*

bright flames waving over their brows, danced among the trees and sang the thrilling songs which stirred them to daring deeds, and drove the fear of death far away from their hearts.

But whilst in the midst of their rejoicings, an arrow comes whizzing through the air. They heed it not, and continue their songs. Another is heard, and another, but the revelry does not cease; now a strain is heard to which the shrill war-whoop is the answer; every bow is strung, and a thousand arrows are sent like the swift lightning back upon the invaders. A fierce battle ensues, many warriors are slain. The enemy flee and are pursued. The air is filled with the shouts of the victors. The ground is covered with the dead.

The next day every warrior returns with a scalp, the trophy of his valor, and the youth, to whose wisdom in council they owe the victory, assembles all the people and announces that his mission is fulfilled. He is about to leave the earth. He has repeated to them his father's instructions. They have learned all the arts of war, and know how to take the scalps of their enemies. He has taught them the song and the dance, and bids them forget not to die like warriors, in battle or at the stake.

The next day they seek him and he is dead.

Now these nations have learned war, and the war-path becomes a beaten trail, so constantly do they go to and fro to take the scalps of their enemies. So they make a trench, and by a law which all agree to obey, pursuit shall not be carried across this boundary. The warrior might come into the enemy's country, but when he was driven back, after he had crossed the line, he should be safe. There they often stood in great numbers, within sight of each other, but neither footsteps nor arrows must go over the trench.

On one occasion, when they were pursuing the enemy, a man ran swiftly up into a tree to escape, and when they looked, behold, he was changed into a bear! His clan was ever after called the Bear Clan. On another occasion, a man who was fleeing descended into a deep ravine, and looking for him as he ascended the opposite side, lo, he was a wolf! thus obtaining for his clan the title of Wolf Clan. After long years of enmity and a thousand battles, it was discovered that these clans which had been so long at war were one nation. They then buried the tomahawk and smoked the pipe of peace.

### MYTHOLOGICAL LEGENDS.

He-no was the Jupiter of the Iroquois, and Ga-oh reminds us of Æolus. Those who are familiar with these mythological personages of the Indian creation, make use of them as the classical student does of the gods of the ancients. When there is a furious storm they say, He-no is in a rage. When a violent tempest shakes the earth, they say, Ga-oh is in a frenzy. But among a great proportion of the reading community, these allusions would have no meaning. A thorough knowledge of Indian history, language and legends, would add a great store of pleasing images to the collections of the poet and novelist, that would be thoroughly American, and add new interest to American literature.

#### THE LEGEND OF HE-NO, THE THUNDERER.

A young maiden residing at Ga-u-gwa, a village above Niagara Falls, at the mouth of Cayuga creek, had been contracted in marriage to an old man of ugly manners and disagreeable person. As the marriage was hateful to her, and by the customs of the nations there was no escape, she resolved upon self destruction. Launching a bark canoe upon the Niagara, she directed it towards the current, and was soon swept over the frightful precipice amid the foaming waters. He-no the Thunderer had his home behind the sheet, and seeing her descend, he caught her in a blanket and carried her behind the fall. One of the servants of He-no being attracted by her beauty desired to marry her, to which she had no objection, and by the voice of the Thunderer they were united.

For many years before this the people of Ga-u-gwa had been visited by an annual pestilence, which destroyed great numbers and for which they could assign no cause. At the end of a year He-no revealed to the maiden the cause, and sent her back to tell the people the remedy. He said a monstrous serpent dwelt under the village, who depended upon the bodies of the dead for sustenance, and in order to obtain his annual supply he went forth once a year and poisoned the river Niagara, and Cayuga creek, so that all who drank of them perished.

The people were directed to move to Buffalo creek, and the young wife was charged to bring up the son of which she would soon become the mother, in retirement, and not mingle in the strifes of war. With those injunctions she departed on her mission.

When the great serpent again poisoned the waters the earth brought him no food, and putting forth his head to discover the cause, he saw the village deserted. He immediately scented the *trail* by which the people had departed, and followed them to their new home. But whilst passing through a narrow channel, He-no discharged upon him a mighty thunderbolt which inflicted a mortal wound. The Senecas still point to a place in the creek where the banks were shelved out in a semi-circular form, which was done by the serpent when he turned to escape.

His body floated down the stream and lodged upon the verge of the Cataract, stretching nearly across the river. The raging waters thus dammed up broke through the rocks behind, and thus the whole verge of the Fall, upon which the body rested, was precipitated with it into the abyss beneath. In this manner, says the legend, was formed the Horse Shoe Fall.

Before this event there was a passage behind the sheet, from one shore to the other. This was not only broken up, but the home of He-no destroyed, so that he removed his habitation to the far West.

The child of the maiden grew up to boyhood, and was found to possess the power of darting lightning at his will. On a certain occasion having been rudely assailed by a playmate, he was transfixed with a thunderbolt. He-no immediately translated him to the clouds and made him assistant Thunderer!

### GA-OH.

Ga-oh was the Spirit of the winds, and is represented in the form of a man, with a face furrowed by age, sitting in solitary confinement, with a tangle of discordant winds ever around him; when he is restless, the rushing noise of the mighty wind is heard, in the forest and upon the sea. On his motions depend the rolling of the billows, and the fury of the tempest. He puts the whirlwind in motion, and bids it again be still. When he is perfectly quiet there is silence over all the earth, and a gentle motion moves the soft fanning breeze. But Ga-oh is subject to the Great Spirit, and ever mindful of his will.

### THE SEVEN STARS.

Seven little boys asked their mothers to permit them

to make a feast; but they were denied. Still intent upon their purpose, they went alone and procured a little white dog to sacrifice, and while dancing around the fire, they were suddenly carried away through the air by some invisible spirit. Their mothers gazed after them with inconsolable anguish, till they saw them take their place in the sky among the starry hosts, where they are dancing still as the seven stars of the Pleiades.

The ancient mythology relates that these stars are the children of Atlas and Pleione, who were thus changed and permitted to shine for ever, because of their amiable virtues and mutual affection.

### THE THREE SISTERS.

Of all the spiritual creations of the Indian, there is none more beautiful than the one concerning the guardians which they imagine to preside over their favorite vegetables, corn, beans, and squashes  Each of these has a spirit, but a separate name is not given to each spirit. They have the forms of beautiful females, and are represented as loving one another as sisters, and dwelling together in perfect unity and happiness. The vines of these vegetables grow in the same soil, and often from the same hill, and cling lovingly around each other, and thus are true representatives of those who watch over them. The maidens are ever young, and are clothed with the leaves of the plants among which they dwell. She who is the guardian spirit of corn, has for her drapery the long tapering leaves of the maize, ornamented with its silken tassels, which also are bound in wreaths about her brow. She whose office it is to guard the bean, has her garments also of its leaves woven together by the delicate tendrils, with a crown of the velvet pods upon her head, interspersed with the blossom which precedes the fruit. The spirit of squashes is also clothed with the productions of the vine under her special care, and all the summer they flit about among the plants, and are called, De-o-ha-ho, Our Life, or Our Supporters.

Corn, the Indians say, was once of easy culture, and yielded far more abundantly than now, the grain being very rich with oil. But the Evil Spirit being envious of this great gift of Ha-wen-ne-yu to man, went forth into the fields and spread over it a universal blight. Since then it has been more difficult to cultivate, and is without its original richness.

When the rustling wind waves the corn leaves, producing a mournful sound, the pious Indian fancies he hears the spirit of corn, in her compassion for the red man, still bemoaning with unavailing regrets her blighted fruitfulness.

I have here given but a few of the innumerable legends which are to be found among the Iroquois, hoping at some future day to devote a volume entirely to this subject. It may not be so interesting, or so valuable a contribution to literature as "Keightley's Fairy Mythology," and it may be many years before such a work will be truly appreciated, even by the antiquarian and the scholar; but it may yet prove a *mite* in the vast treasure house of traditional lore, and will some day be considered not entirely unworthy a place beside the fairy castles of Merrie England, Scotia's sylvan temples, and the grottos of Italian nymphs.

# CHAPTER VII.

A CAPTIVE'S LIFE AMONG INDIANS, ILLUSTRATED BY THE LIFE OF "THE WHITE WOMAN."

To be taken captive by the Indians, was among the early colonists considered the most terrible of all calamities; and it was indeed a fearful thing to become the victim of their revenge. But those who were enduring the actual sufferings of captives, or suffering still more from terror of uncertain evils, thought little of the provocation given by our own people. The innocent often suffered for the guilty, and however persevering the efforts of the government to be just, in its infancy, in a wild unknown country, it was impossible to control unprincipled marauders. Some atrocious act was first committed by white men, which drove the Indian to retaliation, and thinking pale faces were all alike, he did not wait till the real offender fell into his hands.

When the white men first came, the Indians looked upon them as superior beings. They were ready to worship Columbus and his little party, and all along on the coast, until their simple trust was outraged beyond endurance they welcomed the strangers—gave them food when they were hungry, and sheltered them when they were cold. It was not till their encroachments became alarming, that the Indian asserted his rights, and if in all cases he had been as justly and kindly dealt with as by the Quakers of Pennsylvania, there would not have been so dark a record of sin and wrong, and torture. If none but men of principle had made treaties with them, and all whose duty it was to observe them, had kept their faith, revenge would not have come out so prominently in Indian-character.

But it was not in obedience to national policy that those who were taken in battle were put to the torture, and burned and flayed. The Six Nations had never found it necessary to build prisons and dig dungeons for their own people. If a man committed murder, they sometimes decided that he should die, and sometimes bade him flee far away where none who knew him could ever look upon his face. But crimes were so rare that they had no criminal code, and when they overcame their enemies, they either adopted them and treated them as friends, or put them immediately to death.

White people have sometimes put Indians to death, and oftener put them in dungeons to waste and starve, but it was no part of their practice to adopt them and call them brethren! Had they sometimes done this, or sent them freely back to their friends unharmed, they might have conciliated where they only made more desperate.

When families were bereaved, they sought to be revenged on those who had bereaved them; and when warriors returned from battle, the prisoners were given up to the friends who were afflicted. With them alone it remained to decide the fate of those who fell into their hands. If they chose, they adopted them in place of the husbands and brothers who were slain; and if they so decided, they were put to death, and in any way they decreed.

If the manner in which their friends had been killed was aggravating and greatly enraged them, they were very likely to decide upon torture, and inflicted it in a manner to produce the greatest suffering. But even in such cases they sometimes showed great magnanimity, and "returned good for evil."

Children were very often adopted, and by a solemn ceremony received into a particular tribe, and evermore treated as one of their own people. We have been in the habit of listening to heart-rending stories of cruelties to captives, but captives who were adopted were never cruelly treated. Those who were immediately put to death experienced great suffering for a few hours, and those who were preserved were subject to hardships which seemed to them unspeakable, but they were such as are necessarily incident to Indian life. They had no written chronicles to tell to all future generations the wrongs and tortures to which they were subjected, but one who sits with them by their firesides, may have his blood frozen with horror at recitals of civilized barbarity.

And there is one species of wrong, of which no captive woman of any nation had to complain when she was thrown upon the tender mercies of Indian warriors. Not among all the dark and terrible records which their enemies have delighted to emblazon, is there a single instance of the outrage of that delicacy which a pure-minded woman cherishes at the expense of life, and sacrifices not to any species of mere animal suffering. Of what other nation can it be written, that their soldiers were not more terrible at the firesides of their enemies than on the battle field, with all the fierce engines of war at their command? To whatever motive it is to be ascribed, let this at least stand out on the pages of Indian history as an ever enduring monument to their honor. A little book, which professes to have been written for the sole purpose of recording and perpetuating Indian atrocities, and dwells upon them with infinite delight, alludes to this redeeming trait in Indian character, but attempts to ascribe it to the influence of superstition, as if it were necessary to find some evil or deteriorating motive for every thing noble or pleasing in Indian character. I have no doubt that it was quite revolting to the general sentiment in an Indian community, to mingle their blood with that of a nation whom they looked up on as a race of evil spirits let loose, and I wonder that they should ever have received them, as they often did, into their families, and to their bosom friendships and confidences. But this hatred in other nations prompts to the very manifestation of which an Indian was never guilty. Their treatment of captives from among Indian nations was the same, and I know not that there has been any satisfactory solution of a characteristic which has been found among only one other civilized, Christian or barbarous nation. A wanderer among the western tribes once asked an Indian why they thus honored their women, and he said, "The Great Spirit taught them, and would punish them if they did not." Among the Germans there existed the same respect for woman, till they became civilized. There may have been some superstitious fear, mingled with a strong governing and controlling principle, but it is not on this account the less marvellous that whole nations, consisting of millions, should have been so trained religiously or domestically, that no degree of beauty or fascination placed under their care, though hundreds of miles in the solitudes of the wilderness, should have tempted them from the strictest honor and the most delicate kindness.

Mary Jewison was eighty years a resident among the Senecas, and in the early part of the time the forests had few clearings, and the comforts and the vices of white men prevailed but little among them. She was born on the ocean, with the billowy sea for her cradle and the tempest for her lullaby. Her parents emigrated from England to this country in 1742, and settled in the unfortunate vale of Wyoming, where date her first remembrances, which were of the woes that fell upon her family—the wail of the sorrow-stricken and the breaking of heart-strings.

The last meal they took together was a breakfast, after which the father and three eldest brothers went into the field, and Mary, with the other little children, were playing not far from the house. They were suddenly startled by a shriek, and knew it must be from their mother. On running in, they found her in the hands of two Indians, who were holding her fast. A little boy ran to call his father, and found him also bound by another of the party, and his eldest brother lying dead upon the earth. The two others fled to Virginia, where they had an uncle, as Mary afterwards learned, and those who remained were made captive and hurried into the woods.

All day they were obliged to march in single file over the rough, cold soil, with no time or permission for conversation, and the lash often applied to quicken their steps. Night found them in the heart of the wilderness, surrounded by their strange captors, and all the horrors of Indian life or Indian death staring them in the face. They had no hope of mercy, whether permitted to live or condemned to die.

The mother thought they would perhaps spare the children, but did not on this account take courage, for it seemed to her better that they should die, than live to become the companions of such a people, and grow up very probably to be like them. Mary was the only one old enough to understand her injunctions, and to her she was allowed to speak before they were separated for the night, and, as she feared, for ever.

She said, "My daughter, you, I think, will be permitted to live; but they will deprive you of your father and mother, and perhaps of your brothers and sisters, so that you will be alone. But endeavor in all things to please the Indians, and they will be more kind to you. Do not forget your own language, and never fail to repeat your catechism and the Lord's prayer every morning and evening while you live." This she promised to do, and having kissed her child, the mother was removed from her sight, and never more saw one of all the little party who were happy in the little cottage together only a few hours before.

Mary was not permitted to ask concerning her friends, and only knew their fate by recognizing their scalps as they were prepared to dry. Her mother's she knew by the long sandy hair, which was neatly combed and braided. Her little brother had soft flaxen curls, which still retained their sunny hue, and hung in glossy waves over the edges of the hoop on which the skin was stretched. She could not restrain the tears, but dared utter no moan that she had been thus cruelly severed from all she loved.

She must at this time have been ten years of age ; but it was less sad for her than if she had been older, for now she could easily assimilate her tastes to those of her new friends, and would naturally soon forget her home and the customs of her people.

She was afterwards told, when she could understand the Indian language, that they should not have killed her parents if the captors had not been pursued, and that a little boy, who was the son of a neighbor, and was also taken, was given to the French, two of whom were of the party.

In the marches of the Indians it was the custom for one to linger behind and *poke up* the grass with a stick, after a party had passed along, to conceal all traces of their foot-steps, so that a pursuit was seldom successful. In deviating from a direct course, in order not to get lost, they noticed the moss upon the trees, which always grew thickest upon the north side, as the south side, being most exposed to the sun, became soonest dry. They also had some knowledge of the stars, and knew from the positions of certain clusters, that were to be seen at certain seasons, which was east and which west.

Mary was carried far down the Ohio, and found her captors to be a party of Shawanese, and by them she was adopted in place of two brothers, who had fallen in battle, and for whom the lamentations had not yet died away.

The ceremony of adoption is very solemn, requiring the deliberations of a council and the formal bestowing of a name, as a sort of baptism, from which time the captive is not allowed to speak any language but the Indian, and must in all things conform to Indian habits and tastes.

It is the custom among them to give children a name which corresponds with the sports and dependence of childhood, and when they arrive at maturity, to change it for one that corresponds with the duties and employments of manhood and womanhood. The first name is given by the relatives, and afterwards publicly announced in council. The second is bestowed in the same way, and by this they are ever afterwards called, except on becoming a Sachem, and sometimes on becoming a chief or warrior, another is taken, and each denotes definitely the new position. Each clan, too, had its peculiar names, so that when a person's name was mentioned it was immediately known to what clan he belonged.

A curious feature in the Indian code of etiquette is, that it is exceedingly impolite to ask a person his name, or to speak it in his presence. In the social circle and all private conversation, the person spoken of is described, if it is necessary to allude to him, as the person who sits there, or who lives in that house, or wears such a dress. If I ask a woman, whose husband is present, if that is Mr. P——, she blushes, and stammers, and replies, "It is my child's father," in order to avoid speaking his name in his presence, which would offend him. On asking a man his name he remained silent; not understanding the reason, the question was repeated, when he indignantly replied, "Do you think that I am an owl, to go about *hooting* my name every where?" the name of the owl in Seneca, corresponding exactly to the note he continually utters.

When Mary Jewison had been formally named *De-he-wa-mis*, they called her daughter and sister, and treated her in all respects as if she had been born among them and the same blood flowed in her veins; or rather they were accustomed to be more kind to captives than to their own children, because they had not been inured to the same hardships. There was no difference in the caresses bestowed, no allusion was made to the child as if it belonged to a hated race, and it never felt the want of affection.

Mary said her tasks were always light, and every thing was done to win her love and make her happy. She now and then longed for the comforts of her cottage home, and wept at the thought of her mother's cruel death, but gradually learned to love the freedom of the forest, and to gambol freely and gayly with her Indian playmates. When she was named they threw her dress away, and clothed her in deer-skins and moccasins, and painted her face in true Indian style. She never spoke English in their presence, as they did not allow it; but, when alone, did not forget her mother's injunction, and repeated her prayer and all the words she could remember, thus retaining enough of the language to enable her easily to recall it when she should again return to civilized society, as she constantly indulged the hope of doing by an exchange of captives.

But when she was fourteen years of age her mother selected for her a husband, to whom she was married according to Indian custom. His name was She-nin-jee, and though she was not acquainted with him previously, and of course had no affection for him, he proved not only an amiable and excellent man, but a congenial companion, whom she loved devotedly. He had all the noble qualities of the Indian, being handsome, and brave, and generous, and kind, and to her ever gentle and affectionate.

Now she became thoroughly reconciled to Indian life, her greatest sorrow being the necessary absences of her husband on the war-path and hunting excursions. She followed the occupations of the women, and tilled the fields, dressed the skins, and gathered the fuel for the winter fires; and though this seems to us unfeminine labor, it was performed at their leisure, and occupied very little of their time.

When the hunters returned they were weary and passive, and seldom were guilty of fault-finding, and so well did an Indian woman know her duty, that her husband was not obliged to make known his wants. Obedience was required in all respects, and where there was harmony and affection, cheerfully yielded; and knowing as they did that separation would be the consequence of neglect of duty, and unkindness, there was really more self-control, and care about little things, than among those who are bound for life, weal and woe, love and hatred, kindness and cruelty. They did not agree to live together through good and through evil report, but only while they loved and confided in one another; and they were therefore careful not to throw lightly away this confidence and affection.

The labor of the field was performed in so systematic a manner, and by so thorough and wise a division of labor, that there were none of the jealousies and envyings which exist among those who wish to hoard, and are ambitious to excel in style and equipage; and before the fire water came among them dissensions of any kind were almost unknown. This has been the fruitful source of all their woes.

It was not till Mary became a mother that she gave up all longing for civilized society, and relinquished all hope of again returning to the abodes of white men. Now she had a tie to bind her which could not be broken. If she should find her friends they would not recognize her Indian husband, or consider her lawfully married; they would not care to be connected by ties of blood to a people whom they despised. Her child would not be happy among those who looked upon her as inferior, and she herself had no education to fit her for the companionship of white people. She looked upon her little daughter and said, "It is Sheninjee's, it is dearer to me then all things else. I could not endure to see her treated with aversion or neglect."

But only a little while was she permitted this happiness—her daughter died, while yet an infant, and when Sheninjee was away. Again the feeling of desolation came over her young spirit, but all around her ministered in every way to her comfort, and became more than ever endeared to her heart. After a long absence Sheninjee returned, and she was again happy for many months. She had a son and named him from her father, to which no objection was made by her Indian friends, and her love for her husband became idolatry. In her eyes he seemed every thing noble and good,—she mourned his departure and longed for his return, for his affection prompted him to treat her with the gentle and winning kindness which is the spirit of true love alone.

But again came the separation, and she must pass another long winter alone. Hunting was the Indian's toil, and though they delighted in it, the pang of parting from his wife and little ones, made it a sacrifice, and spread a dark cloud over a long period of his life. And now it became dark indeed to Mary, for she waited long and Sheninjee came not. She put every thing in order in his little dwelling—she dressed new skins for his couch, and smoked venison to please his taste; she made the fire bright to welcome him, hoping every evening when she lay down with her baby upon her bosom, that ere the morning sun the husband and father would gladden them by his smile, but in vain; winter passed away, and the spring, and then came the sad tidings that he was dead. She was a widow and her child was fatherless. Very long and deeply did she mourn Sheninjee, for it seemed to her there was none like him; but again the sympathies of his people created new links to bind her to them, and she said she could not have loved a mother or sister more dearly then she did those she stood in this relationship to her, and soothed her by their loving words.

Not for four years was she again urged to marry, and during this time there was an exchange of prisoners, and she had an opportunity to return to her kindred. She was left to do as she pleased. They told her she might go; but if she preferred to remain, she should still be their daughter and sister, and they would give her land for her own, where she might always dwell. Again she thought of the prejudice she should every where meet, and that she could never patiently listen to reproaches concerning her husband's people. It would not be believed that he was noble, because he was an Indian,—she should have no near relatives, and those she had might reject her if she should seek them. So she came to the final conclusion, and never more sighed for the advantages or pleasures of civilized life. She came with the brothers of Sheninjee to the banks of the Genesee, where she resided the remaining seventy-two years of her life.

Her second husband, Hiokatoo, she never learned to love. He was a chief and a warrior, brave and fearless, but though he was always kind to her, he was a man of blood. He delighted in deeds of cruelty and delighted to relate them, and now the fire-water had become common, and the good were made bad and the bad worse, so that dissensions arose in families and in neighborhoods, and the happiness which had been almost without alloy, was no longer known among these simple people.

She adds her testimony to that of all travellers and historians concerning the purity of their lives, having never herself received the slightest insult from an Indian, and scarcely knowing an instance of infidelity or immorality. But when they had once tasted of the maddening draught, the thirst was insatiable, and all they had would be given for a glass of something to destroy their reason. Now they were indeed converted into fiends and furies, and sold themselves to swift destruction. Hiokatoo hesitated at no crime, and took pleasure in every thing that was dark and terrible, but this was a small trial compared to those which Mrs. Jewison was called upon to endure from the intoxication and recklessness of her sons.

Her oldest, the son of Sheninjee, was murdered by John, the son of Hiokatoo, who afterwards murdered his own brother Jessee, and came to the same violent death himself by the hands of others. When they came to be in the midst of temptation there was no restraining principle, and even after they grew up, her house was the scene of quarrels and confusion in consequence of their intemperance, and she knew no rest, from fear of some calamity from the indulgence of their unbridled passions.

The chiefs of the Seneca nation, to which her second husband belonged, gave her a large tract of land, and when it became necessary that it should be secured to her by treaty, she attended the council and plead her own case. The commissioners, without inquiring particularly concerning the dimensions of her *lots*, allowed her to make the boundaries, and when the document was signed, and she was in firm possession, it was found that she was the owner of nearly four thousand acres, of which only a deed in her own handwriting could deprive her. But though she was rich, she toiled not the less diligently, and forsook not the *sphere of woman* in attending to the ways of her household; and also true to her Indian education, she planted, and hoed, and harvested, retaining her Indian dress and habits, till the day of her death.

During the revolutionary war, her house was made the rendezvous and head-quarters of British officers and Indian chiefs, as her sympathies were entirely with her red brethren, and the cause they espoused was the one she preferred to aid. It was in her power to sympathize with many a lone captive; she always remembered her own anguish at the prospect of spending her life in the wilderness, the companion of Indians, and though she had learned to love instead of fearing them, and knew they were, as a people, deserving of respect and the highest honor, she understood the feelings of those who knew them not.

Her supplications procured the release of many from

torture, and her generous kindness clothed the naked and fed the starving.

Lot by lot, and acre by acre, the Indians sold their lands, and at length the beautiful valley of the Genesee fell into the hands of the white man, except the domain of "The White Woman," as she was always called, which could not be given up without her consent. She refused at the time of the sale to part with her portion, but after the Indians removed to the Buffalo Reservation, and she was left alone, though lady of the manor, and surrounded by white people, she preferred to take up her abode with those whom she now called her people. Most emphatically did she adopt the language of Ruth in the days of old—"Entreat me not to leave thee, or return from following after thee, for whither thou goest I will go, and where thou lodgest I will lodge; thy people shall be my people, and thy God my God. Where thou diest, I will die, and there will I be buried."

She was as thoroughly Pagan as the veriest Indian who had never heard of God, and exclaimed with him, that their religion was good enough for her, and she desired no change.

She was ninety years old—eighty years she had been an exile from the land of her birth—she had forgotten the prayers her mother taught her, and knew nothing of the worship of her fathers, when one morning she sent a messenger to tell the missionaries she wished to see them. She had ever before refused to listen to them if they came to her dwelling, but they hastened to obey the summons, glad to feel that they should be welcome, though quite uncertain concerning the nature of the interview she proposed. She was literally withered away. Her face was scarcely larger than an infant's, and completely checkered with fine wrinkles; her teeth were entirely gone, and her mouth so sunken that her nose and chin almost met; her hair not silvery, but snowy white, except a little lock by each ear, which still retained the sandy hue of childhood; her form, which was always slight, was bent, and her limbs could no longer support her. She had revived the knowledge of her language since she had dwelt among white people, but " Oh," said she, as the ladies entered, " I have forgotten how to pray; my mother taught me, and told me never to forget this, though I remembered nothing else." And then she exclaimed, " Oh God, have mercy upon me!" This expression she had heard in her old age, and now uttered it in the fulness of her heart. There had come a gleam of light through all the dark clouds of superstition and Pagan blindness, and this spark was kindled at the fireside of that little cottage home, and fell upon her heart from a mother's lips, and now revived at the remembrance of a mother's love and her dying blessing. It was eighty years since she had seen that mother's face, as she breathed out her soul in anguish, bending over her in the silent depths of the wilderness— eighty years since she listened to " Our Father who art in Heaven," from Christian lips, and now the still small voice which had so long been hushed, spoke aloud, and startled her as if an angel called. She tried to stifle it, and for many days after it awoke in her bosom heeded it not, but it gave her no rest. No earthly voice had since reminded her that her heart was sinful, and needed to be washed in order to be clean. The seed which had been sown in it when she was a little child had just sprung up— the snows of eighty winters had not chilled it—the mildews of nearly a century had not blighted it, and the heavy hand of a hundred calamities had left it unharmed. She had not been in the midst of corruptions, therefore it had not been destroyed. The little germ was still alive, and proving that it had not been planted in vain.

The aged woman sat pillowed up in bed with her children and children's children of three generations around her, and lifting her withered hands and sunken eyes to heaven, once more repeated, "Our Father, who art in heaven," while a new light, like a halo, overspread her face, tears flowed in floods down her cheeks, and in the dark eye of every listener there glistened the tear of sympathy in her new-found happiness.

For many years she remembered her mother's injunction, and repeated the words of the prayer and the catechism; but as she became more thoroughly familiar with the language, and could join in the thanksgivings of her new people, she ceased to care for the faith of her fathers. Yet it was the connecting link between her and those who were called Christians, and the sole means of enabling her to revive and easily acquire the knowledge of her native tongue. Without this the missionaries could not have communicated with her, as they had not then learned the Seneca, and those around her who understood both, cared very little, and knew scarcely more than she, of the Redeemer of whom she wished to hear.

When asked if she regretted that she had not consented to be exchanged, and returned to her mother's friends, she still said, no. She loved the Indians—she loved them better than white people. They had been kind to her, and provided generously for her youth and her old age, and her children would inherit an abundance from the avails of the lands and herds and flocks which were her sole possessions. Alas! she did not know that the money she had deposited in the hands of the agent to be invested for the benefit of her family, was wickedly squandered by him, so that not a single cent ever reached their hands.* She was rich, but they were miserably poor, and he who thus defrauded her was of the same blood, and hesitated not to take advantage of her because she had grown up among an unsuspicious people, who knew not how to redress their wrongs. Her adopted brethren had honored her above the women of their own nations—she had received good, and not evil, all the days of her life; she belonged to a race they had every reason to hate—a race who had trampled them as their legend said the mammoth buffaloes trampled the forests in their march, and yet they had respected her, and loved her, and honored her. And hers was not the only instance of such kindness; it is not she alone who bears testimony to their virtues, to their magnanimity, their truly Christian spirit of forgiveness, their purity, their meekness, their long-suffering, and their brotherly love, ere they were wronged and contaminated by the vices of their enemies.

A few days after the new light dawned upon her spirit, in the year 1833, Mrs. Jewison was numbered with the dead. She had embraced the faith which makes no difference between those who come at the first and the eleventh hour; and those who were present at the dissolution of soul and body, doubted not Jesus had whispered to her the same consolation that fell upon the heart of the thief upon the cross, "This day shalt thou be with me in Paradise."

She was buried in the mission burial-ground, near Buffalo, where the dead are a strange concourse; for it seems once to have been the site of an ancient fort, and afterwards to have become the repository of the dust of

---

* This has since been refunded by the Government.

people of many nations, and is to the historian, the Christian, and the traveller, an interesting spot.

Not many years ago, the family of the mission were awakened from their midnight slumbers by the piteous cry of an infant. It was November, and the plaintive moan of the little one, mingled with the wailing of the night wind when all else was still, came with startling sadness to their ears. At first, they thought some lone mother, in her desolation, had come to them for relief, and hastened to open the door to the houseless wanderer. But when they looked out into the darkness, they could see nothing; still the little voice came up, though it grew fainter, as if its strength was failing. Again they searched, and found upon the door-step a tiny band-box, in which was snugly curled a baby—a little baby! All around was dark; there was no mother, no friend; the little thing was there alone—alone, unconscious of its loneliness.

A little opening had been made in the top of the box, through which they peeped, and saw a tiny hand move, and then the blue eyes opened to the light; but when they brought it to the fire it was stupefied by the effects of cold and some drug it had taken to keep it quiet, and scarcely showed signs of life for a day. Then it awoke, and on its face there rested a smile that seemed a beam from heaven. Never more was it alone. Hearts had become linked to its little heart, and all the household looked upon it as a treasure and not a burden. Its coarse blanket and faded frock, proved that it had not been cast out from the dwellings of the rich, and the few words which were written on a torn and soiled bit of paper, in a fair hand, proved that its mother was not ignorant, though poverty-stricken.

"Farewell my little baby! Thy mother must desert thee, but may God take care of thee and find thee friends!"

Then it was blistered with tears, and placed among the folds of the blanket.

Why did the mother thus desert her child? Must its innocent name be stained by some dark sin; or was it wretched poverty alone that drove her to such a sacrifice? There had evidently been sundered a heart-string, and the bosom on which it was born to rest was neither cold nor hard. Yet it was a cast-away.

That night a wagon was seen slowly winding its way toward the mission-house, and from a neighboring window observed to stop in front of the path that led to the door. At the same time a child, evidently very young, was heard distinctly to cry for a few moments, and then ceased, and the wagon moved on toward the great city. This is all its new-found friends ever learned concerning it. But it became a very sunbeam in their dwelling, and was beautiful as a cherub. Its ruby lips never failed to curl with that same sunny smile, whenever the tones of a pleasant voice fell on its ear, and its gleeful playfulness awoke in every heart an echo. But it was one of those bright leaves which decay and dazzle and then depart.

Those upon whose hands it was thrown, helpless and dependent, thought, how could they keep and nourish it? They too, were poor, and it would be a burden.

In less than a year, the bright flower faded and died. Twined around it was every heart-string, and it had found a nestling place in every bosom, when it grew cold, and shut its eyes on them for ever. They must wrap it in a shroud, and give it back to earth.

To show their love, they made its grave beneath a spreading walnut, where the green mound would be sheltered from the burning sun, and the footsteps of love might linger, and the heart-broken water it with their tears.

The sod was removed and the dark earth thrown up, and soon they came to the crumbling bones of a man. It was probably a warrior's grave. But they laid the little strange baby upon his breast, and covered them, to be again disturbed perhaps in some far-off century, by another people and ruder hands.

Near by is another little one, whose grandfather was taken captive nearly a century before on the banks of the Juniata; whose mother and grandmother were Indian women, and who was given when an infant to the mission family to be their own. It was a little girl, whom they named Louisa Maria, and who, though she died in early childhood, lived long enough to become a bud of promise, yes, a blossom of Christian love, and hope, and faith, a lamb of Christ's flock. She belonged to the class of those who always die in infancy, "whose names are all on gravestones." They are perfected without the discipline of earth's trials, and transplanted to bloom as spring flowers in the gardens above. Life would be a dreary pathway without the little ones, and there would be discord in the heavenly choir without the soft melody of infant voices. A little while before she died, lying still upon the bed, there came a sweet smile upon her face, and she said, " I see them, ma, angels, angels all round me, come to carry me away!" and then she kissed each friend as if she were bidding them good-by, to return again, and immediately soared away where angel-children dwell.

In the same inclosure, under the same spreading tree, was buried a little Indian boy, whose mother had been long a member of the mission church.

It was a cold day in January when he came in a little sad from his play, and said, " Mother, I do not feel well; will you take care of me?"

His mother was busy and did not answer, and soon he said again, "Will you put your hand upon my head, mother; it aches? I think I shall be sick and die; but I shall go to heaven, where God lives, and be happy."

He had never before talked of death, and it was not known that he had ever particularly thought of it. But now he often said, "I am going to Jesus, you must give *up me*, mother. I am not afraid, I am happy." A quick consumption soon wasted his form and destroyed the bloom upon his rosy cheek, but he thought only of the bright world to which he was going.

Their home was a rude Indian cabin, but the mother was a refined Christian woman. She knew not how to read, but she had learned the language of prayer. Her heart, too, was swelling with a mother's love. She knew not how to give him up. A few moments before he died, in great distress he said, "Now mother, pray." She knelt alone beside him, and in her own rich language poured out her heart to God. When she had finished he said, "Some one has come in—how pleasant he looks." No one had entered, but still he gazed as if looking upon some beautiful object, then slowly drooped the lid over the brightly-kindled eye, and he was gone.

In the gateway of this entrance to the city of the dead was buried a distinguished pagan chief, and all around sleeps the dust of Indian warriors and chiefs, sad relics of those who fell in bloody battles long before the red man has any tradition concerning the spot. Here, too, are many captives, borne from Christian firesides in childhood, to become the brethren of the children of the wilderness, and be laid to rest away from their kindred in a strange land, and here are old men and aged women who, at the eleventh hour, came up to labor in the vineyard of the Lord.

An old lady used to come tottering to meeting when it seemed impossible her feeble limbs could support her. When surprise was expressed that she should come when the weather was cold, and she had so far to walk, she said with great earnestness, "Oh! I shall always come as long as I can get here, and when my poor body is too feeble to attempt it longer, *I shall bow my head this way as often as the season of prayer returns.*"

Her dust is now mingling with the strange group in this strange place, and yet it is still but a few years since the messengers of a better faith came among them. The fruits have been rich and abundant, among those who belonged to the generation already passed away, and among those who are still living useful and honored in the Church and the community, rejoicing the hearts of those who have diligently and faithfully labored, as stewards of Him who is Lord of the vineyard, and who sent them forth.

May they live to see the wilderness become a fruitful field, and the desert a garden under their fostering care, and richly will they be rewarded when they too shall cross over Jordan.

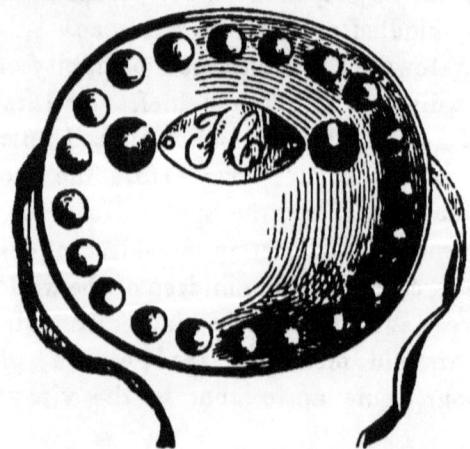

# CHAPTER VIII.

ELOQUENCE AMONG THE IROQUOIS — RED JACKET, OR SA-GO-YE-WAT-HA.

BRAVERY and every warlike trait, characterized all the Indian races, but oratory was heard only among the Iroquois; and the Forum in the palmy days of Rome, the Parliament-house of England, or the Senate-chamber at Washington, never echoed more thrilling strains than the sylvan temple in which were assembled the red children of the wilderness, to listen to the eloquence of their most distinguished Chief, Sa-go-ye-wat-ha,—or as his people were accustomed to call him, the " Young Prince of the Wolf Clan,"—in the days when trials and bitter wrongs stirred the deepest and the loftiest emotions in the bosom of the untutored Indian.

The name which Red Jacket received in his infancy was O-te-tiana, and signified ALWAYS READY. According to the custom of his people, when he became chief he took another, Sa-go-ye-wat-ha, which means HE KEEPS THEM AWAKE. The insignificant one which he always bore after his acquaintance with white people, was given him on account of the red jacket in which he was always seen, and which was presented him by a British officer as a reward for some special service. It was richly embroidered, and he took great pride in wearing it. When one was worn out, another was presented him, so that it became a mark to distinguish him, and acquired him the name.

RED JACKET.

As the government and whole construction of the Iroquois confederacy was a pure democracy, few were born to titles. All honors must be earned. Sometimes families gained a kind of distinction by their wisdom in council, or their bravery in war, as did that of Brandt, the great Mohawk chief; but Red Jacket had an humble origin, even in the estimation of his own people.

His birth-place was Canoga, west of Cayuga Lake, in 1750. It has been the universal testimony of books that he was a coward; and this inference has been drawn very naturally, perhaps, from the fact that he opposed war, and seldom wielded the tomahawk. But the old men of his nation who knew him, and the motives from which he acted, deny the charge. The Mohawk Chieftain held him in great contempt, and was in the habit of repeating various anecdotes to bring his courage into disgrace among his people. Among the old men now living who knew him, there are many who assert that he was brave, and not at all lacking in the qualities they admire in the warrior. They assign other reasons for his persevering opposition to war, and maintain that his superior sagacity led him to see the consequences of war to the Indian. In the Revolutionary contest, the red men enlisted on the side of the British, believing it to be for their interest. They could not understand any thing of the real nature of the controversy between the two rival powers, and were justifiable in studying their own interest alone. When the war was over, they saw themselves deprived of their territory, and obliged still to flee before their pursuers. The Mohawks removed to Canada, and the remnants of the other nations fell back to Western New York. Red Jacket saw that the Indians were only used as instruments for promoting the interest of the white men. Why should they be torn asunder and scattered to the four winds, in order to fight the battles of their enemies? Their warriors fought and bled, but what was their reward? To be driven from the land they defended. Let them alone, said the wise man and the orator. Let us remain upon our lands and take care of ourselves. So they called him coward; but when his prophecies had been fulfilled, they saw the wisdom of his decrees. He saw the end from the beginning, but with all his eloquence he could not stay the tide which was swallowing them up. He was a Cayuga on his father's side, and the Cayugas claim to have been a thoughtful and far-seeing people. His eloquence has never been disputed; and that he was an ORATOR, was his own peculiar pride and boast.

Cicero was accused of cowardice, and Cæsar was certainly timid, and both were charged with treachery; but their voices have echoed through the world. Red Jacket has been placed side by side with them on this platform, and had he spoken a language which the learned could understand and correctly translate, his fame might have equalled theirs.

It is asserted by others that an orator must necessarily be a coward. His is a moral courage alone; and the enthusiasm, emotion, and fine feeling which are necessary to the orator, make physical courage and strong nerves impossible. It is not necessary to ascribe every species of greatness to one man, and Red Jacket had plenty of gifts without those which constitute the warrior.

Of his childhood we, of course, know nothing; and like many another, he owed his celebrity to the troublous times in which he lived. The powers of the orator can only be exhibited on occasions of great interest; and the mighty intellect of Red Jacket could not have exercised itself upon theology, or law, or philosophy, for the Indian was a stranger to all these things.

One of the first forensic efforts of the young Chief was in behalf of the women of his people, who, as I have said, were permitted to exert their influence in all public and important matters. In the year 1791, when Washington wished to secure the neutrality of the Six Nations, a deputation was sent to treat with them, but was not favorably received, as many of the young Chiefs were for war and sided with the British. The women, as is usual, preferred peace, and argued that the land was theirs, for they cultivated and took care of it, and, therefore, had a right to speak concerning the use that should be made of its products. They demanded to be heard on this occasion, and addressed the deputation first themselves in the following words: "Brother:—The Great Ruler has spared us until a new day to talk together; for since you came here from General Washington, you and our uncles the Sachems have been counselling together. Moreover, your sisters, the women, have taken the same into great consideration, because you and our Sachems have said so much about it. Now, that is the reason we have come to say something to you, and to tell you that the Great Ruler hath preserved you, and that you ought to hear and listen to what we, women, shall speak, as well as the Sachems; *for we are the owners of this land*, AND IT IS OURS! It is we that plant it for our and their use. Hear us, therefore, for we speak things that concern us and our children; and you must not think hard of us while our men shall say more to you, for we have told them."

They then designated Red Jacket as their speaker, and he took up the speech of his clients as follows:

"BROTHERS FROM PENNSYLVANIA:—You that are sent from General Washington, and by the thirteen fires; you have been sitting side by side with us every day, and the

Great Ruler has appointed us another pleasant day to meet again.

"Now listen, Brothers:—You know it has been the request of our head warriors, that we are left to answer for our women, who are to conclude what ought to be done by both Sachems and warriors. So hear what is their conclusion. The business you come on is very troublesome, and we have been a long time considering it; and now the elders of our women have said that our Sachems and warriors must help you, for the good of them and their children, and you tell us the Americans are strong for peace.

"Now, all that has been done for you, has been done by our women; the rest will be a hard task for us; for the people at the setting sun are bad people, and you have come in too much haste for such great matters of importance. AND NOW, BROTHERS, you must look when it is light in the morning, until the setting sun, and you must reach your neck over the land to take in all the light you can to show the danger. And these are the words of our women to you, and the Sachems and warriors who shall go with you.

"Now, Brother from Pennsylvania and from General Washington, I have told you all I was directed. Make your minds easy, and let us throw all care on the mercy of the Great Keeper, in hopes that he will assist us."

So there was peace instead of war, as there would often be if the voice of woman could be heard! and though the Senecas, in revising their laws and customs, have in a measure acceded to the civilized barbarism of treating the opinions of women with contempt, where their interest is equal, they still cannot sign a treaty without the consent of *two thirds of the mothers!*

On another occasion the women sent a message, which

Red Jacket delivered for them, saying that they fully concurred in the opinion of their Sachems, that the white people had been the cause of all the Indians' distresses. The white people had pressed and squeezed them together, until it gave them great pain at their hearts. One of the white women had told the Indians to repent; and they now, in turn, called on the white people to repent—they having as much need of repentance as the Indians. They, therefore, hoped the pale-faces would repent and wrong the Indians no more.

At the termination of hostilities between the United States and Great Britain, the Indians, who were the allies of the English, were left to take care of themselves as best they could. Though they had fought desperately in their own way, and inflicted every species of suffering upon our people, Washington extended to them the hand of friendship and offered them protection. His kindness won him the gratitude of the Indian, and procured for him a boon they have bestowed upon no other white man, except William Penn. He is permitted to enter paradise, though not within the sacred inclosure where the red man dwells. Near the entrance to Heaven is fitted up a beautiful garden, where bloom the most beautiful flowers, and the grandest trees of the forest wave their boughs. In this glorious Eden, Washington is the only inhabitant, and walks to and fro in the flowery paths, dressed in his soldier's uniform, and perfectly happy, though no word ever passes his lips. The Indian, on his way to his own Heaven, is permitted to look upon the man whom the Great Spirit has thus honored, but no sign of recognition is made, as nothing must disturb his meditations, or mar the perfect felicity which he is to enjoy through eternity in his celestial residence.

Though we hope he has gone to a happier and more

delightful abode than this, the Indian has conferred upon him the greatest honor it was in his imagination to conceive, and the highest proof of his confidence in his goodness and belief in his benevolence; and it is gratifying to us to record this of our beloved Washington, among all the wrongs which this simple people have to relate concerning those in whose power it was to awaken similar emotions, and who preferred to fill them with indignation and revenge.

Red Jacket was one of fifty Chiefs who went to confer with Washington at the seat of government, where they were treated with great attention, and professed to be satisfied with the provisions made for their people, and to be convinced that peace and civilization were now their only hope.

When they were about to leave, Washington presented Red Jacket with a large silver medal, bearing his own likeness, which he wore till his death, and of which he was very proud. During this visit, General Knox presented each of the Chiefs with a military suit of clothes, with a cocked hat as worn by the officers. When Red Jacket's suit was offered him, he said, as he was not a war Chief he could not consistently wear such a dress, and requested that a different suit might be given him, more suitable to his station. But when the plain dress was brought, he declined giving up the regimentals, coolly remarking, that though as a Sachem he could not wear a military uniform in time of peace, yet in time of war the Sachems joined the warriors, and he would, therefore, keep it till war broke out, when he could assume a military dress with propriety.

Once on being invited, with several of his people, to dine at the house of an officer, he ate very voraciously of many kinds of meat; and seeing the surprise of the host, he remarked that he belonged to the Wolf Clan, and "wolves were always fond of meat."

"I am an orator; I was born an orator," was all the boast Red Jacket could make with the certainty of being at that time appreciated; and to all future generations his name will descend, enrolled on the list with Demosthenes and Cicero in ancient, and Pitt and Randolph and Webster in modern times; and though a Pagan, and belonging to a rude, uncultivated race, his vices were no greater than those of men who lived all their lives under Christian influences, and professed to be believers in the pure gospel of the Redeemer, and to govern their lives by His holy will and example.

He strenuously opposed every effort to introduce Christianity among his people, for he could not understand how it could be so valuable or necessary, when he saw how little it influenced the conduct of white men, and the wrongs they inflicted in the name of their God upon the red man. He could not make the distinction between those who possessed religion and those who professed it; and as he came in contact with very few who walked uprightly, he naturally concluded that a religion which did no more for its followers was not worth adopting. He believed that the Great Spirit had formed the red and white man distinct; that they could no more be of one creed than one color; and when the wars were over and there was nothing more for them to do, he wished to be separated entirely from white men, and return as much as possible to their old customs.

He saw his people wasting away before the pale-faces, as he once said in a speech before a great assemblage:

"We stand a small island in the bosom of the great waters. We are encircled,—we are encompassed. The Evil Spirit rides upon the blast, and the waters are dis turbed. They rise, they press upon us, and the waves once settled over us, we disappear for ever. Who, then, lives to mourn us? None! What marks our extermination? Nothing! We are mingled with the common elements."

If historians have rightly judged, the first missionaries sent among the Senecas were not very judicious, and did not take the wisest course to make their religion acceptable to any people, and especially to a wronged and outraged race.

In 1805, a young missionary was sent into the country of the Six Nations, by the name of Cram. A council was called to consider whether to receive him, and after he had made an introductory speech, Red Jacket made the following reply:

"FRIEND AND BROTHER:—It was the will of the Great Spirit that we should meet together this day. He orders all things, and has given us a fine day for our council. He has taken his garment from before the sun, and caused it to shine with brightness upon us. For all these things we thank the Great Ruler, and HIM *only!*

"BROTHER:—This council-fire was kindled by you. It was at your request that we came together at this time. We have listened with joy to what you have said. You requested us to speak our minds freely. This gives us great joy, for we now consider that we stand upright before you and can speak what we think. All have heard your voice, and can speak to you as one man. Our minds are agreed.

"BROTHER:—Listen to what we say. There was a time when our forefathers owned this great island. Their seats extended from the rising to the setting sun. The Great Spirit had made it for the use of Indians. He had created the buffalo, the deer, and other animals for food. He had made the bear and the beaver. Their skins served us for clothing. He had scattered them over the country, and taught us how to take them. He had caused the earth to produce corn for bread. All this He had done for His red children, because He loved them. If we had some disputes about our hunting-ground, they were generally settled without the shedding of much blood. But an evil day came upon us. Your forefathers crossed the great water, and landed upon this island. Their numbers were small. They found friends, and not enemies. They told us they had fled from their own country on account of wicked men, and had come here to enjoy their religion. They asked for a small seat. We took pity on them, granted their request, and they sat down amongst us. We gave them corn and meat; they gave us poison (rum) in return.

"The white people, BROTHER, had now found our country. Tidings were carried back, and more came amongst us. Yet we did not fear them. We took them to be friends. They called us brothers; we believed them, and gave them a larger seat. At length their numbers had greatly increased. They wanted more land; they wanted our country. Our eyes were opened, and our minds became uneasy. Wars took place. Indians were hired to fight against Indians, and many of our people were destroyed. They also brought strong liquor amongst us. It was strong and powerful, and has slain thousands.

"BROTHER:—Our seats were once large, and yours were small. You have now become a great people, and we have scarcely a place left to spread our blankets. You have got our country, but are not satisfied; you want to force your religion upon us.

"BROTHER:—Continue to listen. You say that you

are sent to instruct us how to worship the Great Spirit agreeably to his mind; and if we do not take hold of the religion which you white people teach, we shall be unhappy hereafter. You say that you are right, and we are lost. How do we know this to be true? We understand that your religion is written in a book. If it was intended for us as well as you, why has not the Great Spirit given to us—and not only to us, but to our forefathers—the knowledge of that book, with the means of understanding it rightly? We only know what you tell us about it. How shall we know when to believe, being so often deceived by the white people?

"BROTHER:—You say there is but one way to worship and serve the Great Spirit. If there is but one religion, why do you white people differ so much about it? Why not all agree, as you can all read the book?

"BROTHER:—We do not understand these things. We are told that your religion was given to your forefathers, and has been handed down from father to son. We, also, have a religion which was given to our forefathers, and has been handed down to us, their children. We worship in that way. It teaches us to be thankful for all the favors we receive; to love each other, and be united. We never quarrel about religion.

"BROTHER:—We do not wish to destroy your religion or take it from you; we only want to enjoy our own.

"BROTHER:—We have been told that you have been preaching to the white people in this place. These people are our neighbors. We are acquainted with them. We will wait a little while, and see what effect your preaching has upon them. If we find it does them good, makes them honest, and less disposed to cheat Indians, we will then consider again of what you have said.

Brother:—You have now heard our talk, and this is all we have to say at present. As we are going to part, we will come and take you by the hand, and hope the Great Spirit will protect you on your journey, and return you safe to your friends."

According to the suggestion of their orator, the Indians moved forward to shake hands with the missionary; but he refused, saying, " There was no fellowship between the religion of God and the Devil." Yet the Indians smiled and retired peacefully.

At another time Red Jacket said, " The white people were not content with the wrongs they had done his people, but wanted to *Cram* their doctrines down their throats."

In a conversation with a distinguished clergyman, who was endeavoring to instruct him on the subject of the Christian religion, not many years before his death, Red Jacket said:

" Brother :—If you white men murdered the Son of the Great Spirit, we Indians had nothing to do with it, and it is none of our affair. If he had come among us, we would not have killed him; we would have treated him well; and the white people who killed him, ought to be damned for doing it. You must make amends for that crime yourselves."

On being invited to see the bridge across Niagara after it was finished, he walked across it and examined every part, evidently struck with admiration at the skill and science displayed in the building; and when he was about to depart, gazed for a moment with an expression no language can convey, and slowly uttered these two words: " D——d Yankee !"

Another attempt was made, several years after the first, to introduce missionaries among his people; but no argument or persuasion could induce him to look upon Christianity with favor.

In another eloquent speech, he painted in glowing colors the curse that seemed to have descended upon all those Indians who had been made the object of pious but mistaken missions. "How imbecile, poor, effeminate, contemptible, drunken, lying, thieving, cheating, malicious, meddlesome, backbiting, quarrelsome, degraded and despised, the victims of civilized instruction had become; having lost all the noble qualities of the Indian, and acquired all the ignoble vices of the white people;" and then adds:

"Brother:—On the other hand, we know that the Great Spirit is pleased that we follow the traditions of our fathers; for in so doing we receive his blessing. The Great Spirit has provided abundance. When we are hungry, we find the forest filled with game; when thirsty, we slake our thirst at the pure streams and springs that spread around us; when weary, the leaves of the trees are our bed—we retire with contentment to rest—we rise with gratitude to the great Preserver. No luxuries, no vices, no disputed titles, no avaricious desires shake the foundations of our society, or disturb our peace and happiness.

"Brother:—We pity you. We wish you to bear to our good friends our best wishes. Inform them, that in compassion to them we are willing to send them missionaries to teach them our religion, our habits, and our customs. We would be willing they should be as happy as we, and assure them if they will follow our example, they would be far more happy than they are now.

"Accept this advice, Brother, and take it back to your friends as the best pledge of our wishes for your welfare. Perhaps you think we are ignorant and uninformed. Go, then, and teach the white people. Select, for example, the people of Buffalo. Improve their morals and refine their habits. Make them less disposed to cheat Indians. Make the white people generally less disposed to make Indians drunk, and to take from them their lands. Let us know the tree by the blossoms, and the blossoms by the fruit. When this shall be made clear to our minds, we may be more willing to listen to you.

"BROTHER :—Farewell."

"A terrible and bitter satire!" and though entirely unjust as far as true religion is concerned, it is quite unanswerable to a heathen mind, and is a stumbling-block in the way of many in enlightened communities.

It was *pagan white people* who poisoned the mind of the great Chief, and prejudiced him against the missionaries and their religion. He thought them the enemies of his people; and those whose interest it was to deceive him, so thoroughly blinded and bewildered him, that he came very near being the destroyer, rather than the saviour, of the little remnant of his race. They, knowing that the missionaries were the true friends of the Indian, and understood their own evil machinations, wished to banish them from the lands. A law was passed that no white people should settle upon the *Reservations*, to which the Indians had been removed, and which had been secured to them by law and treaty; and though it was no part of the design that missionaries and teachers should be excluded, the companies who wished to obtain the lands and drive the Indians beyond the Mississippi, took advantage of the law, and urged the pagan Chiefs to insist upon their departure. In order to obey the strict letter of the law, they were obliged to go. As soon as the law could be revised, they returned again; and there are few now, among Chiefs or people, who do not recognize them as their best friends, and acknowledge their influence to be for their true interest, temporal as well as spiritual; and they are fast becoming so enlightened by the Gospel and by universal education, through their untiring zeal, as to be in no future danger from designing and unprincipled speculators.

Before he died, Red Jacket began to discriminate truly between his friends and foes, and to understand the disinterested friendship of the missionaries.

He had always great confidence in the Quakers; owing, we presume, to the fact that no land-shark ever belonged to this sect. In their early intercourse with the Indians, they were, fortunately, more judicious in the measures they took towards advancing them in all the arts of cultivated life. As the great Chief once said: "They give us ploughs, and show us how to use them; they counsel us in our troubles, and instruct us how to make ourselves comfortable; they do us great good—we are satisfied with what they do."

Witchcraft was punishable with death by the laws of the Six Nations, and it often happened that persons were accused of exercising the powers of sorcery upon individuals, when sickness could be accounted for in no other way, and their arts produced no effect in healing. A case of this kind was the occasion of one of Red Jacket's most sarcastic speeches.

A woman was accused of causing the death of an Indian, whose lingering illness they could not understand, and by their laws condemned to die. He who was appointed to be her executioner, faltered in the hour of trial, and another, who was more bold, stepped forward and drew the knife across her throat. The Indians were not subject to the laws of the United States as far as their own internal affairs were concerned, and had the right to administer justice as they pleased; but some of their neighbors, being shocked at these summary proceedings, arrested the murderer and put him in prison. A trial was had, and every effort made to procure the condemnation, and of course the hanging, of the accused, whose name was Tommy Jemmy; but the Indians insisted that the woman had been as judicially condemned and executed as Tommy Jemmy would be if he was given up to them, and if it was murder in the one case, it would be murder in the other.

Red Jacket, seeing that their belief in witches was the theme of ridicule, answered in these words:

"What! do you denounce us as fools and bigots, because we still believe what you yourselves believed only two centuries ago? Your black-coats thundered this doctrine from the pulpit; your judges pronounced it from the bench, and sanctioned it with the formalities of law, and you would now punish our unfortunate brother for adhering to the faith of his fathers and of yours! Go to Salem! Look at the records of your own government, and you will find that hundreds have been executed for the very crime which has called forth the sentence of condemnation against this woman, and drawn down upon her the arm of vengeance. What have our brothers done more than the rulers of your people have done? And what crime has this man committed, by executing in a summary way the laws of his country and the command of the Great Spirit?"

It is said his looks were far more terrible than his words; and his eye, when aroused by indignation, was fearful in its blaze. He gained his cause, and the prisoner was liberated.

## CHAPTER IX.

SARCASM AND SAGACITY—RED JACKET, OR SA-GO-YE-WAT-HA.

An interesting interview is related in Mr. Stone's Life of Red Jacket, as having taken place between Rev. Dr. Breckenbridge and the great Indian orator, and I transfer it, as given by this author, in the words of him who wrote it:

"The first opportunity I ever enjoyed of seeing that deservedly celebrated Indian Chief, Red Jacket, was in the year 1821, at the residence of General Porter, Black Rock, New York. Being on a visit to the General and his family, it seemed a peculiarly fit occasion to become acquainted with the great Seneca orator, whose tribe resided within a few miles of Black Rock. General Porter embraced the Indian warriors who fought with us on that line during the late war with Great Britain in his command. From this cause—from his high character—his intimate acquaintance with the Chiefs, and his known attachment to those interesting people, he had great influence over them; and his lamented lady, who, it is not indelicate for me to say, was my sister, had by her kindness won the rugged hearts of all their leading men. So that their united influence, and my near relationship to them, secured to me at once access to the Chiefs and their entire confidence.

"I had not only a great desire to see Red Jacket, but also to use this important opportunity to correct some of his false impressions in regard to Christianity and the missionaries established in his tribe. To this end it was agreed to invite Red Jacket and the other Chiefs of the Senecas to visit Co-na-shus-tah, and meet his brother at his house. The invitation was accordingly given, and very promptly and respectfully accepted.

"On the appointed day they made their appearance in due form, headed by Red Jacket, to the number of eight or ten besides himself. He wore a blue dress, the upper garment cut after the fashion of a hunting-shirt, with blue leggins, a red jacket, and a girdle of red about his waist. I have seldom seen a more dignified or noble looking body of men than the entire group. It seems— though no such impression was designed to be conveyed by the terms of the invitation—that some indefinite expectation had been excited in their minds of meeting an official agent on important business. And they have been so unworthily tampered with, and so badly treated by us, as a people, and many of their most important treaties have been so much the result of private and corrupting appeals, that they very naturally looked for some evil design in every approach to them, however open and simple it may be. So it was on this occasion. As soon as the ceremonies of introduction were over, with the civilities growing out of it, the old orator seated himself in the midst of the circle of Chiefs, and after a word with them, followed by a general assent, he proceeded in a very serious and commanding manner—always speaking in his own nervous tongue, through an interpreter—to address me, in substance, as follows:

"'We had a call from our good friends (pointing to the General and his lady), to come down to Black Rock to meet their brothers. We are glad to break bread and drink the cup of friendship with them. They are great friends to our people, and we love them very much. Co-na-shus-tah is a great man, and his woman has none like her. We often come to their house. We thank them for telling us to come to-day. But as all the Chiefs were asked, we expected some important talk. Now here we are, what is your business?'

"This, as may readily be supposed, was an embarrassing position to a young man just out of college. I paused. Every countenance was fixed upon me, while Red Jacket in particular seemed to search me with his arrowy eye, and to feel that the private and informal nature of the meeting, and the extreme youth of the man, were hardly in keeping with the character and number of the guests invited; and his whole manner implied, 'that but for the sake of the General and his good friends, I should have waited for you to come to me.' With these impressions of his feelings, I proceeded to say, in reply:

"'That I should have thought it very presumptuous in me to send for him alone—and still more, for all the Chiefs of his tribe—to come so far to see me; that my intention had been to visit him and the other Chiefs at his town; but the General and his lady could not go with me to introduce me; nor were we at all certain that we should find him and the other Chiefs at home; at any rate, the General's house was most convenient. That as to myself, I was a young man, and had no business with them, except that I had heard a great deal of Red Jacket, and wished to see him and hear him talk; and that I would return his visit, and show him that it was not out of disrespect, but out of regard for him, and great desire to see him, that we had sent for him—this being the way the white men honor one another.'

"Mrs. Porter immediately confirmed what I had said, and gave special point to the hospitality of the house, and the great desire I had to see Red Jacket. Her appeal, added to the reply, relaxed the rigor of his manner and that of the other Chiefs, while it relieved our interview of all painful feelings.

"After this general letting down of the scene, Red Jacket turned to me familiarly and asked: 'What are you? You say you are not a government agent; are you a gambler (meaning a land speculator), or a black-coat—or what are you?'

"I answered, 'I am yet too young a man to engage in any profession; but I hope some of these days to be a black coat.'

"He lifted up his hands, accompanied by his eyes, in a most expressive way; and though not a word was uttered, every one fully understood that he very distinctly expressed the sentiment, 'What a fool!' But I had been too often called to bear from those reported 'great and wise' among *white* men, the shame of the cross, to be surprised by his manner; and I was too anxious to conciliate his good feelings to attempt any retort. So that I commanded my countenance, and seeming not to have observed him, I proceeded to tell him something of our Colleges and other institutions.

"A good deal of general conversation ensued, addressed to one and another of the Chiefs, and we were just arriving at the hour of dinner, when our conference was suddenly broken up by the arrival of a breathless messenger, saying that an old Chief, whose name I forget, had just died, and the other Chiefs were immediately needed to attend his burial. One of the Chiefs shed tears at the news; all seemed serious, but the others suppressed their feelings, and spent a few moments in a very earnest conversation, the result of which Red Jacket announced to us. They had determined to return at once to their village, but consented to leave Red Jacket and his interpreter. In vain were they urged to wait till after dinner, or to refresh themselves with something to eat by the way. With hurried farewell and quick steps they left the house, and by the nearest foot-path returned home.

"This occurrence relieved me of one difficulty: it enabled me to see Red Jacket at leisure alone. It seemed, also, to soften his feelings, and make him more affable and kind.

"Soon after the departure of the Chiefs, we were ushered to dinner. Red Jacket behaved with great propriety in all respects; while his interpreter, though half a white man, after a few awkward attempts at the knife and fork, found himself falling behind; and repeating the adage, which is often quoted to cover the same style among our white urchins, of picking a chicken bone, '*that fingers were made before forks,*' he proceeded with real gusto and much good humor to make up his lost time upon all parts of his dinner. It being over, I invited Red Jacket into the General's office, where we had four hours' most interesting conversation on a variety of topics, but chiefly connected with Christianity, the government of the United States, the missionaries, and his loved lands."

It was during this interview that the objects of speculators were so explained to him, that he understood their evil designs; and the true nature of the missionary enterprise was made clear to his comprehension, so that his enmity was never afterward so bitter.

When assured that by the course he was pursuing, he was doing more than any one else to break up and drive away his people, and that the effect of the teachings of the missionaries was to preserve them, he grasped the hand of the speaker and said: "If this is so, it is new to me, and I will lay it up in my mind (pointing to his noble forehead), and talk of it to the Chiefs and the people."

Dr. B. continues: "Red Jacket was about sixty years old at this time, and had a weather-beaten look, which age, and more than all, intemperance had produced; but his general appearance was striking, and his face noble. His lofty and capacious forehead, his piercing black eye, his gently curved lips, fine cheek and slightly aquiline nose—all marked a great man; and as sustained and expressed by his dignified air, made a deep impression on all who saw him. All these features became doubly expressive, when his mind and body were set in motion by the effort of speaking—if effort that may be called which flowed like a stream from his lips. I saw him in the wane of life, and heard him only in private, and through a stupid and careless interpreter. Yet, notwithstanding these disadvantages, he was one of the greatest and most eloquent orators I ever knew. His cadence was measured, and yet very musical; and when excited, he would spring to his feet, elevate his head, expand his arms, and utter with indescribable effect of manner and tone, some of his noblest thoughts."

General Porter speaks of him as a man endowed with great intellectual powers, and who, as an orator, was not only unsurpassed, but unequalled by any of his contemporaries. Although those who were ignorant of his language could not fully appreciate the force and beauty of his speeches, when received through the medium of an interpreter,—generally coarse and clumsy,—yet such was the peculiar gracefulness of his person, attitudes and action, and the mellow tones of his Seneca dialect, and such the astonishing effects produced on that part of the auditory who did fully understand him, and whose souls appeared to be engrossed and borne away by the orator, that he was listened to by all with perfect delight. His figures were frequently so sublime, so apposite and so beautiful, that the interpreter often said the English language was not rich enough to allow of doing him justice.

Another gentleman says: "It is evident that the best translations of Indian speeches must fail to express the beauty and sublimity of the originals—especially of such an original as Red Jacket. It has been my good fortune to hear him a few times, but only in late years, when his powers were enfeebled by age and intemperance; but I shall never forget the impression made on me the first time I saw him in council. The English language has no figures to convey the true meaning of the original, but though coming through the medium of an illiterate interpreter, I saw the dismembered parts of a splendid oration."

On one occasion he used the following figurative language in speaking of the encroachments of the white people:

"We first knew you a feeble plant, which wanted a little earth whereon to grow. We gave it you; and afterward, when we could have trod you under our feet, we watered and protected you; and now you have grown to be a mighty tree, whose top reaches the clouds, and whose branches overspread the whole land, whilst we, who were the tall pine of the forest, have become a feeble plant, and need your protection.

"When you first came here, you clung around our knee and called us *father*; we took you by the hand and called you brothers. You have grown greater than we, so that we can no longer reach up to your hand; but we wish to cling around your knee, and be called your children."

Of the domestic character and habits of the great Indian orator, we of course know very little. It has not been the custom of civilized or Christian people to relate this portion of the life of any who became eminent among them, and we have no means of learning much concerning the home life of Indians.

We know that Red Jacket separated from his first wife after she had become the mother of several children, and that her infidelity was the alleged cause. The repugnance which he ever afterwards manifested towards her, is in accordance with his known moral purity of character.

That he had a father's love for his children, we may see in the following beautiful language which he used in answer to a lady, who inquired if he had any living, as she knew that several had been taken away.

Fixing his eyes upon her with a mournful expression of countenance, he replied:

"Red Jacket was once a great man, and in favor with the Great Spirit. He was a lofty pine among the smaller trees of the forest. But after years of glory, he degraded himself by drinking the fire-water of the white man. The Great Spirit has looked upon him in anger, and his lightning has stripped the pine of its branches."

Had he hated the white men sufficiently to resist their temptations, he might have been the glory and the saviour of his people. The word which in Seneca is used to express strong drink, very truly and emphatically describes it as *the mind destroyer*. This was its office, and if the noble mind of Red Jacket had not been destroyed by its agency, he would have seen clearly through the dark plots of his enemies, and been able to counter-plot to their destruction, and thus rescued his people from the grasp of their pursuers. His fall is often quoted as a proof of the weak and vicious propensities of the race, which it is useless to attempt to place on a level with the Anglo-Saxon.

It may be necessary to concede that the Saxon is superior to all others, inasmuch as all the others fall back and waste away before it. But this superiority will not entitle them to claim for themselves more virtues than many others can boast. I know it is customary for us to pride ourselves upon our success as conquerors and destroyers, but yet it is lamentable that our national traits are far from being Christian ones. It is by making use of cruel and revolting means, that we obliterate the traces of whole nations and blot out kingdoms, as water obliterates blood. A nation of CHRISTIANS, of whatever name, could not thus conquer and destroy. If only the warrior had been cut off, and the tomahawk and scalping-knife buried, the pages of Indian history would not be so dark. But they are stained with something worse than blood. They are reeking with the slime of falsehood, avarice, treachery, drunkenness, and every species of debauchery. When Indians adopt civilization, there is no greater proportion of the whole number who become the slaves of vice, than takes place among white people.

Red Jacket became intemperate,—but how many of the members of every Senate and House of Representatives, since the formation of our government, have become the same? How many of the brightest names on our historic scroll would be blotted out, if only the virtuous were allowed to remain?

I cannot learn that he was addicted to any other debasing vice.

As one of the proofs that the Indian had an intuitive

perception of propriety, may be related an incident which occurred whilst a gentleman was travelling with a party of Indian Chiefs and their interpreter. Red Jacket was one of the party, but he was uniformly grave. The others were much inclined to merriment, and during an evening when they were gathered around the fire in a log cabin, the mirth was so great and the conversation so jocular, that Red Jacket was afraid the stranger, who could not understand their language, would think himself treated with impoliteness, and infer that their sport was at his expense. He evidently enjoyed their happiness, though he took no part; but after awhile he spoke to Mr. Parish, the interpreter, and requested him to repeat a few words to Mr. Hospres, which were as follows:

"We have been made uncomfortable by the storm; we are now warm and comfortable; it has caused us to feel cheerful and merry; but I hope our friend who is travelling with us, will not be hurt at this merriment, or suppose that we are taking advantage of his ignorance of our language, to make him in any manner the subject of mirth."

On being assured that no such suspicion could be entertained of the honorable men who were present, they resumed their mirth and Red Jacket his gravity.

When Lafayette was an officer in the Revolutionary army, he met Red Jacket at the treaty of peace at Fort Stanwix, in 1787, where the Indian orator eloquently opposed "burying the tomahawk." When he again visited this country, in 1825, they met at Buffalo, and General Lafayette remarked, that time had wrought great changes upon both since their first meeting. "But," rejoined Red Jacket, " he has not been so severe with you as with me. He has left you a fresh countenance, and hair to cover your head; while to me —— behold!" and taking the covering from his head, he disclosed that he was nearly bald. But Lafayette did not leave him to think thus harshly of time, but proved to him that the ravages had been nearly the same upon both, by removing a wig and exposing a head almost as bald as the Chief's; upon which he remarked with much pleasantry, that a scalp from some bystander would renew his youth in the same manner!

A young French nobleman visited Buffalo a few years before this, and having heard much of the fame of Red Jacket, sent him word that he wished to see him, inviting him to come the next day. Red Jacket received the message, and affected great contempt, saying, "Tell the *young man* if he wishes to visit the old Chief, he will find him with his nation, where other strangers pay their respects to him, and Red Jacket will be glad to see him." The Count sent back word that he had taken a long journey and was fatigued; that he had come all the way from France to see the great orator of the Seneca nation, and hoped he would not refuse to meet him at Buffalo.

"Tell him," said the sarcastic Chief, "that having come so far to see me, it is strange he should stop within seven miles of my lodge."

So the young Frenchman was obliged to seek him in his wigwam; after which he consented to dine with the Count, at Buffalo, and was pronounced by him a greater wonder than Niagara itself.

On one occasion he was visited by a gentleman who talked incessantly, and to little purpose, and who would go very near the person he was addressing, and chatter about as intelligibly as a magpie. Red Jacket, receiving the message that a stranger wished to see him, dressed himself with great care, and came forth in all his dignity. One glance was sufficient to his keen eye to understand the character of his guest; and listening a few moments with contempt in all his features, he went close to him and exclaimed, "Cha! cha! cha!" as fast as he could speak, and turned on his heel towards his own cabin " as straight as an Indian," nor deigned to look behind him while in sight of the house tenanted by the gentleman, who stood for once speechless!

His vanity was very conspicuous. He was fully aware of his importance, and disposed to make others aware of it on every possible occasion. Colonel Pickering was often employed by the government to negotiate treaties, and would take down the speeches on the occasion in writing. At one time, when Red Jacket was the orator, he thought he would note the words of the interpreter whilst the Chief was himself speaking. He immediately paused, and on being requested to proceed said, "No, not whilst you hold down your head."

"Why can you not speak whilst I write?"

"Because, if you look me in the eye, you will know whether I tell you the truth."

At another time, he turned his head to speak to a third person, when Red Jacket very haughtily rebuked him, saying, "When a Seneca speaks, he ought to be listened to with attention, from one end of this great island to the other."

When he returned from Philadelphia, he was in the habit of using his oratorical powers to embellish the manner of his reception, and would collect around him the Chiefs and people of his nation, and, dressed in his uniform, with the cocked hat under his arm, would personify the President, and bow to all present as if they were the company in the great saloon, imitating the manners and gestures of the original with true grace and dignity, and then entertain his audience with the compliments and attentions which had been bestowed upon him.

When invited to dine, or be present on any occasion of social festivity among white people, he conformed with wonderful tact to the customs to which he was a stranger —never manifesting any surprise or asking any questions, till he could consult some friend whose ridicule he did not fear. It was after returning from Philadelphia, where he had dined with General Washington, that he asked the following explanation.

He said a man stood behind his chair, and would, every now and then, run off with his plate and knife and fork, and immediately return with others. "Now," said Red Jacket, "what was this for?" He was told that there was a variety of dishes on the President's table, and each was cooked in a different way, and for every new dish the guests were helped to a new plate. "Oh," said he, musing a moment, "is that it? You must then suppose that the plates and knives and forks retain the taste of the cookery?" On hearing the affirmative, he said, "But I should suppose the taste would remain on the palate longer than on the plate." That, he was told, they were in the habit of washing away with wine. "Oh," said he, "I now understand it. I thought, for so general a custom, you must have some good reason, and now regret that I did not know it when I was in Philadelphia; for the moment the man ran off with my plate, I would have drank wine till he returned with the other—for though I am fond of eating, I am more fond of drinking."

We are accustomed to think the blanket of the Indian a sign of barbarity, and any thing but dignified and graceful. Yet the *toga* of the Roman orator was never folded about his noble figure with more grace or dignity, than the homely mantle of the Seneca Chief, when he arose to address an Indian audience. The adjustment of his dress was always the signal by which it was known that he was about to rise. A gentleman who knew him intimately for half a century, says he was the most graceful public speaker he ever heard. His stature was above the middle size; his eyes fine, and expressive of the intellect which gave them fire; he was fluent, without being too rapid; and dignified and stately, without rigidity. When he arose, he would turn towards the Indians, and ask their attention to what he was about to say in behalf of the commissioner of the United States. He would then turn towards the commissioner, and with a slight but dignified inclination of the head, proceed. Decorum was at all times the characteristic of an Indian council. If the orator omitted what was considered by any one present important to be dwelt upon, he would place himself very near the speaker, and in a quiet and most delicate manner whisper his suggestion. As they had no written documents, their memories were the tablets on which were engraven all important events, and these were often more faithful than the scrolls of the learned.

In a council which was held with the Senecas by General Tompkins, of New York, a discussion arose concerning some point in a treaty made several years before. The agent stated one thing, and the Indian Chief another, insisting that he was correct. He was answered that it was written on paper, and must be so.

"The paper then tells a lie," said the orator, "for I have it written here (placing his hand upon his brow). You Yankees are born with a feather between your fingers, but your paper does not speak the truth. The Indian keeps his knowledge here; this is the book the Great Spirit has given him, and it does not lie."

On consulting the documents more particularly, it was found that the Indian record was, indeed, the most correct!

Although fond of good things, Red Jacket had a great contempt for the sensualist. When speaking of an Indian, whose name was *Hot bread*, and who was known to be indolent and gluttonous, he exclaimed, "Waugh! big man here (laying his hand upon his abdomen), but very small man here," bringing the palm of his hand with significant emphasis across his forehead.

That he shrank from spectacles of human suffering, may have been the reason of his aversion to the war-path. He did not like to look on blood.

At one time, when three young men were to suffer death by hanging, and multitudes were rushing towards the spot, he was met hurrying in an opposite direction. When asked why he did not go to witness the execution, he answered, "Fools enough there already; the battle-field is the place to see men die." One would certainly think, to witness the throngs which crowd around the gallows, that neither Christian nor human feeling filled the breasts of civilized beings.

The efforts were for a long time fruitless to induce Red Jacket to sit for his portrait. "When Red Jacket dies," he would say, "all that belongs to him shall die too." But at length, an appeal to his vanity availed, and on being assured that his picture was wanted to hang with those of Washington and Jefferson, and other great men in the National Galleries, he consented; and having once broken his resolution, no longer resisted, and was painted by several artists. The one by Weir is considered best, and was taken during a visit of the Chief to New York, in 1828, at the request of Dr. Francis. He dressed himself with great care in the costume he thought the most becoming and appropriate, decorated with his brilliant war-dress, his tomahawk, and Washington medal. He then seated himself in a large arm-chair

while around him groups of Indians were reclining upon
the floor. He was more than seventy years of age at the
time, but tall, erect and firm, though with many of the
traces of time and dissipation upon his form and countenance. He manifested great pleasure as the outlines of
the picture were filled up, and especially when his favorite
medal came out in full relief; and when the picture was
finished, started to his feet and clasped the hand of the
artist, exclaiming, " Good! good!"

One who knew him remarks, " That his characteristics
are preserved to admiration, and his majestic front exhibits an altitude surpassing every other I have ever seen
of the human skull."

His early youth was spent in the beautiful valley of
the Genesee; there were his favorite hunting-grounds,
and there his memory loved to linger. During the strife
of wars, and the more bitter strife of treaties, he had indulged very little in his favorite pastime; and when a
day of comparative quiet came, he, in company with a
friend, took his gun and went forth, in hopes to find a
deer for the sport of his rifle. They had gone but a little
distance, when a *clearing* opened before them. With a
contemptuous sneer, the old man turned aside and wandered in another direction. In a little while he came to
another, and looking over a fence, he saw a white man
holding a plough, which was turning up the earth in dark
furrows over a large field. Again he turned sadly away,
and plunged deeper in the forest, but soon another open
field presented itself; and though he had been all his life
oppressed with the woes of his people, he now for the
first time sat down and wept. There was no longer any
hope,—they had wasted away.

Red Jacket was decidedly aristocratic, and disposed
to *stand upon his dignity*. No person who knew him

would venture upon familiarity with him, and he did not like to have his children mingle freely with all whom they might meet in the streets. But he never considered the manners and habits of living among white people as worthy of imitation; and after chairs and tables were introduced by his wife into his own dwelling, he scorned to use them, and took his meals, as in the olden time, sitting on the floor, or a rude bench, cushioned with deer-skin. Yet he would not eat alone. Though he talked very little, he liked to be surrounded by his family. His second wife was his favorite, and he treated her with the most affectionate kindness, except in leaving free her religion; and then he scarcely reproached her—only saying that in embracing it, she was countenancing the wrongs committed upon her people, which he could not, and if she persisted he should leave her; and knowing her affection for him, he probably thought she would not hesitate between her husband and Christianity. When he found she would not renounce her new faith, he departed and lived several months at Tonnewanda. His enmity was evidently entirely political. He understood nothing of the real nature of Christianity, and was not willing to learn any thing concerning it from those who had been guilty of the grievous wrongs the red man had suffered, whenever those calling themselves Christians had come among them.

But he was not happy separated from those he loved, and those he left were not happy without him. He missed the caresses of the children, and especially the youngest daughter, of whom he was very fond. She used to sit upon his knee, with her little arms around his neck and her soft cheek resting upon his, and play with his silver locks. When he was gone she mourned for him, and gave her mother no rest till she promised to take her to where her father lived.

They went together; but the mother, with true womanly delicacy, entered not his dwelling, and refused to see him. She was willing to gratify her children, and cultivated their affection and respect for him who had deserted her, but she would not seek him.

The little girl, who is now a Christian woman, and herself told me the story, threw her arms around her father's neck, and kissed him; and he pressed her to his bosom, weeping tears of joy, and perhaps of true sorrow and repentance, and told her he was coming home; that he was sorry he had left her mother, and did not think her religion had done her any harm. He said he had bought her some broadcloth and beads, and would bring them when he came. When she left him he went with her to the door of the house where her mother lodged, but did not enter, and with many sobs and tears she bade him good-bye, and returned home.

In a little while he followed. He came into the house and humbly addressed his wife, saying he had come back again to live with her, if she would receive him; that he had done wrong, and was very sorry, and had been very unhappy. The injured wife did not answer a word, but threw her shawl around her, and went to the missionary to ask him if it would be right to receive him now, and what she should do. The missionary told her it was best to welcome him kindly, and encourage him to stay, if he made no opposition to her new mode of worship.

On hastening back, she, in a dignified manner, expressed her joy at seeing him, and her unchanged regard; but said she could not consent to his remaining, unless he would permit her to go to the Mission Church on Sunday, and in no way interfere with her religious duties. To this he assented, saying he knew she was a better woman than before she became a Christian, and he would never again molest her.

The children were rejoiced at the reconciliation, and all were again happy. He never violated his promise; and though he could not join the family in their mode of worship, not a word of disapprobation, or a look of contempt, reminded them that he liked it not.

And often on Sabbath morning, the old Chief would rise early and awake the daughters, saying, "Come, it is Sunday, you know; get up and have the work all done, so as to go to meeting with your mother; always go with your mother." Before he left her, his wife was obliged to steal away when he did not know it. She would have her house in order, and her blanket ready somewhere outside the dwelling, and when the bell rang, would go quietly out, take her blanket, and run. But now, when the bell rang for Sabbath, or evening meeting, he said, "Go;" and though he disliked to be left alone, he murmured not, and made himself as comfortable as he could till she returned. He had a great respect for her, and knew she was worthy of his confidence.

Though so eloquent in the council-chamber, Red Jacket seldom opened his lips in the wigwam. Among his own people he was not social, and never entered into familiar conversation upon ordinary topics. He was always ready to discuss the affairs of the nation with Chiefs or distinguished strangers, but was not given to story-telling, and seldom entered the houses of his neighbors. All the latter years of his life, he was sad on account of the woes the Indian had experienced, and the woes he predicted were still in store for them. He would lie upon his couch for hours, with his hands crossed upon his breast, and seem in deep distraction, and wish no interruption.

When he had been drinking, he was sometimes merry and talked very silly; but gravity was his prevailing mood,—though this is not the prevailing mood of Indians generally, as some people imagine.

When he meditated a speech, he would often repeat it to himself, and sometimes rehearse it to the interpreter, in order to be sure it would sound well. But his incapacity for business, and his degeneracy in consequence of his intoxication, procured for him the general dislike of his people. Many were beginning to see that the missionaries were their real friends, and to understand the distinction between reality and pretension, and wished Christianity to be encouraged. Red Jacket was constantly disturbing the councils by his bitter opposition and sarcasms, and was so unrelenting, that there seemed no hope of changing his opinions; and it finally began to be whispered, and then boldly proposed, that he should no longer be numbered among the Chiefs of the nation. A council was called, and formal resolutions drawn up, declaring the reasons why he was not fit for his office, and signed by twenty-six Chiefs. When it became known to him, he was greatly grieved, and resolved not to submit to such an indignity. Arousing his slumbering energies, he made a journey to Washington, to talk with the President. He called on Colonel McKenney, who was in charge of the Bureau of Indian Affairs; and as he had been informed by agents of all that had transpired among the Senecas, he recapitulated the state of affairs, and advised the Chief to return, and endeavor better to understand the nature of the missionary work; and, at least, to allow those who differed from him in opinion, the same liberty he demanded for himself—those who preferred to be Pagans, could remain so; and those who wished to change, should have the privilege.

The old man listened with the deepest attention till the speaker had finished, and then said, pointing to him and then in the direction of his people: "Our father has got a long eye." He endeavored to justify himself, and poured forth volumes of epithets upon the "black-coats," whose professions of disinterestedness he could not understand. But on returning home, he became more quiet, and seemed convinced of the policy, if not of the justice, of the advice he had received, and commenced in earnest to retrieve his position. "It shall not be said of me," thought he, as the fire of his youth again kindled his eye—"It shall not be said that Sa-go-ye-wat-ha lived in insignificance, and died in dishonor. Am I too feeble to revenge myself of my enemies? Am I not as I have been?"

Another council was called, on which occasion his sense of wrong and humiliation inspired him with something of his former pathos and earnestness, and he said:

"BROTHERS:—You have been correctly informed of an attempt to make me sit down, and throw off the authority of a Chief, by twenty-six misguided Chiefs of my nation. You have heard the statements of my associates in council, and their explanations of the charges brought against me. I have taken the legal and proper way to meet those charges. It is the only way in which I could notice them. They are charges which I despise, and which nothing could induce me to notice, but the concern many of the respected Chiefs of my nation feel concerning their aged comrade. Were it otherwise, I should not appear before you; I would fold my arms, and sit quietly under these ridiculous slanders. The Christian party have not even proceeded legally, according to our usages, to put me down. Ah! it grieves my heart when I look around and see the situation of my people—in old times, united and powerful—now, divided and feeble. I feel sorry for my nation. When I am gone to the other world—when the Great Spirit calls me away—who among my people can take my place? Many years have I guided the nation."

He was restored to his former rank, but the excitement of the occasion being over, he sank into a state of almost imbecility and stupor, and was never again the Sa-go-ye-wat-ha of old, nor ever again exhibited the fire and energy of former days.

He was taken suddenly ill in the Council House, of cholera morbus, where he had gone that day dressed with more than ordinary care, with all his gay apparel and ornaments. When he returned he said to his wife, "I am sick; I could not stay till the council had finished. I shall never recover." He then took off all his rich costume and laid it carefully away; reclined himself upon his couch, and did not rise again till morning, or speak except to answer some slight question. His wife prepared him medicine which he patiently took, but said, "It will do no good. I shall die." The next day he called her to him, and requested her and the little girl he loved so much to sit beside him, and listen to his parting words.

"I am going to die," he said. "I shall never leave the house again alive. I wish to thank you for your kindness to me. *You* have *loved* me. You have always prepared my food, and taken care of my clothes, and been patient with me. I am sorry I ever treated you unkindly. I am sorry I left you, because of your new religion, and am convinced that it is a good religion and has made you a better woman, and wish you to persevere in it. I should like to have lived a little longer for your sake. I meant to build you a new house and make you more comfortable, but it is now too late. But I hope my daughter will remember what I have so often told her—not to go in the streets with strangers, or associate with improper persons. She must stay with her mother, and grow up a respectable woman.

"When I am dead, it will be noised abroad through all the world—they will hear of it across the great waters, and say, 'Red Jacket, the great orator, is dead.' And white men will come and ask you for my body. They will wish to bury me. But do not let them take me. Clothe me in my simplest dress—put on my leggins and my moccasins, and hang the cross which I have worn so long, around my neck, and let it lie upon my bosom. Then bury me among my people. Neither do I wish to be buried with Pagan rites. I wish the ceremonies to be as you like, according to the customs of your new religion if you choose. Your minister says the dead will rise. Perhaps they will. If they do, I wish to rise with my old comrades. I do not wish to rise among pale-faces. I wish to be surrounded by red men. Do not make a feast according to the customs of the Indians. Whenever my friends chose, they could come and feast with me when I was well, and I do not wish those who have never eaten with me in my cabin, to surfeit at my funeral feast."

When he had finished, he laid himself again upon the couch and did not rise again. He lived several days, but was most of the time in a stupor or else delirious. He often asked for Mr. Harris, the missionary, and afterwards would unconsciously mutter—"I do not hate him—he thinks I hate him, but I do not. I would not hurt him." The missionary was sent for repeatedly, but did not return till he was dead. When the messenger told him Mr. Harris had not come, he replied, "Very well. The Great

Spirit will order it as he sees best, whether I have an opportunity to speak with him." Again he would murmur, "He accused me of being a snake, and trying to bite somebody This was very true, and I wish to repent and make satisfaction."

Whether it was Mr. Harris that he referred to all the time he was talking in this way could not be ascertained, as he did not seem to comprehend if any direct question was put to him, but from his remarks, and his known enmity to him, this was the natural supposition. Sometimes he would think he saw some of his old companions around him, and exclaim, "There is Farmer's Brother; why does he trouble me—why does he stand there looking at me?" then he would again sink into a stupor.

The cross which he wore was a very rich one of stones set in gold, and very large; it was given to him, but by whom his friends never knew. This was all the ornament which he requested should be buried with him. It was a universal custom among the Indians to make funeral feasts. No family was so poor that they did not endeavor to honor the dead in this manner. If a cow was all they possessed, it was slaughtered on this occasion. Red Jacket commanded that there should be nothing of the kind for him. A pagan funeral for a distinguished person is a very pompous affair. It continues for ten days, and every night a fire is kindled at the grave, and around it the mourners gather and utter piteous wails. It is foolish and heathenish, too, but scarcely more so than the custom among the ultra refined of spending a little fortune upon a peculiar dress, to be worn so many days or years —and it is not very long since Christian people thought it a testimony of their regard for the dead, or a necessary and solemn warning to the living, to place *death's heads* around the grave yard. It is all a relic of barbarism.

It certainly was a great step in the march of progress, that Red Jacket should abjure these pagan rites. After a life of sworn enmity to Christianity, that the example, the quiet unobtrusive example of a Christian woman in her household, should so influence him concerning Christianity, that he requested a Christian burial, and voluntarily and formally expressed to her his approbation of her religion, and his desire that she and her children should embrace it and live in accordance with its requirements. If he had come in contact with none but truly Christian men, he might in early life have been, not only a nominal, but an experimental Christian, and all his noble gifts consecrated to the elevation and redemption of his people.

The wife and daughter were the only ones to whom he spoke parting words or gave a parting blessing; but as his last hour drew nigh, his family all gathered around him, and mournful it was to think that the children were not his own—his were all sleeping in the little churchyard where he was soon to be laid—they were his stepchildren—the children of his favorite wife. It has been somewhere stated that his first wife died before him, but it is a mistake. She was living at the time of his death. He never went to see her but once after he left her, and that was about six months after their separation. He always asserted that he did not condemn her upon suspicion, that he was satisfied of her guilt before he deserted her. But he went once again to see her, thinking he might be able to forgive her, and receive her again as his companion for his children's sake, but found it impossible. He revolted from the thought of again calling her wife, and turned away never to see her more.

So there were none around his dying bed but stepchildren. These he had always loved and cherished, and they loved and honored him, for this their mother had taught them. The wife sat by his pillow and rested her hand upon his head. At his feet stood the two sons, who are now aged and Christian men, and by his side the little girl, whose little hand rested upon his withered and trembling palm. His last words were still, "Where is the missionary?" and then he clasped the child to his bosom, while she sobbed in anguish—her ears caught his hurried breathing—his arms relaxed their hold—she looked up, and he was gone. There was mourning in the household, and there was mourning among the people. The orator, the great man of whom they were still proud, while they lamented his degeneracy, was gone. He had been a true though mistaken friend, and who would take his place!

He had requested that a vial of cold water might be placed in his hand, when he was prepared for the burial, but the reason of the request no one could divine. It was complied with, however, and all his wishes strictly heeded. The funeral took place in the little mission church, with appropriate but the most simple ceremonies; and he was buried in the little mission burying-ground, at the gateway of what was once an old fort, around him his own people—aged men, sachems, chiefs and warriors, and little children.

A simple stone was erected to mark his grave, and the spot became a resort for the traveller from far and near. Soon it began to be desecrated, and his name disappeared from the marble, defaced by those who wished to carry away some memento of having visited the chieftain's tomb. Some among those who knew and honored him, wished to remove his remains to the new cemetery at Buffalo; but knowing or understanding the tenacity of his friends concerning his being buried among white people, they caused him to be disinterred and placed in a leaden coffin, preparatory to a burial in a new spot. But ere their desire was accomplished, his family had heard of what they considered the terrible sacrilege, and immediately demanded that he should be given up. They had removed from the Buffalo to the Cattaraugus reservation, and therefore did not wish to bury him again in the mission church-yard, so they brought every particle of the precious dust to their own dwelling, where it still remains unburied. They almost felt as if he would rise up to curse them, if they allowed him to lie side by side with those he so cordially hated. He did not wish *to rise with pale-faces;* and though, if we should meet him on the resurrection morn, we should probably be able to discover no marked difference between his complexion and our own, it is not strange he did not even wish to mingle his red dust with that of his white foes.

It was one of his most emphatic predictions, that the "craft and avarice of the white man would prevail;" and in less than nine years after his death, every foot of "the ancient inheritance of the Senecas was ceded to the white men, in exchange for a tract west of the Mississippi." Through the intervention of the Friends, as I have elsewhere stated, this calamity was averted, and for the first and only time, the Indians recovered their land, after it had been fraudulently obtained.

There seemed for a time every prospect that the prophetic assertion of the historian would be fulfilled—that "Red Jacket was the last of the Senecas." But there have been wise men and orators among them since, and the present just and liberal policy of the State of New York, will soon place education and cultivation within the reach of all, and they are abundantly disposed to improve and enjoy the good gifts which are bestowed upon them.

Schoolboys and collegians may find some other theme

for their eloquence, than "the last of the Mingoes wending his way towards the setting sun," for there is no longer any room to fear this dire calamity.

The following is the inscription upon the stone at the head of his grave :

SA-GO-YE-WAT-HA,<br>
HE KEEPS THEM AWAKE.

RED JACKET,<br>
CHIEF OF THE<br>
WOLF TRIBE OF THE SENECAS.<br>
Died, Jan. 20, 1830.<br>
Aged, 78 years.

## CHAPTER X.

DIGNITY OF CHARACTER AMONG THE IROQUOIS, ILLUSTRATED BY THE LIFE OF FARMER'S BROTHER AND YOUNG KING.

RED JACKET has been most conspicuous among the Chiefs of the Seneca Nation, because he excelled in those qualities which his enemies were willing to allow were great. He was not a warrior but an orator, and however marvellous his speeches and cutting his sarcasms, it did them no great harm in those points where their interest was most concerned. What he said was true, and pierced like a sword, but it fell powerless so far as preventing the wrongs of which he complained, or preserving his people from the doom which avarice had marked out. So even those who felt most keenly his *home thrusts*, were willing to applaud and crown him with honor.

But the warrior was more dangerous, and courage, and fortitude, and skill, in an Indian, did not receive these names. His bravery was savage desperation, his fortitude sullenness, and his successful stratagems treachery. When a war of extermination was planned by white men, it was said to be in self-defence, but they could not understand that Indians might be influenced by the same motive. A wrong to one individual or clan was more essentially a wrong to the whole, among a people who were comparatively so few and scattered, than among flourishing communities. The death of a few distinguished warriors or chiefs, was a loss which could not be easily supplied; when their forests were cut down and their villages were laid waste, there was nothing left but starvation for themselves and families, or else to bid for ever farewell to the hills and valleys, and rocks and streams, which were hallowed by the legends of centuries,—the birth-place and burial-place of their fathers. They appreciated every thing that was beautiful in scenery, and loved their native wilds as we love the spot where we were born. When they went forth to defend them, it was not in cold blood, but with enthusiasm—an enthusiasm kindled by the purest and loftiest sentiments which can animate the human soul. On the field of battle, they were bewildered and maddened by the pompous array and the flashing fire, and when overcome they were desperate, sullen and revengeful.

Farmer's Brother might have shone in the council, but he preferred the war-path. He had all the gifts of Red Jacket, and some which the great orator had not. He was truly noble, possessing the virtues which command respect in the world, and endear to the heart in social and domestic life. By one who knew him intimately as a companion on the war-path and in the camp, he is said to be " the most noble Indian in form and mould—in carriage and in soul, of that generation of his race." He led the warriors of his nation in the war of 1812, during which they were remarkable for magnanimity and kindness—for listening to the dictates of humanity, where even the rules of civilized nations would have sanctioned a different course. During the revolutionary war he was a faithful ally of the British; and is said to have been in the bloody battle in which Braddock lost his life and the flower of the British army in the old French war.

As almost his whole life was on the war-path, there is

very little to be said of him as a private man. During the wars with the Western Indians, he made several speeches which were remarkable for power and eloquence, but so early as that period it was not the custom to preserve the speeches of the Indians, and no portion of these remain. But he made one in behalf of two white men, who had been taken captive in their childhood and adopted by the Indians, and to whom they wished to give a tract of land, to be theirs and their children's for ever. As this donation could not be made without the consent of the State, at the convening of the General Assembly this petition was sent by the Chiefs, Sachems and warriors, and written by Farmer's Brother. It is another proof of the consideration shown to captives by the Indians. Mr. Jones and Mr. Parish had been interpreters for the Six Nations, and always true and faithful to the Indian interests.

"The Sachems, Chiefs, and warriors of the Seneca nation to the Sachems and Chiefs assembled about the great Council Fire of the State of New York:

"BROTHERS:—As you are once more assembled in council for the purpose of doing honor to yourselves and justice to your country; we, your brothers, the Sachems, Chiefs and warriors of the Seneca nation, request you to open your ears and give attention to our voice and wishes.

"BROTHERS:—You recollect the late contest between you and your father, the great King of England. This contest threw the inhabitants of this island into great tumult and commotion, like a raging whirlwind which tears up the trees, and tosses to and fro the leaves, so that no one knows from whence they come, or where they will fall.

"BROTHERS:—This whirlwind was so directed by the Great Spirit above as to throw into our arms two of your

infant children, Jasper Parish and Horatio Jones. We
adopted them into our families and made them our children. We loved them and nourished them. They lived
with us many years. AT LENGTH THE GREAT SPIRIT
SPOKE TO THE WHIRLWIND, AND IT WAS STILL. A clear and
uninterrupted sky appeared. The path of peace was opened, and the chain of friendship was once more made bright.
Then these our adopted children left us to seek their relations. We wished them to return among us, and promised
if they would return, and live in our country, to give each
of them a seat of land for them and their children to sit
down upon.

"BROTHERS:—They have returned, and have for several years past been serviceable to us as interpreters. We
still feel our hearts beat with affection for them, and now
wish to fulfil the promise we made them, and to reward
them for their services. We have therefore made up our
minds to give them a seat of ten square miles of land,
lying on the outlet of Lake Erie, about three miles below
Black Rock, beginning at the mouth of a creek known by
the name of Scoy-gu-quay-des Creek.

"BROTHERS:—We have now made known to you our
minds; we expect and earnestly request that you will permit our friends to receive this our gift, and will make the
same good to them according to the laws and customs of
your nation.

"BROTHERS:—Why should you hesitate to make our
minds easy with regard to this our request? To you it is
but a little thing, and have you not complied with the request, and confirmed the gift of the Oneidas, the Onondagas and Cayugas, to their interpreters? And shall
we ask and not be heard?

"BROTHERS:—We send you this our speech, to which

we expect your answer before the breaking up of your great council fire."

Mr. Jones, who is alluded to, was taken captive at the age of sixteen, on the banks of the "Blue Juniata," and conveyed to the Genesee Valley, where he was adopted into an Indian family, and remained five years, when he was made interpreter for the Six Nations by General Washington.

He was the favorite interpreter of Red Jacket; and having secured the perfect confidence of the Indians, had great influence over them.

He married an Indian wife, and his son became one of the most respected among the Seneca chiefs; he married the step-daughter of Red Jacket, and left an interesting family of children, one of whom was presented by the dying mother to the missionaries, who adopted it for their own. It was a little girl, whom they named Louisa Maria, and who, though she died in early childhood, lived long enough to become a bud of promise; yes, a blossom of Christian love, and hope and faith, a lamb of Christ's flock. She belonged to the class of those who always die in infancy, "whose names are all on gravestones." They are perfected without the discipline of earth's trials, and transplanted, to bloom as spring flowers in the gardens above. Life would be a dreary pathway without the little ones, and the heavenly choir would not make so sweet melody without the music of their voices.

Mr. Parish was born in Connecticut, and afterwards emigrated to Pennsylvania. His home was the Vale of Wyoming, and he experienced the fate of so many of its children. He was taken captive when he was eleven, and adopted with the usual ceremonies, being transferred from one nation to another, and experiencing all the vicissitudes of Indian life during seven years, when he was released.

He could speak five of the Indian dialects fluently, and was interpreter for the Six Nations thirty years.

Farmer's Brother, at one time on a visit to Philadelphia, was presented with a silver medal by Washington, which bore his own likeness, and of which the chief was very proud, wearing it suspended from his neck, and saying he would lose it only with his life.

During the war of 1812 he was often associated with Captain Worth, who was a great favorite with the Indians. At one time he was very sick for several weeks, and the Indians lingered about his tent, expressing the greatest anxiety, ready for any service, and Farmer's Brother was in the habit of sitting by his bedside several hours every day.

On one occasion, a Chippewa Indian crossed over from Canada, and joined a little party near the quarters of Captain Worth, pretending that he had deserted. But Indians of any nation were not in the habit of deserting, so his new companions did not believe his story. Still they did not molest him, and he mingled with them freely, listening to their stories and relating his own, till one day an indiscretion betrayed him. The Americans and some of their red allies were boasting of the number of redcoats they had killed, when the Chippewa, forgetting his disguise, also boasted, but it was of the Yankees and Senecas he had slain. Ah, yes! he was a spy; and quickly was he arraigned to answer for his sin.

Farmer's Brother was by his sick friend, but hearing the noise without, he sallied forth to learn the cause. The poor Chippewa was surrounded by warriors, that he might not make his escape, and pointed out to the old chief with great contempt as an enemy in their midst. He learned the particulars, and then stepped up to the Chippewa, with a word or two, which he alone understood; and immediately the culprit drew his blanket over his head, and coolly received a blow from the war-club, which sent him staggering to the ground.

For a moment he was stunned and motionless, but suddenly he sprung to his feet, rushed through the circle, and fled. To shrink from pain or fear death, was an everliving disgrace to an Indian, and he had not gone far when the taunts of the Senecas stung him more than would a thousand barbed arrows. He stopped, deliberately retraced his steps, and entered again the circle. Yes, he would die with all the heroism of an Indian warrior; and the Athenian philosopher did not more coolly swallow the poison mixed by his enemies, than the dauntless Chippewa seated himself upon the ground, and drew again his blanket over his head, to receive the death blow. Now they permitted him to be shot, and Farmer's Brother discharged the contents of his faithful rifle in his breast.

During the same war, a fugitive Mohawk, from the enemy, had endeavored to pass for a Seneca, and came among those who were led by this famous chief, who immediately recognized him.

"I know you well," said he; "you belong to the Mohawks. You are a spy. Here is my rifle, my tomahawk, my scalping knife; say which shall I use; I am in haste."

The young Mohawk knew there was no hope, and said he would die by the rifle. He was ordered to lie down upon the grass, and with one foot upon his breast, the chieftain shot him through the head.

Some of my readers will be ready to exclaim, "How heartless and barbarous!" and thoroughly savage, too, perhaps; but I shall only have to refer them for a parallel, to English and American history only a few years before, when young Hale was hung in an English camp for being a spy, and the gallant Major Andre in an American camp for the same reason; and no petitions or pleadings could procure for them a more honorable death. "Only permit me to be shot, and I will glory in my death," plead the brave young man who was risking life, and honor too, in the service of his country, and whose only sin was that he dared too much for the cause he had espoused. But even Washington would not relent, and the noble youth was hung like a common felon.

The simplicity of the Indian in money matters, and especially concerning the interest of sums deposited in banks, was very amusing. At one time there was ceded a tract of land including four millions of acres, for which they were to receive one hundred thousand pounds; the Indians being told that the interest of the money would be more useful than so much unproductive land, and this interest should be paid them annually. It was very difficult at first for them to comprehend the nature of a bank, and how money could be made to grow, knowing as they did that it was not placed in the earth to produce like corn. They saw that it was planted and produced a crop, but the place and the process were a great mystery. But those on whom devolved the business soon made themselves masters of the science, and knew very quick if the crop was not the full amount, though the uninitiated would sometimes ask what the prospect was in a season like that? The figure was adopted, and is still used in their language, of saying the money is planted and grows. They have planted a certain sum, and it has grown to a great amount. As few of them could count more than a hundred, it was a long time before they could reckon a hundred thousand; and their first lesson was given by filling a cask with dollars, and then another, and showing them how many casks would be required to contain the whole, and how many horses would be necessary in order to draw it.

It was in the making of this treaty that Red Jacket was guilty of a duplicity which left a dark stain upon his name for ever, and sowed enmity between him and the honest Farmer's Brother and Cornplanter, which was never entirely removed.

When they heard that there was trouble about the interest of the money that had been deposited in the bank, as it might fail, Farmer's Brother wrote a letter expressing the fears and misunderstandings of the people, addressed to the Secretary of War.

"BROTHER:—The sachems and chief warriors of the Seneca Nation of Indians, understanding you are the person appointed by the great council of your nation, to manage and conduct the affairs of the several nations of Indians with whom you are at peace and on terms of friendship, come at this time as children to a father, to lay before you the trouble which we have on our minds.

"BROTHER:—Listen to what we say. Some years since we held a treaty at Bigtree, near the Genesee River. This treaty was called by our great father, the President of the United States. At this treaty we sold to *Robert Morris*, the greatest part of our country; the sum he gave us was one hundred thousand dollars. The commissioners who were appointed on your part, advised us to place this money in the hands of our great father, the President of the United States. He told us our father loved his red children, and would take care of our money, and plant it in a field where it would bear seed for ever, as long as trees grow, or waters run. Our money has heretofore been of great service to us, it has helped us to support our old people and our women and children; but we are told the field where our money was planted is become barren.

BROTHER :—We do not understand your way of doing business. The thing is very heavy on our minds; we hope you will remove it."

On the reception of this letter the fund was transferred from the bank to the Government of the United States, which has ever since paid the Indians the interest faithfully. From the sale of other lands in the State they receive several thousand dollars, and in all about ($16,500) sixteen thousand five hundred dollars. This is divided equally among men, women, and children. The infant of two days old receives as large a sum as the greatest Chief. It would be infinitely better for them, now, if this money could be appropriated to educational purposes, or devoted to the public benefit in some other way; but there is not yet a sufficient number who appreciate the importance of educational and other improvements, to consent to a change in the distribution of their annuities. Unless they save it every year, they would think they did not have it. Yet there are many who fully understand and strongly advocate a *better way*, and I doubt not ere long it will be adopted, and schools and agricultural interests be the first to receive the benefit; for these they are fast learning to value.

The following extract from the journal of Mr. Savery, one of a deputation sent in 1794, by the Quakers, to learn the condition and wants of the Indians, will give a glimpse of him in his forest home.

" After dinner we went to view Farmer's Brother's encampment, which contained about five hundred Indians. They were located by the side of a brook, in the woods; having built about seventy or eighty huts, by far the most commodiously and ingeniously made of any we have yet seen. The principal materials are bark and the boughs of trees, so nicely put together as to keep the family nice and warm. The women as well as the men appeared to be mostly employed. In this camp there are a large number of pretty children, who, in all their activity and buoyancy of health, were diverting themselves according to their fancy. The vast numbers of deer they have killed, since coming here, which they cut up and hang around their huts inside and out to dry, together with the rations of beef which they had drawn daily, give the appearance of plenty to supply the few wants to which they are subjected. The ease and cheerfulness of every countenance, and the delightfulness of the afternoon, which these inhabitants of the woods seemed to enjoy with a relish far superior to those who are pent up in crowded and populous cities, all combined to make this the most pleasant visit I have yet made to the Indians; and induced me to believe that before they became acquainted with white people, and were infected with their vices, they must have been as happy a people as any in the world. In returning to our quarters we passed by the Indian Council, where Red Jacket was displaying his oratory to his brother chiefs. He afterwards made us a visit with his wife and five children, whom he had brought to see us. They were exceedingly well clad, agreeable in their manners, and the best behaved and prettiest Indian children I had ever met with."

In closing the report he says, that during a sojourn of seven weeks among the Indians, they had frequent opportunity of observing the melancholy and demoralizing effects resulting from the supply of ardent spirits furnished them by white people; and the difficulties and hardships to which these poor people, once a free and independent nation, are now subjected, appeared to them loudly to claim the sympathy of friends and others, who have grown opulent upon the land which was their former inheritance.

Farmer's Brother never yielded to the temptation of the fire-water. He lived and died a sober man. "He was a noble instance of a great and magnanimous mind. No one who looked upon him could imbibe feelings of disgust or hatred; and all who knew him well, felt esteem and veneration. He was never guilty of meanness, littleness, or intrigue; but was ever open, dignified, and fearless. He was a fine specimen of the Indian form, and trod the earth like a king, with the impress of integrity and honor upon his face as it was thoroughly stamped upon his character."

"'He was one of nature's noblemen,
——the front of Jove himself,
An eye like Mars to threaten and command:
A station like the herald Mercury.'"

"None who saw him will fail to recollect his majestic mien and princely bearing, much less will they who have heard him in council, forget the power and deep-toned melody of his voice—his natural and impressive gestures, and the unaffected and commanding dignity of his manner. Unrivalled as a warrior, and only equalled by Red Jacket in eloquence, speaking in the verity of sober prose, it may be said that his was

"'A combination and a form indeed,
To give the world assurance of a man.'"

"His influence with his nation was very great; and his true glory, his open-heartedness, his fidelity to truth, and his generous magnanimity, secured for him the admiration and respect of every white person who had the honor of his acquaintance. He was a firm friend where he promised fidelity, and a bitter enemy to those against whom he contended; and would lose the last drop of blood in his veins sooner than betray the cause he had espoused. He lived to be ninety years of age, dying in 1814, and continued a Pagan to the day of his death, as thoroughly opposed to Christianity and all the inroads of civilization as Red Jacket himself."

### YOUNG-KING.

The Indian names fall strangely, and sometimes harshly on *ears polite*, and when belonging to persons of dignity, convey to us any thing but an idea of the true qualities of those who bore them. Yet *Big-Kettle* was a truly great and noble man; and every time I find myself in company with Indians, I am introduced to those whose names bring a smile to my lips in spite of all my attempts at gravity; like Mr. Silver-heels, Mr. Sun-down, and Mr. Tall-Chief. Young-King was a chief of the Seneca Nation, and one of whom the people were very proud on account of his bravery in war, his wisdom in council, and his mild, pacific character in social life. He was born at Canandaigua, which signifies in their language "The Chosen City," and indicates far more to them than it does to us of beauty in scenery and location, and was to the Indian one of his most loved spots, among all the smiling valleys and fruitful fields which dotted their favorite hunting-grounds, on the borders of the lakes and rivers which stretch from the Hudson to Niagara, and from the St. Lawrence to the Ohio. Oh! the cruel desolation which swept them away!

Young-King was one of those who fled before the American army under General Sullivan, who was sent to destroy their settlements in 1777. But he was only a boy, being, as he thought, ten or twelve years of age—as his mother gave him a frying-pan to carry on their flying route to Canada, where they went to seek the protection of the British, in whose service their warriors had fought,

"And in their cause bled nobly."

He was the son of "Old Smoke," one of the most distinguished sachems of the Six Nations, and though not equal to his father, was the keeper of the council-fire, and ever won the respect of enemies and the love of friends.

As I read over volumes of history in order to glean the truth from the great mass of details, I cannot help being struck with the different manner in which massacre and bloodshed are represented when Indians are spoken of, and when the same things are recorded of white men. The villages of Wyoming and Cherry Valley were devastated and destroyed by British and Indians, and the shocking story is repeated and dwelt upon as unparalleled in atrocity. The Indian is called a barbarian and bloodthirsty assassin—the personification of cruelty and revenge. But when it is recorded of the American army that "they were sent in every direction to overrun and lay waste Indian settlements, cut down their orchards, destroy their provisions and crops, kill their cattle and horses, and apply the besom of destruction to every thing that could give shelter or sustenance to man or beast;" and it is added, that "they meted out the full measure of destruction and desolation upon every settlement that came in their way, and actually destroyed forty Indian villages, one hundred and sixty thousand bushels of corn, vast quantities of beans and other vegetables, a great number of horses, and all farming utensils, and indeed every thing that was the result of labor or the produce of cultivation; all this being the unmolested and unremitting employment of five thousand men for three weeks;" and to close their labors of destruction, applied the torch to the ancient metropolis of the Seneca Nation, which contained one hundred and twenty-eight houses—many being killed and many taken prisoners, and all obliged to flee—men, women, and children—through the wilderness, strewing the way with the dead and dying—it is called "gallant," a "brilliant achievement," a "glorious exploit!" That Indian mothers see their children murdered before their eyes, or starving, or wasting from sickness, is nothing to excite pity or call forth compassion. That the horses, and cows, and sheep of Indians are burnt, and all their pleasant fields laid waste, is matter of rejoicing. Their homes were far more dear to them than were the homes of those who had occupied them but for a few years; for they were living with the legends and sweet associations of centuries. They were deprived of their birthright. I have listened with horror as I have heard old men relate the tales of hunger, and sickness, and misery to which thousands were reduced by an act which gained for the victors immortal honors and not a single censure.

The Indians were the allies of the English, and faithful to their plighted word. They fought according to their rules of warfare, and fought for their homes and their firesides, their wives and their children, and fought in vain. Theirs, too, were happy homes, where love and domestic virtue dwelt; and their freedom from envyings and jealousies, and strife and malice, might put many Christian homes to shame. Instead of wondering that they hated white people, I only wonder that the wounds they received should ever have healed—that they do not rankle for ever, and produce utter detestation and unconquerable enmity to every thing with a pale skin.

This has been the case with many, and made it almost impossible for the missionaries to convince them that a religion taught by such a people, could have in it any good thing. And only by living among them, and exemplyfying its principles by long and intimate intercourse, could induce them to listen to the Gospel messages.

Young-King was one of the first among the Seneca chiefs to see the good influence of education and the Christian religion upon his people; and his influence was very great, standing as he did so high as a warrior and chief.

Like too many, too, he partook of the *fire-water*, and for many years was a victim of the lowest intemperance. In a drunken brawl he lost an arm, and a finger from the remaining hand; but after he became a Christian, not a drop ever wet his lips. At one time, on a journey, he was thrown from his carriage, and badly injured. When the physician came, he was groaning upon the floor in a neighboring hut; but the whiskey-bottle stood upon the table, and was an irresistible temptation; he must drink before he could attend his patient. When Young-King observed it, he asked "What you drink?" The doctor answered, "Whiskey, and it will do you good; come, take a glass!" "No," said the chief, "and you no bleed me, you no bleed me!" and though in the most intense suffering, he would not allow any thing to be done for him by a man who drank whiskey.

He was the first man who built a rod of fence on the Buffalo Reservation, where the missionaries first resided; and often, in the cold winter days, would be seen on Saturday, crossing the creek in his little canoe, to see if the church were supplied with fuel for the Sabbath; and if it

10

were not, with his one hand wielded the axe, and chopped the little pile, which he also carried to the door, to be sure that it was ready for the morning service, saying, he came so late into the vineyard, he must work diligently in order to accomplish any thing before he was called away. He enjoyed very little direct instruction, and could not read; yet he seemed to understand clearly the history of redemption, and the nature of the atonement, as well as the intricate workings of the human heart.

His manners were very refined and gentlemanly; and his deportment, at all times, that of one who had been well-bred and accustomed to cultivated circles; and the old-fashioned hospitality which characterizes his people, was kept up at his fireside; the poor were welcome, the hungry were fed, and the friendless made to feel that there was still in store for them sympathy and the kindness of cordial friendship.

He early lost the wife of his youth, but in the wife of his old age he had a genuine helpmate, who participated in his desire to do good among his people, encouraged his hospitality, and set an example of prudence and dignity at the head of her household.

They united with the little mission church on the same day, and reminded one of disciples at the feet of Jesus, when they listened to the words of the preacher, so childlike were their manners, and so trusting the expression of their countenances as they drank at the fountain of knowledge.

The punishment of children in the schools often caused much trouble among parents, and Young-King proposed that there should be a committee appointed among the chiefs to visit the schools regularly, and encourage the teachers, by talking to the children of the necessity of obedience and order, and the importance of education;

proving in all times of trouble an able and faithful counsellor, and a support in every good cause.

Wicked white men often tempted him, in order to overcome his temperance resolutions and lead him into sin; but he was always firm, and brought no dishonor, in any way, upon the cause which he had espoused.

During the last war, he was on the side of the United States, and the remainder of his life received a pension of two hundred dollars a year, as compensation for his bravery, and a wound which he received in performance of his meritorious services.

He died in 1835, and lies in the Mission Burial-Ground, about four miles from Buffalo, where are also most of the distinguished men and women of the nation who have died in the last half century. It is a consecrated spot indeed to the Indian and to the mission, for there are the lost and loved ones of their own little families, and the first fruits of their labors among a pagan people, who received Christian burial. It was once a fort, and the soldiers' graveyard; and warriors of many nations, and Christian pilgrims, and little children, whom Jesus took in his arms and blessed, now mingle their dust beneath the same green mounds; and some of them will awake at the sound of the last trump on the resurrection morn, and enter together the New Jerusalem.

# CHAPTER XI.

INDIAN MAGNANIMITY ILLUSTRATED BY THE LIFE OF CORN-PLANTER.

Wars develope warriors, and give an opportunity to the brave to display their heroism. Had there been no American Revolution, Washington would probably have remained a quiet farmer on his estates, unknown to fame; and had not war been the most glorious occupation in which men could engage, thousands of others would have gone down to the grave unhonored and unsung.

With the Iroquois, war and oratory being the only fields of distinction, it is only the lives of orators and warriors that we have to record, in writing Indian history

Cornplanter was scarcely less famous than Brandt, as his feet were, all his life, upon the war-path. The year of his birth cannot be ascertained with accuracy, but must have been as early as 1735. Like Farmer's Brother, he was in the battle which ended so disastrously for the British in Braddock's defeat, in 1755; and to the Indians alone the French owed all their victories, in the "old French war," as in an Indian country, with the primitive inhabitants so numerous as they were then, he who secured their alliance, must be morally certain of securing victory. Allowing Cornplanter to have been twenty years old at that time, and he could scarcely have been younger, his

CORN PLANTER.

birthday was three years later than that of Washington. His father was a white man, and his mother an Indian of the Seneca nation, and his birthplace Conewango, in the valley of the Genesee River. There is very little for me to relate of him, though he lived more than a hundred years, and was ever on the alert, because I cannot follow him to the battle ground, and he lived in a time when it was thought little else was worth relating concerning a great man, except his great deeds.

In a speech which he once wrote to the Governor of Pennsylvania, he says of himself:

"When I was a child, I played with the butterfly, the grasshopper, and the frogs; and as I grew up, I began to pay some attention, and play with the Indian boys in the neighborhood; they took notice of my skin being a different color from theirs, and spoke about it. I inquired of my mother the cause, and she told me that my father was a resident in Albany. I still ate my food out of a bark dish. I grew up to be a young man, and married me a wife, and I had no kettle or gun. I then knew where my father lived, and went to see him, and found he was a white man, and spoke the English language. He gave me food while I was at his house, but when I started to return home, he gave me no provisions to eat on the way. He gave me neither kettle nor gun."

It was the fate of all those who had as much white as red blood in their veins, to be rejected by the white parent; and they therefore had no alternative but to wed themselves to Indian customs, and be Indians in name, if not in reality. This sometimes infused a bitterness into their spirits, and made them doubly ferocious, when called to defend themselves against white enemies.

During all the revolutionary war, Cornplanter was the ally of the British; but when the hatchet was buried, and especially when the Indian was deserted by those for whom he had so faithfully fought, he became the friend of the United States, and never after wavered in his loyalty to the Republic. In one of his war excursions, he sought his father's dwelling, and surprising him, made him a prisoner. The old man was in terror at falling into the hands of an Indian; and, perhaps, would have feared more, if he had known that his captor was his son. But he did not recognize him till Cornplanter, after obliging him to march ten or twelve miles into the forest, leaving him all the while to imagine his fate, stepped up before him and said:

"My name is John O. Bail—commonly called Cornplanter. I am your son! You are my father! You are now my prisoner, and subject to the customs of Indian warfare. But you shall not be harmed—you need not fear. I am a warrior! Many are the scalps I have taken! many prisoners I have tortured to death! I am your son! I was anxious to see you, and greet you in friendship. I went to your cabin and took you by force. But your life shall be spared. Indians love their friends and their kindred, and treat them with kindness. If now you choose to follow the fortunes of your red son, and to live with our people, I will cherish your old age with plenty of venison, and you shall live easy. But if it is your choice to return to your fields, and live with your white children, I will send a party of my trusty young men to conduct you back in safety. I respect you, my father; you have been friendly to Indians, and they are your friends."

The father, of course, preferred his home and his white children; and the promise was faithfully fulfilled, of escorting him in safety back to his cabin. One can easily imagine that the young Cornplanter intended to "heap coals of fire on his head," though he had never heard the Scripture injunction; and in this instance, certainly acted according to the golden rule, of doing as he would be done by. His father had rejected him; had never performed the parent's duty of sheltering him, or giving him food or clothes, or bestowed upon him a word of affection, or manifested in him any interest. That he had a son among them, may have softened his feelings towards Indians, and prompted him to befriend them; but our impressions concerning the promptings of Indian blood, would lead us to expect retaliation for such neglect. We might expect him to ask, Why should the father love and cherish his white children, and leave him to run wild in the forest? Very likely these thoughts passed through his mind, but no Christian mother ever more thoroughly inculcated the precept, "Honor thy father and thy mother, that thy days may be long in the land which the Lord thy God giveth thee," than the untaught Indian woman in the wilderness. If Cornplanter had fallen upon his white brethren and sisters in anger, and meted out to them vengeance, on account of their being the Benjamins of their father's household, we should have called it consistent with Indian character. But though he had it in his power at any time to cause them to be slain, or taken captive, he left them by their firesides in safety and peace. That he sometimes thought of the injustice he was experiencing, is evident from the ironical allusions he made to the peculiar embarrassment of neglected children, in his speeches.

At one time, he, with several other Chiefs, was at a great dinner, given upon the ratification of a long-pending treaty. Wine being part of the entertainment, Cornplanter took his glass and said:

"I thank the Great Spirit for this opportunity of

smoking the pipe of friendship and love. May we plant our own vines, *be the fathers of our own children, and maintain them!*"

The Indian name of Cornplanter was Ga-ne-o-di-yo, or Handsome Lake; and he had a half-brother, who became distinguished among the Iroquois as the founder of a new religion. Having spent his youth in dissipation, he suddenly reformed, and announced that he had been commissioned by the Great Spirit as an apostle, endowed with supernatural gifts, and having a new revelation. At the time of his *conversion*—if such it may be termed—he resided with Cornplanter, in a little village on the Alleghany River, in the State of Pennsylvania.

During a severe illness, he pretended to have had a vision, and to have visited the world of spirits, where he was shown tortures inflicted upon the wicked, and also the happiness of the good. He was successful in obtaining the credence, not only of the people, but of the Chiefs; and through his new doctrines, operated upon the superstitious tendencies in the minds of those whom it was his office to reform, and was really the means of great good. He rejected some of the ancient Pagan ceremonies, and adopted new ones in their stead, and promulgated a code of morality, suited to their new condition and temptations.

The Indians had a superstitious fear of conforming to the customs of white people—believing it would not be right for them to build similar houses, or wear similar clothes, or eat the same food.

The new teacher convinced them that it would be impossible for them to live longer in their old way, and that the Great Spirit had commissioned him to tell them they might now adopt the customs of pale-faces. But he threatened them with all the tortures which the evil-minded could inflict, if they did not cease to drink the fire-water; and so thoroughly did he inspire them with respect for himself, and faith in his divine mission, that there was soon visible a great change in the moral condition of the people.

Among his inventions for working upon their fears, were the particular torments designed for offenders of various classes.

He saw in the House of Torment a drunkard, obliged to drink a red-hot liquid, as this was an article he had always loved. After drinking, there issued from his mouth a stream of blaze. He was slowly consuming with his tortures.

A man, who was in the habit of beating his wife, was led to the red-hot statue of a female, and requested to treat it as he had done his wife. He commenced beating it, and the sparks flew out and were continually burning him, but yet he would not consume. Thus would it be done to all who beat their wives.

Those who sold fire-water to the Indians, would have their flesh eaten from their arms.

Those who sold land to white people, would be for ever employed in removing heaps of sand, grain by grain.

In a large field of corn, overrun with weeds, women were at work pulling them up; but as fast as they were removed, they grew again—thus their work was never done. These were women who had been *lazy*, and thus all indolent women would be punished.

There was an appropriate punishment for those who were unkind to the aged and to children; and he who instituted this new order of things, went from village to village, "preaching and exhorting;" and among all the unchristianized Indians, he was favorably received, few doubting his divine authority.

By many, the scheme is thought to have originated

with Cornplanter, and is certainly worthy his sagacious mind. But he who executed the plan, must have been a man of no ordinary genius They probably saw their race running to swift destruction, and thought to devise a way to arrest the destroyer. There was little hope of bringing them so speedily under the influence of Christianity, as to produce the desired effect; and in no way would there be much hope, but by appealing to their superstitious fears.

The successor of the apostle is So-se-ha-wa, who is a sincere believer in the divine nature of the mission of Ga-ne-o-di-yo. At the convening of the mourning and religious councils, he repeats the message first delivered to the author of the new religion, and earnestly entreats all the people to heed his instructions. He is a man eminent for his virtues, and full of zeal in the performance of what he believes to be the duties of his holy office. He is a grandson of Ga-ne-o-di-yo, and nephew of Red Jacket. His birthplace was Ga-no-wau-ges, near the town of Avon, in 1774; and his present residence, Tonawanda, in the county of Genesee.

Cornplanter had for many years the enmity of a large portion of his people, on account of the course he took in selling lands and making treaties. His superior sagacity led him to see, that unless by formal treaty they parted with a portion, and secured to themselves another portion by the same means, they would again be involved in war, and be deprived of the whole. His motives were afterwards appreciated; but during the trial he was often in danger of losing his life, so exasperated were the Indians at seeing their beloved country thus readily yielded up to their enemies. Cornplanter mourned as sincerely as they, but a wise policy dictated the course he pursued. In one of his appeals concerning a small territory, bordering upon Pennsylvania, occupied by Halftown and his people, which had been ceded by the treaty of Fort Stanwix, and which they wished restored, he used the following language:

"They grew out of the land, and their fathers grew out of it, and they cannot be persuaded to part with it. *It is a very little piece.* We, therefore, entreat you to restore to us this little piece of land."

It reminds one of the prayer of Lot: "*Is it not a little city?*" but it was not successful. Halftown and his people were obliged to move, and again fell trees and till new fields. It is not strange they were discouraged, and retrograded, instead of advancing in civilization.

In 1790 Cornplanter visited Philadelphia in company with Rev. Mr. Kirkland, the celebrated missionary among the Iroquois, and Bigtree and Halftown. During the frequent interviews of the missionary with the great chief, the Christian religion was the theme of conversation, and Mr. Kirkland inclined to the opinion that Cornplanter became a believer in its doctrines, and also experienced the faith and indulged the hopes of the Christian.

In Sparks' American Biography, I find the following extract from his journal concerning the event.

"I do not now regret my journey. I think I never enjoyed more agreeable society with any Indian than Cornplanter has afforded me. He seems raised up by Providence for the good of his nation. He exhibits uncommon genius, possesses a very strong and distinguishing mind, and will bear the most mental application of any Indian I was ever acquainted with. When the business he came upon did not require his immediate attention, he would be incessantly engaged in conversation upon the subject of divine revelation. He appeared anxious as well as curious, in his inquiries for the evidences of the Scripture account of creation, the Christian scheme of doctrine, and the effects Christianity would produce upon the various nations of the earth, under the administration of the Son of God. No subject seemed to animate his mind, and excite his inquiries more, than the universal peace and harmony which should take place in the latter day. He would many times not leave the subject short of three or four hours' conversation. For the last week I was with them, he would not allow the Sachems and warriors to sit down at meal-time, without having me ask the divine blessing upon the food, and has never been intoxicated once during the whole course of his life. At our parting he observed to me, that his business with Congress was settled to his entire satisfaction, and he believed it would gratify every wish of his nation, and he should return home well stored with provisions by the way; but through the wonderful good providence of God, he had a richer store of spiritual food, out of which he could take a portion for his mind to feed upon, and digest every day through his long journey; and that he could not sufficiently thank the Great Spirit for giving him this opportunity of being so long with me."

The Indians were accustomed to call Washington "The Town Destroyer," on account of the destruction his armies caused wherever they went; but after he became President, his patient attention to their appeals, and promptness in redressing their grievances, acquired for him the title of Father, and gained for him the love of the Indians, that was like the love of children.

The following extracts are from a long appeal, made to Washington by Cornplanter and other chiefs, setting forth their wrongs, and asking justice.

The speech of Cornplanter, Halftown, and Bigtree,

chiefs and councillors of the Seneca Nation, to the Great Councillor of the Thirteen Fires.

"FATHER :—The voice of the Seneca nation speaks to you, the great councillor, in whose heart the wise men of all the Thirteen Fires have placed their wisdom. It may be very small in your ears, and we therefore entreat you to hearken with attention; for we speak of things which are to us very great. When your army entered the country of the Six Nations, we called you the TOWN DESTROYER; and to this day when that name is heard, our women look behind them and turn pale, and our children cling to the necks of their mothers. Our councillors and warriors are men, and cannot be afraid; but their hearts are grieved with the fears of our women and children, and desire that it may be buried so deep as to be heard no more. When you gave us peace we called you FATHER, because you promised to secure us in the possession of our lands. Do this, and so long as the lands shall remain, that beloved name shall live in the heart of every Seneca."

Then follows a long and particular account of the treaty by which the Indians had given up their land; how they had been deceived, and were threatened with war if they did not comply with all that was demanded—and proceeds:

"Upon this threat, our chiefs held a council, and they agreed that no event of war could be worse than to be driven with our wives and children from the only country which we had any right to.

"Astonished at what we heard from every quarter, with hearts aching with compassion for our women and children, we were compelled to give up all our country north of the line of Pennsylvania, &c.

"FATHER :—You have said that we were in your hand, and that by closing it you could crush us to nothing. Are you determined to crush us? If you are, tell us so; that those of our nation who have become your children, and have determined to die so, may know what to do.

"In this case, one chief has said he would ask you to put him out of pain. Another, who will not think of dying by the hand of his father or his brother, has said he will retire to the Chateaugay, eat of the fatal root, and sleep with his fathers in peace.

"Before you determine on a measure so unjust, look up to God, who has made *us* as well as *you*. We hope he will not permit you to destroy the whole of our nations.

"The Chippewas and all the nations westward, call us and ask us,—'Brothers of our Fathers, where is the place you have preserved for us to lie down upon?' You have compelled us to do that which has made us ashamed. We have nothing to answer to the children of the brothers of our fathers.

"FATHER:—We will not conceal from you that the Great God, and not man, has preserved the Cornplanter from the hands of his own nation. For they ask continually, 'Where is the land which our children and their children after them, are to lie down upon?' He is silent, for he has nothing to answer. When the sun goes down he opens his heart before God, and earlier than the sun appears upon the hills, he gives thanks for his protection during the night; for he feels that among men, become desperate by their danger, it is God only who can preserve them. He loves peace, and all that he had in store, he has given to those who have been robbed by your people, lest they should slander the innocent to repay themselves. The whole season which others have employed in providing for their families, he has spent in his endeavors to preserve peace; and at this moment his wife and children are lying on the ground, and in want of food; his heart is in pain for them, but he perceives that the Great God will try his firmness in doing what is right.

"FATHER:—The game which the Great Spirit sent into our country for us to eat, is going from among us; we thought that He intended that we should till the land with the plough, as the white people do, and we talked to one another about it. But before we speak to you concerning this, we must know from you whether you mean to leave us and our children any land to till.

"FATHER:—Innocent men of our nation are killed one after another, and our best families; but none of your people who committed the murders have been punished.

"FATHER:—These are to us very great things. We know that you are very strong, and we have heard that you are wise, and we wait to hear your answer to what we have said, that we may know that you are just."

It was not in the power of Washington to perform all the Chiefs asked, but he promised that all he could do should be done, and expressed the kindest sympathy in their sufferings, saying:—

"The merits of Cornplanter, and his friendship for the United States, are well known to me, and shall not be forgotten; and, as a mark of esteem of the United States, I have directed the Secretary of War to make him a present of two hundred and fifty dollars, either in money or goods, as the Cornplanter shall like best."

So they returned home soothed and comforted. In the answer which Cornplanter made he said:—

"FATHER:—Your speech written on the great paper, is to us like the morning to the sick man, whose pulse beats too strongly in his temples, and prevents him from sleep. He sees it and rejoices, but is not cured.

"FATHER:—You give us leave to speak our minds concerning the tilling of the ground. We ask you to teach us to plough and to grind corn; to assist us in building saw-mills, and to supply us with broadaxes, saws, augers, and other tools, so as that we make our houses more comfortable and more durable; that you will send smiths among us, and, above all, that you will teach our children to read and write, and our women to spin and weave."

Whilst Cornplanter was absent several murders were committed among his people by white men, and some, of the best families, were destroyed. He then made another appeal for protection, and did all in his power to quiet the revengeful feelings of those who had been injured; thus proving that he was sincere in his professions of friendship and love of peace.

At the very time that he was about to depart as an ambassador of peace to the Western Indians, "three of his people were travelling through a settlement upon the Genesee, and stopped at a house to light their pipes. There happened to be several white men within, one of whom, as the foremost Indian stooped down to light his pipe, killed him with an axe, another of the party was badly wounded with the same weapon whilst escaping from the house."

When Cornplanter heard of this, he did not plan revenge, and instigate his men to slay the first white men they met in return; but commanded his warriors to let their tomahawks remain sheathed, and only said, ". It is hard, when I and my people are trying to make peace for the white people, that we should be thus rewarded. I can govern my young men and warriors better than the Thirteen Fires can theirs."

This was a magnanimity worthy of a Christian, and had it originated with a Grecian or Roman conqueror, or in any other than an Indian bosom, would have been written in letters of gold, and presented by every mother to her son as a worthy example. But how few are there yet that ever heard of an Indian who thought of any thing but revenge for injuries.

When Washington was about to retire from the Presidency, Cornplanter made a special visit to the seat of government to bid him farewell, and again ask his attention to the condition of his people. After stating the several points which he wished him to consider, he concludes: "Father, I congratulate you on your intended repose from the fatigues and anxiety of mind, which are constant attendants on high public stations, and hope that the same good Spirit which has so long guided your steps as a father to a great nation, will still continue to protect you, and make your private reflections as pleasant to yourself as your public measures have been useful to your people."

This was the last interview between the two chiefs of a widely different people, both richly endowed by nature, to be so variously favored by fortune. Washington lived but a little while longer, and went down to the grave amid the lamentations of a nation, with a name on which has been bestowed the homage of a world; and Cornplanter retired to his secluded cabin in the forest, to live forty years, devoted to humble efforts for the elevation of his people; to die alone, with a name which has been almost forgotten.

The remainder of his life Cornplanter lived very quietly, always on friendly terms with white people, and earnestly engaged in promoting agriculture, and all the arts of civilization among his people. He was a professing Christian, and always welcomed the clergymen and teachers to his humble abode. In 1816 he was visited by Rev. Mr. Alden, President of Alleghany College, who speaks with delight of the improvements which had been made under the fostering care of the old chief,—of the large fields of buckwheat, corn, and oats; the great number of sheep, oxen, and horses that seemed at home, and perfectly domesticated on Indian lands. Cornplanter testified his joy at seeing Christian friends, by performing the offices of servant himself, and going into the field and mowing the grass for their horses. He was the owner at that time of thirteen hundred acres of land on the banks of the Alleghany, and six hundred were occupied by Indians, whose comfortable dwellings and cultivated fields formed a thriving village.

The following is an appeal to the Society of Friends by Cornplanter, imploring their aid in promoting agriculture and education among his people.

"BROTHERS:—The Seneca nation see that the Great Spirit intends they should not continue to live by hunting, and they look around on every side, and inquire who it is that shall teach them what is best for them to do. Your fathers dealt honestly by our fathers. They have engaged us to remember it, and we wish our children to be taught the same principles by which our fathers were guided.

"BROTHERS:—We cannot teach our children what we perceive their situation requires them to know. We have too little wisdom among us. We wish them to be instructed to read and write, and such other things as you teach your children—especially the love of peace."

He died March 7th, 1836, and was buried beneath a spreading tree in his own field, but no stone or monument marks his grave. A century hence, when it is too late, a proud and peerless nation will wake up to their guilt, and their duty to a peculiar, if not a chosen people:

"But they will all have passed away,
The noble race and brave;"

and then will commence the lamentations, that those who had it in their power should have looked so indifferently on whilst they wasted away.

Cornplanter had a son, "a boy of fine spirit and promise," who was sent to Philadelphia for the benefit of an English education, under the care of the Quakers, who placed him in a suitable school and directed his studies.

He was not only received into good society, but caressed. On one occasion, being at a ball, while dancing with a beautiful girl, the jealousy of one of the young gentlemen present was excited, and he gave vent to his vexation by muttering the dislike he felt at seeing the young lady "dance with a damned Indian." The quick ear of young Henry caught the sound, and after the figure was ended, having invited the young swain to the head of the stairs, he thrust him out, and gave him a push which sent him headlong down. "There," said he, "you may now boast that you have been kicked down stairs by a damned Indian."

But Henry had been too long the wild boy of the mountains, to be pleased with confinement, or bear patiently his monotonous exercises. He wasted and pined till he became pale and emaciated. He was very courteous in manners, and had the suavity peculiar to the forest Chieftain. "My sister," he would say,—"my sister is not here, and there is another who is not with me." He thirsted for the bright waters of his native valley, and longed to breathe once more the pure air of the Alleghanies. The crowded streets of the city had no charms for him. He stayed but a few months, and bursting from his confinement, bounded back with the alacrity of a wounded deer, to the green mountain haunts of his boyhood, the sweet tones of his sister, and the gentle cooings of his forest dove.

The following year Mr. N——, a gentleman from Philadelphia, who had known the Chief there, came on an errand of agency to our country, where he has since resided. Having no acquaintance here, and feeling a deep interest in his young friend, he penetrated through the dark wilds of Potts and McKean, and soon found himself at the village of the Cornplanter. Henry welcomed him cordially, presenting him to his father, his sister, and his friends; but there was a sadness visible in his countenance, a quick restlessness in his movements, which betrayed how deep were the workings within. Mr. N—— then asked him for the gentle dove he had described to him in days gone by. "She is gone," said he, and led him to her grave. Here, Harry, after the custom of white people, had planted flowers, not the forget-me-not, nor the rose, nor the myrtle, but pale spring violets, refreshing them with his tears, and breathing from this hallowed spot his invocations to the Great Spirit.

He was in the war of 1812, and a gallant soldier under General Porter, but very sorrowful is the story of his after life, and dark indeed was the day of his death; but I will not relate it, to become an instrument of universal accusation against his people, who have been too long and too often judged by individual instances of degeneracy.

# CHAPTER XII.

REFINEMENT AND SENSIBILITY IN INDIAN CHARACTER, ILLUSTRATED IN THE LIFE OF LOGAN.

THE Indian name of Logan has scarcely been heard or written, as the one by which he was familiarly known was given him in childhood by his father, in memory of a dear friend, a white man, Charles Logan. His Indian name was Tal-ga-yee-ta, and his father was a Cayuga Chief, whose house was on the borders of Cayuga Lake.

There has been much dispute about the events of Logan's life, and the speech which has rendered his name immortal, has been ascribed to others—even to a white man. But Mr. Jefferson, who first gave publicity to this proof of his eloquence, and to his sorrows, has taken special pains to verify his narrative, and proved that the words which have thrilled a million of heart-strings, were uttered by Logan, and by no other.

He inherited his gifts and his noble nature from his father, who was ever the friend of peace, and who was ever the white man's friend. His wigwam was known far and near, as the abode of hospitality, and friendship, and kindness. It was a wigwam, but there was something of the halo about it which invested a feudal castle, in the days of English chivalry and romance. Those who gathered around the cordial fire, which was lighted for every stranger, by the forest chieftain, felt the independence which the lone traveller did in some old baronial hall; and he who presided at the feast, to which all were welcome, was not less noble, or less dignified than an English lord. Had there been a pen to record his hospitality and *table talk*, there would most probably have been seen in it more of wisdom than entered into the discourse of many a prince or potentate. But alas! for forest eloquence, it was wafted only by the breeze, and its echoes died away in the forest.

Logan moved in early life to the banks of the Juniata, which is a beautiful river, flowing through a wild romantic country, watered also by the Susquehanna. In a pleasant valley he built his cabin, and married a Shawnee wife. Thus he became identified with the Shawnese and Delawares, though belonging to the Six Nations. And it was thus that he became the victim of those lawless marauders, who believed Indians every where lawful prey, when they could slaughter them with impunity.

Logan had listened in boyhood to the instructions of the Moravian missionaries, and their gentle manners and soothing words, had probably influenced his character. Whether he was a Christian, I know not; but there are many who bear the name, in whom there is far less exemplification of Christian principle. There was about him a quiet and softened dignity, a refinement of sentiment and delicacy of feeling, which characterizes none but the lofty, and exhales from none but the pure. His house, like his father's, was the Indian's and the white man's home, the dwelling-place of love. Alas! that the milk of human kindness in his bosom, should ever have been turned to gall, by bitter and corroding wrongs. In his childhood, a little cousin had been taken captive by white men, under aggravating circumstances, but for this he did not become the white man's foe. "Forgive and forget," was his motto, in all things that could be forgiven and forgotten; and he lived to be an aged man, before vengeance took possession of his soul.

In all the country where he dwelt he was known, and to every cottage Logan was welcome; terror did not creep into the heart of woman, nor fear fall upon the little child, when his footsteps were heard at their doors. And this, as was afterwards proved, was not because he had not all the traits which make a brave warrior, but from a settled principle that all men were brothers, and should love one another.

He set forth at one time on a hunting expedition, and was alone in the forest. Two white hunters were engaged in the same sport, and having killed a bear in a wild gorge, were about to rest beside a bubbling spring, when they saw an Indian form reflected in the water. They sprang to their feet and grasped their rifles, but the Indian bent forward and struck the rifles from their hands, and spilt the powder from their flasks. Then stretching forth his open palm in token of friendship, he seated himself beside them and won his way to their hearts. For a week they roamed together, hunting and fishing by day, and sleeping by the same fire at night. It was Logan, and henceforth their brother. He pursued his way over the Alleghanies, and they returned to their homes, never again to point the gun at an Indian's heart.

Some white men on a journey stopped at his cabin to rest. For amusement a shooting match was proposed, at which the price was to be a dollar a shot. During the sport Logan lost five shots, and when they had finished, he entered his lodge and brought five deer-skins for the redemption of his forfeit, as a dollar a skin was the established price in the market, and the red man's money. But his guests refused to take them, saying they had only been shooting for sport, and wished no forfeit. But the honorable Indian would take no denial, replying, "If you had lost the shots I should have taken your dollars, but as I have lost, take my skins."

Another time he wished to buy grain, and took his skins to a tailor, who adulterated the wheat, thinking the Indian *would not know*. But the miller informed him, and advised him to apply to a magistrate for redress. He went to a Mr. Brown, who kindly saw that his loss was made up, for Logan came often to his house, and he knew his noble heart and grieved to see him wronged. As he was waiting the decision of the magistrate, he played with a little girl, who was just trying to walk, and the mother remarked that she needed some shoes, which she was not able to purchase for her.

The child was very fond of Logan, and loved to sit upon his knee, and when he went away was ready to go too. He asked the mother if he might take her to his cabin for the day, and she, knowing well the attention which would be bestowed upon her in the Indian's lodge, consented. Towards night there was some anxiety about the little one, but the shades of evening had scarcely begun to deepen, when Logan was seen wending his way to the cottage with his precious charge; and when he placed her in her mother's arms, she saw upon her feet a tiny pair of moccasins, neatly wrought, that his own hands had made. Was this not a delicate way of showing gratitude, and expressing friendship? Was it a rude and savage nature that prompted this attention to a little child, to make glad a mother's heart? Not all the refined teachings of civilization could have invented a more beautiful tribute of sympathy and grateful affection.

Logan was never tempted by friend or foe to touch the *fire-water* to his lips, till after wrongs kindled revenge in his soul.

He adopted few of the customs, and rejected all the vices of civilization. This dignity and politeness were Indian characteristics, and are found universally among his people.

But in an evil day the enemy found his way to the peaceful cabin in the forest, and darkness shrouded all the remainder of the good man's life.

Had Logan remained farther north, and preserved his identity with the Six Nations, he would probably have been spared the woes which fell so thickly upon him. The Iroquois were still formidable, and neither armies nor individuals ventured to insult them without provocation. If it had been known that he was a Sachem, and one of the chief men of his tribe, he would have been left unmolested. But the sin would have been as great of desolating a home, the inmates of which were peaceful unoffending women and children.

A little company of military men were on their way to the west, and encamped in the vicinity of Logan's cabin. Not by the authority of their captain, but unknown to him, two or three set off in the night to inflict any injury which might be in their power upon the Indians they had heard were near. The husband and father was absent, but they lured one brother into the forest, and murdered him in cold blood, and then returned to destroy another as cruelly, and then shot the mother and little ones, leaving all upon the floor weltering in blood. Logan returned to find his cabin tenanted only by the dead, and vengeance for the first time was kindled in his bosom, and burned like a raging flame in his soul. Now he became the white man's foe, and incited every son of the forest to slay without mercy their common enemy. Thus commenced the long and frightful Indian war which filled the whole land with terror, and for ten years stained our historical records with Indian atrocities, unparalleled in our colonial or national experience. The quiet peaceful homes of white men were invaded, and women and children either killed or carried away captive; but then it was not known why these outrages were committed. They were ascribed to Indian love of war, and carnage, and bloodshed; but wherever Indian cruelty may be traced, it will be found to have been preceded by acts more cruel and heartless on the part of white men

> Stranger,—there are who think and write
> The Indian's soul untouched with light,
> And that to him belongs the guilt
> For all the blood his hand hath spilt!
> Like mine, his friendly homes among,
> They would have known God never made,
> A heart all darkness, and how long
> The Indian bore aggressive wrong.
> Old Logan was the white man's friend;
> But injuries forced his love to end;
> Of children, wife, and kindred shorn,
> None left for him to joy or mourn,
> He rose in calm, vindictive ire,
> Beside his nation's council fire,
> And bade them, by their fathers slain,
> No more in voiceless peace remain,
> But lift the brand, and battle cry,
> For vengeance, if not victory!

"Welcome, Englishmen! welcome, Englishmen!" was the pleasant greeting our fathers heard on the shores of New England; and a similar hospitality was extended to all who came, by this unsuspicious and trusting people.

In 1774, a deputation was sent to treat with the Sachems and chiefs, and to endeavor to appease their revenge. But Logan was a long time in yielding. No persuasion could induce him to attend a council that was to treat of peace. He would not talk with white men of peace. It was useless to contend longer, he knew—they might as well submit. There was no hope for the Indian but to flee before the armed legions which were pursuing them, but he would never be their friend.

At length Gen. Gleson, who was one of the deputation, followed him into the depths of the forest; and there, seated upon a fallen tree, with Cornstalk, the venerable Shawnee chief by his side, he was induced to sign the treaty which all the other Sachems had signed before him, but not till he had repeated the heart-rending story of his wrongs, and the wrongs of his people. It was like wringing out his heart's blood to see them thus wasting away. They fell in thousands before the sword, and tens of thousands before the still more desolating scourge of the fire-water; and while he talked, the tears coursed down his furrowed cheeks, and his keen sensibilities were quickened to the intensest suffering. Here it was that he made the speech which is familiar to every English tongue.

The name of Cresap appears in the speech, as Logan thought he was with the men at the time of the murders. The details of the transaction vary in almost every account given of them, but as I have no room for discussions, I give the best authenticated narrative, and transcribe the speech as it first appeared in "Jefferson's Notes on Virginia," in which he challenges all the authors of antiquity to produce any thing superior.

### SPEECH OF LOGAN.

"I appeal to any white man to say, if ever he entered Logan's cabin hungry, and he gave him no meat; if ever he came cold and naked, and he clothed him not. During the course of the last long and bloody war, Logan remained in his cabin, an advocate for peace. Such was my love for the whites, that my countrymen pointed as they passed, and said, 'Logan is the friend of white men.' Col. Cresap, the last spring, in cold blood, and unprovoked, murdered all the relations of Logan, not even sparing my women and children. There runs not a drop of my blood in any living creature. This called on me for revenge. I have sought it. I have killed many. I have fully glutted my vengeance. For my country I rejoice at the beams of peace. But do not harbor a thought that mine is the joy of fear. Logan never felt fear. He will not turn on his heel to save his life. Who is there to mourn for Logan? Not one."

Never again did Logan possess a HOME. He wandered about for many years from settlement to settlement, restless, moody, and unhappy, and finally laid himself down in the forest to die. "There were none to mourn for Logan;" but very truly Jefferson remarks, "his talents and misfortunes have attached to him the respect and commiseration of a world."

## CHAPTER XIII.

#### THE DARKEST PAGE OF INDIAN HISTORY.

THE history of TREATIES is by far the darkest of all the pages of Indian history. War and bloodshed are terrible,—terrible indeed; the stories of massacres chill the blood in our veins; and the bitter strife of war is revolting to all the finer feelings of our nature. But there has been a far more bitter strife of treaties, at which the heart bleeds, and the spirit moans.

When the Six Nations were fairly subdued, and settled on the free reservations which were left to them in the western part of New York, if they could have remained undisturbed, and experienced no more wrong or dishonor, they would soon have adopted the arts of civilization; and, through the instructions of the missionaries, have become a Christian people.

But the echo of the warwhoop and the booming cannon had no sooner died away, than there came among them an army of serpents in human form, wearing the semblance of angels of light. These were land speculators; and there is no species of bribery or corruption within the power of man to which they did not resort, in order to drive the Indians entirely from our borders.

By this means they were kept in a constantly unsettled state, so that for many years the labors of the missionaries seemed utterly in vain. Some of the chiefs would now and then yield to bribery, and some to deception, and conclude to give up all they possessed, and remove beyond the Mississippi. And, as late as 1846, an emigration party was formed, and more than a hundred departed to the western wilds, where more than half of them perished before the end of a year.

By a gross and wicked fraud, the Buffalo reservation was finally obtained, so that the Indians were all obliged to move from their comfortable homes and well-tilled fields, and commence anew in the forests to fell trees, and plough, and plant, and sow. By a similar fraud, the Tonawanda reservation was claimed; but the chiefs and people would not remove, saying the treaty had never been signed by any member of those who had the power to make contracts, and they had no desire to part with another acre of their lands to white men. So the case is still in the courts, where thousands of dollars have been spent in an offensive and defensive war of words and quibbles. But the Indians now have lawyers among themselves, and firm friends and able counsellors among white people, and it is hoped the right will yet prevail.

During these troublous times there were many affecting appeals made to societies and the Government, which, one would think, might melt hearts of stone, and prove, too, that eloquence did not die with Red Jacket or Cornplanter.

These troubles, too, rallied around them many friends, especially among the Quakers, and awakened sympathy and renewed effort in their behalf. A few extracts from letters, written by those who defended them in the hour of their calamity, and from the speeches of some of their Chiefs, a few of whom are still living, will give some idea of what the Indian is in a civilized state, when *literally* seated by his fireside.

Extract from a Report, made by a deputation of Friends, to investigate the true nature of the differences between the land speculators and the Indians:—

"It has been common for those who would deprive the Indians of their lands, first to describe them as ignorant, or stupid, or savage; and then, 'for such worthy cause, to deem them as their lawful prey,' to put them out of the pale of civilization, and then shut upon them the gate of mercy.

"But it is not true, that these remnants of the Six Nations are either barbarous or vicious. On the contrary, they are an innocent and improving people. Feeling their own weakness they have been forced to yield to oppression and injury; but they are neither quarrelsome nor vindictive. They are the remnant of a bold, warlike, and highly gifted race; fallen indeed from the dizzy height of a tremendous political and physical power, but bearing that fall with patience and dignity; inspiring respect, and rendering them objects of intense interest to the philanthropist and philosopher.

"These New York Indians, like all other communities of mankind, present great varieties of character and grades of intellect, but as a people, perhaps none of the aborigines of North America have equalled them in all the manifestations of mental power. They have not had the use of letters to store their minds with knowledge, or to record their own achievements; yet we know that they have had many great and talented men among them, who, making a very moderate allowance for the want of education, would not suffer by comparison with the greatest of European competitors. They have from the earliest times been considered a very extraordinary race, distinguished from all the surrounding nations by their capacity for negotiation, eloquence, and war. Remarkable for the love of liberty, they scorned submission to foreign control. Baron La Houtan says of them, 'They laugh at the menaces of kings and governors, for they have no idea of dependence—the very word to them is insupportable. They look upon themselves as sovereigns, accountable to none but God, whom they call the Great Spirit.'

"De Witt Clinton in his history of the Six Nations informs us, that they held supremacy over a country of amazing extent and fertility, inhabited by warlike and numerous nations, which must have been the result of unity of design and system of action, proceeding from a wise and energetic policy, continued for a long course of time. That in eloquence and dignity, and in all the characteristics of personal policy, they surpass an assembly of feudal barons.

"Their territory was estimated at 1,200 miles long by 700 broad, including the great lakes or inland seas which bound our possessions to the north. Among their orators they had a Garangula, a Cornplanter, a Red Jacket, and a Big Kettle, of whom an elegant writer has said, 'they were men whose majesty of mind shone with a lustre that no belittling appellations could bedim.' President Jefferson says, 'I may challenge the whole orations of Demosthenes and Cicero, and of any more eminent orator, if Europe has furnished more eminent, to produce a single passage superior to the speech of Logan; yet this Logan was the son of a Cayuga chief, a Sachem of the New York Indians.'

"When the news spread among them that the treaty was signed, and their land sold, there was unutterable sorrow. To the poor Senecas it was 'a day of darkness and of gloominess, of clouds and of thick darkness,' through which a ray of gladness could not penetrate.

Consternation and gloom covered their settlements. Their women were seen on all sides weeping in their houses—along their roads—as they passed to their occupations, and in the fields whilst engaged in their labors. One of their chiefs, in a speech on the occasion said, ' It seems as if we should be worn down. When we see our fields covered with grain, and our orchards loaded with fruit, it only increases our sorrows.' The settled and expressive gloom that was manifested upon their countenances and deportment attested the reality of their sorrows.

"The cruelty of the attempt to drive the Indians away at this time was enhanced by the consideration that within the last half century, under the care of Friends, they had made great advances in civilization. They had good houses, barns, horses, wagons, horned cattle, sheep, swine, and farming utensils. They had places of worship and schools, many of them could read and write, and had books and private libraries. They had good farms, and some skill in agriculture. It would be far less cruel to drive the surrounding white population into the deserts beyond the Missouri, than to send there the Seneca Indians. The former would soon gather around them all the comforts of life—the latter would soon scatter, or perish for ever."

The following is a communication to the Society of Friends at Baltimore, from twenty Chiefs of the Seneca Nation, making known their troubles.

Cattaraugus in Council, Oct. 5, 1845.

To THE COMMITTEE OF FRIENDS,

"BROTHERS:—We are informed you are soon to hold a great Council in Baltimore, on the subject of our affairs. We pray the Great Spirit may strengthen you, and give you wisdom and direct you aright in all your deliberations.

11*

"BROTHERS:—We know you love us; the Great Spirit has taught you to do so. Your ears have been open to hear our cries, and your hearts inclined to help us in our distress. We cannot reward you; we have nothing to give you in return but our love and gratitude. This you have full and complete.

"BROTHERS:—When your fathers were weak and ours were strong, the Great Spirit led them to believe you were their friends; they helped you in your childlike condition. Things have changed! You have become great and strong, and we poor and weak. You are now paying us for what our fathers have done.

"BROTHERS:—Our troubles are great indeed. This you are sensible of, and have done much to relieve us in our distress; but the chains of the white men have grown, and continue to grow tight upon us at the loss and expense of our substance. They multiply, and become too heavy for us to endure.

"BROTHERS:—We have none (on earth) to look to for aid and protection, but you. When you forsake us, all is lost. Our wives and daughters wet their pillows with their tears, and pray the Great Spirit to keep your ears open that you may hear their cries.

"BROTHERS:—We have but little to say; our mouths are almost closed. Our hopes are in you. Farewell."

Extract from an address to the Committee of the Four Yearly Meetings of Friends of New York, Philadelphia, Baltimore and Genesee, by several Indian Chiefs.

"When we turn our faces backward, and look over the histories of the past, we find that more than fifty winters have gone by since the Iroquois, or Six Nations, first selected the Society of Friends *as their friends*, upon whom they could repose confidence without fear of being betrayed.

"The selection was made from the sects and denominations of those who styled themselves Christians, at the time when war had diminished the members of the Iroquois braves—when the Iroquois bowstring had been broken—when his council fires were nearly put out by the blood of his people, and the loud thundering voices of the big iron guns of the pale faces caused the ground to tremble beneath his feet, and his council house to shake to its very foundation—when oppression crushed the Iroquois, and cruelty made his heart bleed—when murder and robbery committed upon the red man, brought bounty to the spoiler committing the foul deed,—when the pale-faces, like hungry hounds, chased the red man from his hunting grounds.

"It was then that the red man's sun was darkened, and the Great Spirit had drawn his sable garment before its shining face, and left his red children to roam in gloom and uncertainty. In looking round, the Iroquois saw none to assist him in his struggles for liberty, his country, and his firesides,—he found no sympathy from the pale-faced Christians, save from the Society of Friends, who, with the true principle of the spirit of Christianity implanted in their breast, guided by the dictation of the Good Spirit, and following the counsel and mandates of HIM WHO NEVER ERRS, came to our relief; not with powder, bullets, or arms, but with sympathy in their bosoms, pity in their hearts, and friendship in their hands; and our tradition informs us, that since the time this alliance was established between the Society of Friends and our people; nothing has occurred to mar our mutual understanding, or tarnish the chain of friendship that bound us together.

"BROTHERS:—We hope that you may teach your children to love and pity the red man; so that when the Master of life and light shall call you hence, your red brothers may still have friends like you, and the good understanding now existing between us, be for ever perpetuated and cherished between your posterity and ours. For the services you have rendered us, accept the gratitude of an injured and oppressed race, and may the Great Spirit watch over and protect you."

There were not at any time more than a fifteenth part of the whole nation in favor of removal, and the consent of those few was obtained by misrepresentation and bribery, for which sums were paid in different ways and at different times to the amount of $32,000. And yet at one time every rood of land was ceded, and the process of removal commenced. It is due to the Society of Friends to state, that it was through their persevering instrumentality that this great calamity was averted.

Among the most noble and venerable of the Seneca Chiefs was

## BIG KETTLE.

In his bosom glowed the loftiest patriotism, and on his brow beamed the purest philanthropy. To him the sorrows of his people were the seeds of death; they ate into his heart, and drank his life-blood. He mourned over their desolation and wept over their sins.

"Oh, is there nothing we can do?" said he one morning to Mr. Wright, the missionary, who remained among them when there was little he could do but encourage them to resist unto the end, and pray that their strength might not fail and who stood by them, ready for any service, in the darkest hours of their adversity. "Is there nothing more we can do? Yes, let us continue to petition," was the answer, and an offer to write whatever he would say.

The result was a remonstrance, which in his own language was pathetic and touching in the extreme. On listening to it, I asked if in the translation it was not embellished; and the reply was, that no translation could do justice to the original. I can make only a few extracts.

"First, as a people, without exception, we love the land of our birth, the place of our fathers' graves; and could we be permitted to retain undisturbed possession of the gifts of God to our people, not one of us would entertain a thought of emigration. We are satisfied with our country, we neither ask nor seek a better one.

"But we are told we can never live in peace here; that the land of the Indians' peace is far towards the setting sun. Let us lay open our hearts to your honorable body. We are troubled. Why should it be said that we can have no peace here? The age, wisdom, and dignity of a great nation are yours. You can resolve our doubts for us. The United States have land enough. You have abundant means of communication. In all your wide country, your steamboats, rail cars, and carriages can bear your people whithersoever they wish to go. Neither have you any lack of wealth, that your people should wish to become rich at our expense. Neither have we given you any ground of complaint against us.

"We have fought by the side of one of your greatest generals. He still lives to bear testimony to our fidelity. Yes, the blood of our chiefs was shed on the battle-field for what you then told us was our common country. It was mingled with the blood of your enemies slain by our hands, and that too at your solicitation, at a time when you said you stood in need of our aid. Why then can we have no peace in a land whose peace we helped to buy at such a price?

"It is true we are now few and weak; you are numerous and mighty, but you are also magnanimous. The great hearts which beat in the bosoms of your chiefs and head men, would not let them oppress the remnant of any nation almost wasted from the earth, much less the remnant of friends who once fought and bled for them.

"It is true, indeed, we are almost wasted away. The smallest of your ten thousand towns has in it more people than our whole nation. And can it then be any satisfaction to the United States to set their foot upon the neck of an old man, even now tottering into his grave? We cannot understand these things. We wish, if we must all go into the grave, and perish from the earth, to lie together in the same dust with our forefathers. The strange, unhallowed earth of other lands will press heavily upon our bosoms. It will be cold—we cannot sleep in such graves.

"We cannot flourish there if our hearts are not there —if we go against our will—if we are driven forth heartbroken and dispirited. No: men will starve and perish in the most luxuriant soil on earth if compelled to take possession of it under such circumstances. We must go contentedly—we must go cheerfully, in order to be benefited by the kind offers of the government; and, above all, we must go unitedly. The bands which held us together have been torn. *Now*, the flames of strife burn high between friends and brethren. If you push us off hastily together, we shall only go to devour each other till we are consumed. And even if we should not absolutely destroy each other, we could not flourish. The oak riven by the thunderbolt will not grow again. A kind, gentle hand might transplant sprout after sprout, and raise up perhaps a forest there. But after the lightning's shock, neither root nor branch retains the power of germinating. What harm can our remaining do you? What is the use of a few thousand acres of land to a nation like the United States? But an honorable name—the love and friendship of those whom God has placed under your care, and, above all, THE CONSCIOUSNESS OF DOING RIGHT, will be of great importance.

"Thus we have laid open our hearts to you. Our warriors, and our women and children will take their own way to make known their concurrence. We hope you will attentively consider what we have said. We have trespassed long upon your patience, but with HOME and COUNTRY,—our fathers' graves, and the honor of the United States at stake, we could not have said less. May the Great Being who controls the counsels and destinies of nations guide you to a right decision."

Big Kettle furnished another gratifying instance that an Indian could resist temptation, and maintain his integrity through the darkest hours of adversity and the most aggravating wrongs. There are many among his own people and among white men, who knew him, who pronounce him a greater man than Red Jacket. He lived to a later day, and felt more keenly, if this were possible, the woes which seemed to fall thicker and faster upon the Indian as years wore on. His head was always clear, for not a drop of the fire-water ever touched his lips. There was a more softened dignity in his deportment and more affability in his manners than was experienced in intercourse with Red Jacket. He had finer sensibilities, and though there is a vein of sarcasm often in his speeches, it was not so bitter as that which ran through almost every thing Red Jacket said. He remained a Pagan to the day of his death, though he seemed to lose some of his interest in Pagan ceremonies. He endeavored earnestly to elevate his people, and promote a true spirit of morality. A distinguished statesman and infidel who proposed establishing a school for propagating infidelity, once fell into company with Big Kettle, and attempted to convince him that there was no God, and to prejudice him against the missionaries, and excite him to bitter enmity against religion; but the Indian's trust in the Great Spirit was not moved, and though he did not understand the Christian's God, his sagacious mind quickly discovered the fallacy of the atheist's arguments, and he was thoroughly disgusted with his coarse manners and conversation, and the want of principle which was manifest in his motives.

He said he was led to abjure the fire-water by witnessing the evil influence of it upon his father, and the misery it introduced into their otherwise happy family.

He literally died of a broken heart. There were some among the chiefs who were in favor of the treaty, and one day in the council house, strife arose to such a height, and discussion became so warm, that tomahawks were unsheathed, and there was danger of something more terrible than a war of words. I have seen the one which gleamed in Big Kettle's hand on that occasion, but it was allowed to do no harm, and it was this that grieved the patriotic old man more than any thing else, to see Iroquois at enmity with one another. It was not so in the days of old. Oh, how changed! The Indians were once all brethren; but now they were divided. To see them wasted was not so sad as to see them broken and degenerate. He mourned and would not be comforted, and like Logan went away into the forest, and shut himself in a lonely cabin to die.

The missionary learned his retreat and visited him, trying to speak comfort to his spirit, but in vain. He tried also to lead him to the Christian's God, and explain to him the Christian's faith. But this too was vain. He said the Great Spirit had not seen fit to give the Indian the good book which white people talked about, and he would not therefore punish him for not knowing what it contained. "Big Kettle," said he, "has never done wrong to his fellow man. Big Kettle has never taken what belonged to another—has never told a lie. The Great Spirit knows Big Kettle loves him, and he will take him to the good place when he dies." So, firm in his trust in the Indian's God, he departed in the year 1830, without a single fear of death, or unwillingness to go, and to the Great Spirit we will leave him. "He alone is judge."

SPEECH OF GAYASHUTA, ADDRESSED TO THE SOCIETY OF FRIENDS.

"BROTHERS:—The sons of my beloved brother Onas.* When I was young and strong, our country was full of game which the Good Spirit sent for us to live upon; the lands which belonged to us were extended far beyond where we hunted; I and the people of my nation, had enough to eat, and always something to give our friends, when they entered our cabins, and we rejoiced when they received it from us; hunting was then not tiresome—it was a diversion—it was a pleasure.

"BROTHERS:—When your fathers asked land of my nation, we gave it to them, for we had more than enough. Gayashuta was among the first of the people to say, 'give

---

* ONAS is the Indian word for *quill*, and by this name they always spoke of William Penn.

land to our brother Onas, for he wants it, and he has always been a friend to Onas and his children.'

"BROTHERS:—Your fathers saw Gayashuta when he was young; when he had not even thought of old age or weakness; but you are too far off to see him now he has grown old. He is very old and feeble, and he wonders at his own shadow—it becomes so little.

"He has no children to take care of him, and the game is driven away by the white people, so that the young men must hunt all day to find game for themselves to eat; they have left nothing for Gayashuta. And it is not Gayashuta only, who is becoming old and feeble—there yet remains about thirty of your old friends, who, unable to provide for themselves, or to help one another, have become poor, and are hungry and naked.

"BROTHERS!—Gayashuta sends you a belt, *which he received long ago from your fathers*, and a writing which he received but as yesterday from one of you. By these you will remember him, and the old friends of your fathers in this nation; look on this belt and this writing, and, if you remember the old friends of *your fathers*, consider their former friendship and their present distress; and, if the Good Spirit shall put it into your hearts to comfort them in their old age, do not disregard his counsel. We are men; and therefore need only tell you that we are old, and feeble, and hungry, and naked; and that we have no other friends but you,—the children of our beloved brother Onas."

There have been attempts to prove that the Friends, as well as others, were guilty of injustice, fraud, and deception towards the Indians, but I can nowhere find these charges substantiated; and it is sufficiently convincing to any unprejudiced mind, that the universal impression among the red men would not be that the Friends were different from other white people, if they had not seen it demonstrated. Whether at the North or the South, the East or the West, the impression of the Indian concerning the pale-faces is the same. The Pequod and the Cherokee, the Seminole and the Dacotah, experience the same treatment, and utter the same sentiment.

The speech of Black Hawk, when, after a long and desperate conflict, he was taken and imprisoned, is the lamentation of all.

"The Sun rose dim on us in the morning, and at night sank in a dark cloud, and looked like a ball of fire. That was the last sun that shone on Black Hawk. His heart is dead, and no longer beats quick in his bosom. He is now prisoner to the white man; they will do with him as they wish. But he can stand torture, and is not afraid of death. He is no coward. Black Hawk is an Indian. He has done nothing for which an Indian ought to be ashamed. He has fought for his countrymen, the squaws, and pappooses, against white men, who came year after year to cheat them, and take away their lands. You know the cause of their making war. It is known to all white men. They ought to be ashamed of it. The white men despise the Indians, and drive them from their homes. But the Indians are not deceitful. The white men speak bad of the Indian, and look at him spitefully. But the Indians do not tell lies; Indians do not steal.

"An Indian who is as bad as a white man could not live in our nation; he would be put to death, and eaten up by wolves. The white men are bad schoolmasters; they carry false looks, and deal in false actions; they smile in the face of the poor Indian, to cheat him; they shake him by the hand, to gain his confidence, to make him drunk, and ruin his wife. We told them to let us alone, and keep away from us; but they followed on, and beset our paths, and they coiled themselves among us like the snake. They poisoned us by their touch. We are not safe, we lived in danger. We were becoming like them—hypocrites and liars, adulterers, and lazy drones.

"There were no deer in the forest; the opossum and the beaver were fled; the springs were drying up, and our squaws and pappooses without food. The Spirit of our Fathers awoke, and spoke to us to avenge our wrongs or die. We all spoke before the council fire. It was warm and pleasant; we set up the warwhoop, and dug up the tomahawk; our knives were ready, and the heart of Black Hawk swelled high in his bosom when he led his warriors to battle. He is satisfied. He will go to the world of spirits contented.

"Black Hawk is a true Indian. He feels for his wife, his children, and friends. But he does not care for himself. He cares for the nation and the Indians. They will suffer. He laments their fate. The white men do not scalp the head; but they do worse,—they poison the heart; it is not pure with them. His countrymen will not be scalped; but they will in a few years become like white men, so that you cannot trust them; and there must be, as in the white settlements, nearly as many officers as men, to take care of them, and keep them in order.

"Farewell my nation! Black Hawk tried to save you, and avenge your wrongs. He has been taken prisoner, and can do no more. His sun is setting, and will rise no more. Farewell to Black Hawk!"

I have not any where made extracts from the bloody records of war, or related instances of Indian barbarity; but if I had, they would have formed a pleasing picture for the mind to dwell upon, compared with the history of the controversy which was waged between a simple, trustful band of Indians, and the thieves and robbers who invaded them with weapons more deadly than tomahawks and scalping-knives—weapons which they could not see, and therefore could not repel. I have given but a glimpse of the long struggle; but I will not dwell upon it longer, for, as far as the Iroquois are concerned, it is ended, we trust, though there is still an effort, and, perhaps, a hope, to weary out the Indians, and thus gain their possessions. But it is futile; they will not part with them but with their blood.

As far as most of them are concerned, those days of clouds and thick darkness have passed away, and with them should vanish the prejudice and mutual distrust to which they gave rise.

Now, the Indians on all these lands are tillers of the soil, and you may ride miles in every direction, and see their fruitful fields and comfortable dwellings, indicating an industrious and an eminently peaceful and happy people. And if you come into this little church, you will see that they are also a Christian people. At first you might smile at the peculiarities in the dress of the women, for they persist, and very properly, I think, in not adopting the dress which we call civilized, but which better deserves the name of barbarous. No screws or lacings mar their forms, and their outer dress is still short and very loose. The elder women sit with uncovered heads, their long black hair tied in braids with gay ribbons down their necks. The younger women have quite universally adopted the gypsy hat with gay streamers, and all wear shawls, generally very tasteful and handsome. This costume, with the rich brown tint of their soft skins, gives them a picturesque and pleasing appearance.

They have large portions of the Bible, a hymn-book, and several school-books in their native tongue, and rich music it is when they all stand up and sing "with the spirit and the understanding," good old-fashioned tunes in their own rich and peculiarly expressive language. There are aged men and manly youths, matrons, maidens, and tiny babies; and all, not excepting the little ones, are very respectful and serious in their deportment.

The sermon to-day is by one of their own people, a chief, and though it is Greek to me, as far as edification is concerned, I listen more attentively than I do sometimes to what I can understand, for there is something very fascinating in the language and in the speaker. He is not a minister, but occupies the pulpit to-day, because both the missionaries are absent to attend an annual meeting at a distant place; but he is superintendent of the Sabbath-school, and though he comes six miles, has been absent but twice I believe in three years. Many who are present have been in the habit of walking eight or nine miles, men, women, and children, and are as sure to be present as the Sabbath bell is to ring.

Here the Indian is the Indian still, and among the youths and maidens of the present generation, there are some noble specimens of this still noble race; and the intermingling of Saxon blood, wherever it has taken place, has caused no deterioration.

As my book is written with the hope of disseminating the truth, and thus removing prejudice, I will give an instance of the prejudice which exists, and doubt not the same incident would have occurred in any city where the trial had been made.

The first Sabbath I attended church, I noticed by my side a fine-looking woman, with the richest tint of clear Mingoe blood upon her cheeks, and her raven hair in soft flowing masses, curving upon her temples, and twined in classic braids behind. Tall and portly in figure, and dignified in deportment, she particularly attracted my attention, and the sweet and intelligent expression of her face told that she was no common woman.

I asked who she was; and learned that she was the step-daughter of their most distinguished chief, Red Jacket, and one of whom he was particularly fond. She was a child when he was an old man, and sat on his knee, and stroked his withered cheek and kissed his brow, and received his most affectionate caresses. Her mother was the second wife of the great orator, and the faithful friend of the missionaries, and a consistent member of the little mission church during all the latter years of her life. The daughter, therefore, has had a Christian education, and is a thoroughly sensible and very interesting woman. But while I listened to this answer and made these remarks, I also listened to a story which made me blush for my people.

A few years ago, when the American Board held their annual meeting in an eastern city, the wife of the missionary, Mrs. Wright, was requested to bring one of the Indian women who could speak English, and was also familiar with her native language, that many more might be interested in their labors by witnessing the fruits. This was the woman she selected to accompany her. There was of course a great crowd of people, and hotels and boarding-houses were more than full. The one where they took up their abode, had the table surrounded with what are termed, in fashionable *parlance, genteel people*, and here the missionaries and the chieftain's daughter of a proud race took their place, as worthy to occupy the same position and receive the same politeness. What was their surprise, to see upon the countenances of those who sat opposite them, indignation and conscious insult, that a lady of a different people, and with a darker hue, should be permitted to dine with them as an equal! No notice was taken of their contemptuous looks and gestures, but what was the surprise of the offending party to find at the next meal that the table was vacated—they were left alone. The hostess then explained the cause of offence, and requested that the *squaw* might take her place at the second table, as they should lose their boarders if she did not. The missionaries answered, that if she sat at the second table they must also; and to this proposition she, without blushing, acceded; and during the remainder of the time, the vulgar gentility of the establishment were not troubled by the presence of two dignified, lady-like, Christian women, as far above their comprehension as the heavens are above the earth. They ate and drank without danger of contamination! It is one of the peculiarities of the Indians never to betray emotion unseasonably, and though it was evident that Mrs. L. understood the designed humiliation, she never by word or look made it manifest. It is also characteristic of them, that when introduced into society, where the customs are different from theirs and entirely new, they manifest no embarrassment or ignorance, but conform with wonderful tact; and while seeming to be indifferent, really observe minutely, and afterward relate every thing that passes.

How the disgraceful and utterly uncivilized conduct of these few who represent a large portion of what is called civilized society, was portrayed by this injured woman to her own people, I know not. I only know that she bore the insult with Christian meekness. She is the woman of whose girlhood I have spoken in the life of Red Jacket, and had he lived his fondest wishes concerning her would have been realized. She grew up to be a woman of whom he might well have been proud. Her husband is the grandson of a British officer, who loved an

Indian maiden, and took her to be his wife. When his erm of service expired he returned to England, but not without using every persuasion to induce his dusky bride to accompany him. She would not consent to go, fearing she might not be recognized as wife when so far away, and claimed the right, which was most reluctantly granted, of retaining their little son. For many years his father annually remembered him, and sent gold and magnificent presents to testify his love, but at length they ceased, and nothing more was ever heard concerning him. As there were no *surnames* among the Indians, the child was not called by his father's name, and it soon became lost to all who ever knew him this side the water. If my Indian friends have any cousins among the lords or nobles of England, they might not care to have me supply the links which would bring them to the knowledge of each other; but I can assure them that the blood of the daughter of an Iroquois Chief has not degraded that of any Peer of the Realm.

## CHAPTER XIV.

### THE EDUCATED INDIAN.

THE following extracts are taken from speeches made by young educated Indians, who are still living and laboring among their people. The first was made before the Historical Society of New York, in behalf of the little company of Cayugas who emigrated beyond the Mississippi, and were reduced to such extreme suffering that a great proportion of them died in less than a year. It was proposed to bring back the remainder, and a speech to excite sympathy and raise funds was made by Dr. Wilson, who obtained ten thousand dollars for this purpose, five hundred of which was given by a member of the Society of Friends in Baltimore.

"The honorable gentleman has told you that the Iroquois have no monuments. Did he not previously prove that the land of Gano-no-o, or the Empire State as you love to call it, was once laced by our trails from Albany to Buffalo—trails that we had trod for centuries—trails worn so deep by the feet of the Iroquois that they became your own roads of travel as your possessions gradually eat into those of my people? Your roads still traverse those same lines of communication and bind one part of the long house to another. The land of Gano-no-o—the Empire State—then is our monument! and we wish its soil to rest above our bones when we shall be no more. We shall not long occupy much room in living; we shall occupy still less when we are gone; a single tree of the thousands which sheltered our forefathers—one old elm under which the representatives of the tribes were wont to meet—will cover us all; but we would have our bodies twined in death among its roots on the very soil where it grew! Perhaps it will last the longer from being fertilized with their decay.

"I have been told that the first object of this Society is to preserve the history of the State of New York. You, all of you know, that alike in its wars and in its treaties the Iroquois, long before the Revolution, formed a part of that history; that they were then one in council with you, and were taught to believe themselves one in interest. In your last war with England, your red brothers—your elder brothers—still came up to help you, as of old, on the Canada frontier! Have we, the first holders of this prosperous region, no longer a share in your history? Glad were your forefathers to sit down upon the threshold of the 'Long House; rich did they then hold themselves, in getting the mere sweepings from its doors. Had our forefathers spurned you from it when the French were thundering at the opposite end, to get a passage through and drive you into the sea, whatever has been the fate of other Indians, the Iroquois might still have been a nation; and I—I—instead of pleading here for the privilege of lingering within your borders—I—I —might have had—a country!"

This was delivered extemporaneously, and was very long, but only these few sentences have been preserved, and for these we are indebted to Mr. Hoffman, who devoted to the author and his subject a long article in the Literary World the next day.

The following was delivered before an enlightened assembly by Mr. Maris B. Pierce.

"It has been said, and reiterated so frequently as to have obtained the familiarity of household words, that *it is the doom* of the Indian to disappear—to vanish like the morning dew before the advance of civilization—before those who belong by *nature* to a different, and by *education* and *circumstances* to a superior race; and melancholy is it to us—those doomed ones—that the history of this country, in respect to *us*, and its civilization, has furnished so much ground for the saying, and for giving credence to it.

"But whence and why are we thus doomed? Why must we be crushed by the arm of civilization, or the requiem of our race be chanted by the waves of the Pacific, which is destined to ingulf us? Say ye, on whom the sunlight of civilization has constantly shone—into whose lap Fortune has poured her brimful horn, so that you are enjoying the *highest* and best *spiritual* and temporal blessings of this world, say, if some being from fairy land, or some distant planet, should come to you in such a manner as to cause you to deem them children of *greater light* and *superior wisdom* to yourselves, and you should open to them the hospitality of your dwellings and the *fruits* of your *labor*, and they should by dint of their *superior wisdom* dazzle and amaze you, so as, for what to them were *toys* and *rattles*, they should gain freer admission and fuller welcome, till, finally, they should claim the *right* to your possessions, and of hunting you, like wild beasts, from your long and hitherto undisputed domain, how ready would you be to be taught of them? How cordially would you open your *minds* to the conviction that they meant not to deceive you further and still more fatally in their proffers of pretended kindness?

"How much of the kindliness of friendship for them, and of esteem for their manners and customs would *you feel*? Would not 'the milk of human kindness' in your breasts be turned to the gall of hatred towards them? And have not *we*, the original and undisputed possessors of this country, been treated *worse* than *you* would be, should any supposed case be transferred to reality.

"But I will leave the consideration of this point for the present, by saying, what I believe every person who hears me will assent to, that the manner in which the white people have habitually dealt with the Indians, makes them *wonder* that their hatred has not burned with tenfold fury against them, rather than that they have not laid aside their own peculiar notions and habits, and adopted those of their civilized neighbors.

"For instances of those *natural* endowments, which, by cultivation, give to the children of civilization their great names and far-reaching fame, call to mind Philip of Mount Hope, whose consummate talents and skill made him the white man's terror, by the display of those talents and that skill for the white man's destruction.

"Call to mind *Tecumseh*, by an undeserved association with whose name one of the great men of your nation has obtained more of greatness than he ever merited, either for his deeds or his character. Call to mind *Red Jacket*, formerly your neighbor, with some of you a friend and familiar, and to be a friend and familiar with whom none of you feel it a *disgrace*.

"Call to mind Osceola, the victim of the white man's treachery and cruelty, whom neither his enemy's arm nor cunning could conquer on the battle field, and who at last was consumed in 'durance vile,' by the corroding of his own spirit. In 'durance vile,' I say. Blot the fact from the record of that *damning baseness*, of that violation of all *law*, of all *humanity*, which that page of your nation's history which contains an account of it must ever be! Blot out the fact, I say, before you rise up to call an Indian treacherous or cruel.

"For an instance of active pity, of deep *rational active pity*, and the attendant intellectual qualities, I ask you to call to mind the story *surpassing romance* of Pocahontas; she who threw herself between a supposed inimical stranger and the deadly club which had been raised by the stern edict of her father, and by appealing to the affections of that father, savage though he was, overcame the fell intent which caused him to pronounce the white man's doom. In her bosom burned *purely* and *rationally* the flame of love, in accordance with the dictates of which she offered herself at the Hymenial altar, to take the nuptial ties with a son of Christian England. The offspring of this marriage have been *with pride* claimed as *sons* and citizens of the noble and venerable State of Virginia.

"Ye who love prayer, hover in your imagination around the cot of Brown, and listen to the strong supplications, as they arise from the fervent heart of Catharine, and then tell me whether

'—the poor Indian, whose untutored mind
Sees God in clouds and hears him in the wind,'

is not capable, by cultivation, of rationally comprehending the *true God*, whose pavilion is the clouds, and who yet giveth grace to the humble.

"The ill-starred Cherokees stand forth in colors of living light, redeeming the Indian character from the foul aspersions, that it is not susceptible of civilization and Christianization. John Ross stands before the American people, in a character both of intellect and heart, which many a white man in high places might *envy*, and yet never be able to attain! A scholar, a patriot, an honest and honorable man; standing up before the 'powers that be,' in the eyes of Heaven and men, now demanding, now supplicating of those powers, a regard for the rights of humanity, of justice, of law—and still a scholar, a patriot, an honest and honorable man; though an Indian blood coursing in his veins, and an Indian color giving hue to his complexion, dooms him, and his children and kin, to be hunted at the point of the bayonet by those powers, for their home, and possessions, and country, to the 'terra incognita beyond the Mississippi.'

"'Westward the star of Empire takes its way,' and whenever that empire is held by the white man, nothing is safe or enduring against his avidity for gain. Population is with rapid strides going beyond the Mississippi, and even casting its eye with longing gaze, for the woody peaks of the Rocky Mountains—nay, even for the surf-beaten shore of the western Ocean. And in process of time, will not our territory there be as subject to the wants of the white people, as that which we now occupy?

"I ask, then, in behalf of the New York Indians, that our white brethren will not urge us to do that which justice, humanity, religion, not only do not require, but condemn. Let us live on where our fathers lived, and enjoy the advantages our location offers us, that we who are converted heathens, may be made meet for that inheritance which the *Father* hath promised to give the Son, our Saviour; so that the deserts and waste places may be made to blossom like the rose, and the inhabitants thereof utter forth the high praises of our God.

"The government instituted by our ancestors many centuries ago, was remarkable for its wisdom, and adapted to the then condition of our nation. It was a republican, and purely democratic government, in which the will of the people ruled. No policy nor enterprise was carried out by the Council of the Grand Sachems of the Confederacy, without the sanction and ratification of the people, and it was necessary that it should receive the consent of the confederate tribes. The consent of the warriors alone was not deemed sufficient, but the women,—the mothers of the nation were also consulted; by this means the path of the wise Sachems was made clear—their hands were made strong, their determinations resolute, knowing full well that they had the unanimous support of their constituents; hence the confederacy of the Iroquois became great and strong, prosperous and happy; by their wisdom, they became statesmen, orators, and diplomatists; by their valor and skill in the war-path, they became formidable—they conquered and subdued many tribes, and extended their territory.

"This was our condition when the pale-faces landed upon the eastern shores of this great island. Every nation has its destiny. We now behold our once extensive domains reduced to a few acres; our territory, which once required the fleetest moons to traverse, is now spanned by the human voice. Yes, the Chiefs under our ancient form of government have reduced our possessions, so that now when we put the seed of the melon into the earth, it sprouts, and its tender vine trails along the ground, until it trespasses upon the lands of the PALE-FACES."

When Colonel McKenney was writing his Indian history, he addressed a letter of inquiry to General Cass, asking whether he ever knew an instance of Indian war or massacre, that was not provoked by the white man's aggression. To this letter he received the following laconic reply:

DEAR COLONEL:—
*Never!* NEVER! NEVER!
Yours truly,
LEWIS CASS.

## INJUSTICE TO THE INDIANS. 273

General Houston, in speeches lately made at Washington and at Boston, has made the same statement; and this, any one thoroughly acquainted with Indian history, will confirm. Had there been nothing more to rouse Indian ferocity, it was enough to see his favorite hunting-grounds devastated, and the desecration of the graves of his fathers. We will not enter into the merits of the question, whether it would have been right to permit so wide an extent of country, capable of supporting millions, to remain in the possession of so few. It is an important question; but when we judge the Indian, we are to look upon the invasion as it appeared to him. In his eyes, the invaders were thieves and robbers,—yes, barbarians and savages. Their mode of warfare, and their system of destroying, were more inhuman and terrible than any thing he had ever witnessed or imagined.

To expect them to yield their territory without a struggle, and a desperate struggle, was an expectation which only an idiot could entertain; and to expect them to lay aside their wild, roving habits, and easy, careless life, for one of toil and drudgery, with none of the advantages of civilization and Christianity apparent to them, was quite as ridiculous. They were every where obliged to yield to the LAW OF FORCE, with only now and then a glimpse of the LAW OF KINDNESS. The good John Robinson, of Plymouth memory, even in his day "began to doubt whether there was not wanting that tenderness for the life of man, made after God's own image, which was so necessary;" and says, "It would have been happy if the early Colonists had converted some, before they killed any."

So early as 1623, it sometimes occurred that "Indians, calling in a friendly manner, were seized and put in irons." "The General Court of Massachusetts once offered one hundred pounds each for ten Indian scalps; and forty white warriors went forth to win the prize, and returned with ten scalps stretched on poles, and received the one thousand pounds!"

The Indian had no other law than an "eye for an eye, and a tooth for a tooth;" but there was, probably, not one among the early Colonists, who had not the Gospel of Christ, as well as the Ten Commandments.

For myself, I have wondered that the fire of revenge and hatred should ever have gone out in a single Indian bosom; that he should have been willing to receive the missionary and school-teacher from among a people who had so forfeited their title to Christian, and practised so contrary to their professions. But whoever will take the trouble to wander among the peaceful valleys of Cattaraugus and Alleghany, will be convinced that the natural and artificial passions of Indians may be lulled, and the gall and wormwood which wrong and oppression have engendered in their hearts, may be converted into the sweetest milk of human kindness. They have learned to distinguish between the possessor and the professor; they have learned to value the good gifts it is in our power to bestow, and are willing to sit at our feet and learn wisdom.

It has become an annual custom among the Senecas to hold a national picnic, to which the people are all invited. The ceremonies are conducted as at similar festivals among other people, and I would like to have had the world, the unthinking, and still inexcusable ignorant world, look upon a scene which was represented not long since in the forest by North American Indians.

Some strangers who happened along here a few months since, exclaimed, "Why, how have you created such a paradise here, and nobody ever has heard of it?" He looked abroad upon the cultivated fields and comfortable dwellings, and could not believe that the Indians had done all this. They are so entirely a distinct and peculiar people, that though living near a great city, and surrounded by an inquisitive and aggressive people, they are less known in the general community than the Chinese or the Laplanders.

What has wrought this great change? The quiet labors and the small still voice of the missionary and the schoolteacher. As well as I could, I have pictured the Indian as he was, and now I wish you to look upon him as he is. Just stand with me upon this little hill, and look upon this gay concourse of people. At our feet is a beautiful grove of elms and oaks and maples, on the borders of a silver stream, so clear that it is a perfect mirror to the shining pebbles upon its bed. It bears still an Indian name, the Cattaraugus, and flows on to mingle its waters with Lake Erie.

There is music in the distance. Look up and you will see a procession. It is heralded by the Seneca National Band, in a costume of red and white, and the tune is Yankee Doodle, though the musicians are all Indians. Then comes the Marshal, who would be singled out by an observer, on any occasion, as a genuine son of a proud race, by his fine figure and noble bearing. With his rich dress, on his caparisoned steed, he is truly princely.

Then follow the children of the six several schools, their soft voices joining in a lively hymn, under the care of their teachers; all with gala dresses and distinguishing badges, and flags waving in the breeze. Another band, "The Sons of Temperance," bring up the rear, and slowly they come marching on, crossing the stream upon a temporary bridge, wheeling about in several military evolutions, and arrange themselves in groups around the platforms wreathed with evergreens, on which the President of the day and the Speaker stand. He who presides is one of the the oldest and most venerable of the chiefs of his people. He is dressed in black, with a broad white silk scarf, terminating in crimson fringes, crossing his breast and falling gracefully at his side. Around him are other venerable men, whose memories easily go back to the time when there was not a Christian in the whole nation. Now the missionary pastor, who has for twenty years labored among them, and can very justly look around him and call what he beholds the fruit of his labors, lifts his voice to crave the blessing of Heaven upon their festal gathering. You will listen to the speaking which follows with interest, though you will not understand the language in which some of the addresses are made. It is not so musical as rich, and falls on the ear like the deep voice of the cataract, rather than the low murmuring rill. But those who think the Indian has no vein of humor and no love of pleasantry, should listen to him when he is surrounded only by his kindred—those who can appreciate him, and whom he can trust. Solemnity, enthusiasm, and mirthfulness, play alternately upon the features of the assembly, but there is in him so great a regard for decorum, that nothing like levity or untimely restlessness ever disturbs an Indian audience. There is the most respectful attention till the orators are seated, and then they gather around the table, which is tastefully and bountifully spread, in the form of a double square. Around it circle the guests, and within stand those who dispense the good gifts prepared for all who come. Here, too, is the order which seldom characterizes so large a number among people of any other name; and happiness, a quiet but soul appreciating happiness, is beaming upon every dusky face.

When the feast is finished, the speakers again mount the rostrum, and as usual after a good dinner, all are more disposed to merriment. Before you are a thousand people of all ages, from the gray-haired man of ninety, to the tiniest baby that ever opened its eyes to the light. You may see there a group of laughing maidens, reclining upon the grass in the shade of a spreading oak, with their gypsy hats and bright streamers, and near by a bevy of matrons, with their raven hair braided in rich tresses, and their mantles gathered in folds about their waists. The musicians fill up the interstices between the speeches with thrilling and plaintive strains, till the daylight begins to fade and the red gleam of the setting sun gilds the forest tops. Then again they form in procession, and march away. The children number about two hundred; and are you realizing all this time that they are what some people still insist upon calling savages, and maintain can never become an educated, refined and cultivated people? really believing that they are incapable of appreciating learning, the arts, Christianity, and civilization? Contending that they ought to be removed far away into the Western forests to roam for ever wild, that the white man may not trample them as he tramples the beast and the reptile in his path? The laborers have been few, far too few for this beautiful vineyard, yet they have accomplished a great work. The population is now on the increase, and schools and churches are multiplying. The people are improving in agriculture, and pretty farms and houses are beginning to dot their hills and valleys. They are becoming a Christian and social people.

I have attended one or two parties, or social gatherings, at the houses of the missionaries, where there were perhaps fifty or sixty, and have seen far less comeliness and propriety of behavior among the same number of the sons and daughters of New England. Indians have remarkable *tact* in conforming to the customs of other people, if they choose to exercise it, and when they are fully convinced that it is best to relinquish their own peculiar habits, they adopt new ones very readily. If land speculators would let them alone, and the State would perform its whole duty, they would soon prove that the last of the Senecas is not yet, nor for a long time to come. They would become a valuable element in our political and social organization—refute the slanders, and blot out the dark pictures which historians have been wont to spread abroad concerning them. May I live to see it done, for most deeply have I learned to blush for my people.

The speech from which I make the following extracts, was made by Mr. N. T. Strong. The President of the day was Henry Twoguns, the step son of Red Jacket, and the Vice President, Dr. Wilson. The Marshal was Mr. M. H. Parker, and the bands were composed entirely of Indians.

His speech also, like the preceding ones, was made in English; and all are in better English than many I have read by foreigners of other nations who have had the same advantages of education.

" LADIES AND GENTLEMEN :—I enter upon the duties assigned me by the committee of arrangements with much distrust. It is a difficult task at all times to speak in a foreign language, and I fear I shall not succeed to the satisfaction of myself or my audience.

" In some respects the present occasion is an extraordinary one—never before did the white man with his women and children meet with the red man and his women and children in a social picnic. It is an occasion to excite our gratitude and make us glad, and I would like for a moment to present the past condition and relationships of the two nations in contrast with the present.

"That the red men were the first occupants of the soil is conceded by all. In this we had the start of the white man, perhaps because John Bull and the Dutchman had not been *Yankeefied* at that time, for we find after this transformation took place the white man had the start of us in every thing!

"In 1647 the confederacy of the Six Nations were able to raise 30,000 warriors. They had a regularly organized government, in which the rights of nations were distinctly defined; but the rights of individuals were not defined. War and the sports of the chase were then the pursuits of the red men. Their clothing was made of the skins of the animals they killed in the chase. Their food was the flesh of wild animals, and the corn and vegetables which were raised by the women, and the labor of the lodge was all performed by them. The conquests of the Iroquois had extended far to the south and west, and the name of the Ho-de-no-son-ne was a terror among all the surrounding nations.

"They roamed from river to river, and from valley to plain in pursuit of the buffalo, the bear, and the elk, and darted across lakes and rivers in their light canoes to find the beaver and otter, in order to take their furs. At appointed seasons they returned to the council fires of the several nations, for the transaction of public business and to keep the annual feasts.

"In 1776, more than a hundred years afterwards, we find them greatly reduced in numbers, though their customs are the same. The Mohawks, who dwelt on the banks of the Hudson, and along the valley which still bears their name, scarcely numbered four hundred souls. The Oneidas, who were situated next west of them, numbered fifteen hundred, and the Onondagas, Cayugas, Senecas, and Tuscaroras, about ten thousand, and could raise two thousand warriors.

"LADIES AND GENTLEMEN:—Let us now look at the white man in the same periods. In 1647 they had, capable of bearing arms, only 300 *all told!* Their pursuits were agriculture and commerce. They had a system of government, and written laws. The rights of nations and the rights of individuals were well defined. Their religion was founded upon the Bible. They were cold and calculating, and knew the value and uses of money. They also knew that land was better than *money!* They therefore made every effort to obtain it. The white man *bought* it of his red brother, and *paid* him little or nothing. He bought furs, too, at his own prices.

"We find him again in 1774 numbering 181,000. Their improvement, in numbers, wealth, and the arts and sciences, has been going steadily onward. The forests fell before the woodsman—the game, and those in pursuit of it, also continued to retreat, till both had nearly disappeared. Thus one of the occupations of the red man, like Othello's, 'was gone.'

"The land of the red man became cultivated—'the wilderness blossomed as the rose.' The white man built cities, towns, villages; he built churches, established colleges, academies, common schools, and other institutions of learning.

"Yes, *you* made canals, railroads, and your electric telegraph transmits news almost with the speed of throught. This is wonderful! The red man can yet scarcely comprehend it. Your commerce has extended over the world. Your ships are on every sea—your steamers on every river. In two hundred years your population has increased from six thousand to three millions.

"Allow me to ask, what price did the red man receive for this broad domain? The public documents testify thus:—'By these presents we do for ourselves and heirs and successors, ratify, confirm, grant, and submit, unto our most Sovereign Lord King George, by the Grace of God, King of Great Britain, &c., defender of the faith, &c., all the land lying between, &c.;' here follows an indefinite description of the premises, including lakes, rivers, &c., *and never paying a cent for it!*

* * * * * *

"LADIES AND GENTLEMEN:—You see from this that your forefathers wronged the red man and took advantage of his ignorance. This you will *now* acknowledge. The red man has a long history of wrongs and griefs; though unrecorded by the hand of man, they are written in the Great Book of Remembrance kept by the Great Spirit, and He will inquire into this at your hands by and by, and He will do justice to his red children.

I have not instituted these comparisons to represent the red man as an inferior, and you as a superior being. No. These results are owing to circumstances in the rise and fall of nations. And you must also bear in mind that the Great God in heaven, whom you profess to worship and adore, governs and directs the affairs of nations as well as individuals. The powerful nations that fall, and the weak that rise, do it alike at His bidding.

"But I appeal to you whether we are not entitled to your sympathy—whether we have not claims upon your assistance, in endeavoring to raise ourselves from the condition in which ignorance and prejudice have sunk our nation.

"The red man is aware of his condition. Yes, he feels it deeply. When he looks at the sun, the light of which enabled his ancestors to look abroad upon a magnificent country, all his own, now peopled by another race, he feels alone—an alien from the commonwealth. There are no monuments to commemorate the deeds of his forefathers, as there are in the old world; but there are the mighty rivers and the eternal hills, which he has named.

"LADIES AND GENTLEMEN:—The Six Nations are now represented before you. The President of the day is a Seneca, and a worthy representative of his nation—the Vice-President on his right is a Cayuga of the *first water*, and on the left a worthy Onondaga. One of your poets has said that 'music has charms even to soothe a savage!' and here is a band of musicians who have delighted us with their sweet strains, composed entirely of the descendants of Senecas and Tuscaroras, and I doubt not they have gratified *even* civilized ears!

"LADIES AND GENTLEMEN:—You perceive we are changed. We already have schools, and books, and churches, and are fast adopting the customs of white men.

"For these improvements we are mainly indebted to the Missionaries of the American Board. Great is our debt of gratitude to these persevering and devoted men and women. And Oh, if you will but continue to extend to us the right hand of fellowship, we shall abundantly reward your efforts, and you will soon see among us a high state of cultivation and refinement.

"The missionaries have not made a great noise concerning their labors by blowing of the trumpet, but quietly and peaceably 'have gone about doing good;' and may they live to see fulfilled their most cherished hopes, and answered their fervent prayers."

Here I have permitted the Indian to speak for himself,

and have given only a few of the proofs which I have of a similar kind, that neither education, nor civilization, nor Christianity enervates the mind or the body of the Indian.

If we had lived when our fathers lived, very probably we should have been like unto them; we should have been guilty of the same errors of judgment, and the same mistakes in practice. But now that we have no fear, and can look back upon the past as a whole, we are able to see clearly, where the actors could only grope in darkness. Yet with the experience of centuries to profit by, we are scarcely more ready to do justice.

We are in undisputed possession of all these fair domains, and we know the paltry price we have paid for them. We know that there is in our midst a remnant of this proud people, whom it is our duty, and whom it is in our power to save; and what have we done, and what are we doing to accomplish their salvation?

## CHAPTER XV.

### THE FUTURE OF THE NORTH AMERICAN INDIAN.

Every historian and prophet who has preceded me, has reiterated the prediction that "the doom of the Indian is extinction!" I shall not contradict it; but I fearlessly say, this ought not so to be. Is it not a libel upon Christianity, that it is not fitted for all the people of the earth? Is it not a libel upon Him, "who made of one blood all nations;" who made the heavens and the earth; that He contemplated the happiness of only one portion, and instituted a system of religion fitted only for a few?

He does not tell us that Christ came into the world, to be crucified and slain for the Saxon and the Norman alone! He died to redeem a world; and He said, "Go and preach the Gospel to all nations." If He created a people incapable of receiving the Gospel and profiting by it, how strange the command that it should be preached to them. We look upon the instances of degeneracy among Indian youth who have been educated, and exclaim, "How fruitless are all our efforts!" without taking into consideration the true causes of this degeneracy, or the inefficacy of any means yet employed for the accomplishment of our ostensible object. Yet it is stated, that as far back as 1846, there were more Cherokees who could read the English or their own tongue, than could be found among the white people, in proportion to the whole number, in any State of the Union!

In 1818, a plan was conceived for educating the Indians of the whole country, by the Superintendent of Indian Affairs, which, though in operation but a few years, proved conclusively that the Indian was capable of any degree of cultivation. He obtained from Congress an appropriation of ten thousand dollars, annually, for his purpose; and with the cordial approbation and co-operation of various missionary and religious societies, established schools among the Indians all along upon our western borders, from Lake Superior to Chattahoochee,—in which were gathered *eighteen hundred children,* "deriving instruction, and making as rapid advances in the various incipient branches of learning, in agriculture and the mechanic arts, as are made in any part of the United States by the children of white people." Then arose a new power; the demons of avarice and selfishness ruled in the councils of our nation. These Indians, who had become a Christian people, with the religion of Christ for their religion—occupying lands, rich with the products of their industry—must be thrust forth, because they were a people of a darker hue than ourselves. So these flourishing schools were broken up; these happy children were deprived of all their means of improvement, and thousands of innocent people were compelled to leave their homes and firesides, and wend their way to the wilderness—leaving the pathway drenched with their tears, and stained with their blood.

And even now, what has the Indian youth to awaken hope, and excite ambition? Not even yet, in the State of New York, is he granted the privileges of citizenship, though his claims, as native American, are prior to those of every Saxon on her soil. He is a land-owner, an agriculturist, an educated, a Christian man—but still treated as if he were an idiot or a brute.

The story of young James McDonald, in whom Colonel McKenney and Philip Thomas took so great an interest, illustrates the feelings of every red man, when he thinks of becoming like his white brethren. This young man was adopted into the family of Colonel McKenney, and being the age of his own son, enjoyed every privilege which he enjoyed. In the family and in the social circle they were equals, and were afforded the same advantages of education. The Indian youth was endowed with all the personal beauty of the noblest of his race, "with a manner the most gracious and winning," said his adopted parent, "and a morality I never saw invaded." Of his progress in study, when he had been only a little while at school, his teacher remarked, that "he came with his lessons better digested, and more Greek and Latin and mathematics in one of them, than the class to which he was attached could get through in a week,—so he was obliged to place him in a class by himself."

When he had finished his academical studies, his benefactor chose for him the profession of the law. But he had begun to think of the difference between the treatment he was then receiving, and that which awaited him when he should go forth in the world, and he exclaimed, "Wherefore! wherefore! Of what use to me will be my present or future attainments? Oh, sir," pressing his hand against his forehead as he continued, "it will be all lost on me. *I am an Indian*, and being an Indian, I am marked with a mark as deep and abiding as that which Cain bore. My race is degraded—trodden upon—despised." He then took from his bosom a letter from his brother, who was a lieutenant in the navy, and whose bitter experience had wrung from him the following words:

"There is only one of two things to do: either throw away all that belongs to the white race and turn Indian, or quit being Indian and turn white man. *The first you can do—the latter it is not in your power to do.* The white man hates the Indian, and will never permit him to come into close fellowship with him, or to be a participator in any of his high prerogatives or distinguished advantages."

When young James was asked if any thing in his experience in the family in which he lived, would justly lead him to such a conclusion, he answered: "No, sir; oh, no; no indeed. But this is an exception, and only serves to prove the rule. You are to me a father. My gratitude to you and your family can never die. I know I am treated with the greatest attention, even to tenderness." The tears came to his eyes; he sat down and pressed his handkerchief to his face, until it was literally wet with weeping.

After awhile he spoke, saying, "Yes, sir; I will go to Ohio and read law with Mr. McLean. I will do any thing that it may be your pleasure for me to do. I should indeed be an ingrate to thwart your kind designs towards me in any thing. *But the seal is upon my destiny!*"

When the time was fixed for him to go, day after day he still lingered, so great was his reluctance to leave home, and father, and mother, and sisters and friends, to become, as he believed, an alien evermore. But he went, and in about half the time usually occupied in acquiring this profession, he was ready for the bar.

He was a Choctaw, and when he had finished his studies he returned to his people, on a visit to his mother. Whilst there he was chosen one of a company of delegates to come to Washington on business, and Mr. Calhoun and others, who were engaged with him in transacting it, were astonished at his powers and his acquisitions. But his adopted parent saw with the deepest anguish that he was endeavoring to blunt his keen sensibilities, and stifle the conflict in his bosom by the intoxicating draught. He could not endure that one so gifted and so beautiful should be thus destroyed, and sought many opportunities of remonstrating with him. At one time he reminded him of the days he had spent under his roof—those days of innocence, and honor, and bliss. He sprang to his feet and exclaimed " Spare, me ! oh, spare me ! It is that thought which makes me so miserable. I have lost that sweet home and its endearments; the veil which was so kindly placed between me and my Indian caste has since been torn away. I have been made to see since that I cannot, whilst such anomalous relations exist, as do exist between the red and the white race, be other than a *degraded outcast.*"

He was invited to go back to that loved spot, and assured that the same welcome awaited him there that he had always experienced; but he said, " Oh, name it not to me, sir ; I can never go there again ! The very thought of those haunts where I was once so happy, and of the kindness shown me there, being met, as they are, and *crushed* by the consciousness of what I now am, distracts me."

But he recovered, in some measure, his former self-reliance and cheerfulness, and returned to open a law office in Jackson, Mississippi, where his prospects were very flattering. Then came disappointed love, to ring again in his ears the doom of the red man, " You are an Indian—you belong to a degraded race." Hope fled and despair took possession of him ; he mounted a high bluff, overhanging the river, and precipitated himself into the water to rise no more. " Wherefore ! wherefore !" He might toil and earn money—riches might be within the reach, even of an Indian; but gold cannot satisfy a noble heart. He must not dream of honors, he must not dream of domestic happiness; and what is gold, aye, what is life, when all this is denied?

Let it suddenly be revealed to all the youth in our colleges, as an unalterable destiny, that they are evermore debarred from distinction, and the hope of one day forming for themselves a home, and being surrounded by a circle of loved ones, and what would there be to allure them up the hill of science? Would not every energy be paralyzed, and should we not with certainty expect to see them go down to perdition? The love of knowledge merely, is a little better than the love of money; but both are very ignoble motives to inspire immortal minds, and support them on the pilgrimage through this world. The desire of the approbation of heaven and of being useful on earth may be good, and perhaps should be sufficient motives; but how many among the most cultivated and Christian would falter, with only these to sustain them?

With a majority of people the idea is entertained that the nature of the Indian is so entirely different from the nature of the Saxon. This is true only in one sense—that education, and centuries of indulgence in peculiar habits, tend to make them *second nature*. The Indian is not alone in loving a wild roving life, free from care and toil.

So late as 1826, restoration to home and kindred was offered to several women who had been made captive and carried beyond Lake Superior, and they rejected the boon. They had become entirely released from the trammels of society, and cared not to be encumbered with them again.

CHATEAUBRIAND relates, that when travelling through the wilds of America, he heard that he had a countryman who had become a resident of the forest. He visited him, not so much with a desire to see his countryman, as of philosophizing upon his condition. After several hours' conversation, he put his last grand question :

"' Phillip, are you happy?'

"He knew not, at first, how to reply. 'Happy?' said he, reflecting—'happy?—yes;—but happy only since I became a savage.'

"'And how do you pass your life?' asked I. He laughed.

"'I understand you,' continued I. 'You think such a question unworthy of an answer; but should you not like to resume your former mode of living, and return to your country?'

"'My country—France? If I were not so old I should like to *see* it again.'

"'And you would not remain there?' The motion of Phillip's head answered my question sufficiently. 'But what induced you,' continued I, 'to become what you call a savage?'

"'I don't know,' said he—'instinct.'

"This expression put an end to my doubts and questions. I remained ten days with Phillip, in order to observe him, and never saw him swerve for a single moment from the assertion he had made. *His soul, free from the conflict of the social passions*, appeared, in the language of the Indian, calm as the field of battle, after the warriors had smoked together their *calumet* of peace."

How many a *trapper* has become wed to a forest life. I never yet heard of one who voluntarily returned to the plough and the anvil. Why, then, should we expect an Indian to seek them? The same necessity must be laid upon him as upon us, ere he will toil, and he must be inspired with the same motives, ere he will prefer knowledge to ignorance.

If there had been no wars in our country, except between the colonists and the Indians, Christianity might have been taught by example as well as precept. But three times since the settlement of America, the red man has been obliged to witness, and take part in bloody conflicts, between the very nations who professed to come to him with the religion which condemned war; and these nations were fighting about the very lands which they were constantly telling the Indian it was wrong for him to defend at the expense of life, though they were his birthright, and dear to him, as the inheritance of his fathers. Their invaders fought to defend what was not their own; why should not he defend what was his all?

It is strange that there have been so many, rather than that there have been so few, who were willing to receive Christianity, and the arts of civilization, from their oppressors. The proud lord of the forest never consented to become subject or slave. When he yielded, it was to stern necessity; and when we remember what he had to give up, and that when we had taken from him his possessions, and all he held most dear, giving him nothing in return, but the privilege of living as best he could, never calling him, or treating him as brother, or freeman; we cannot fail to see that he has done exactly as we should have done in the same circumstances.

As it was, the labors of Eliot and Mayhew, of Kirkland and Brainard, and many more in modern times, have not been without their reward. Mayhew wrote the lives of between one and two hundred "Christian men and women, and godly ministers," and there is exhibited no difference between Indian Christians, and Christians of other nations.

What a beautiful illustration of Christian principle was the famous Oneida Chief, Shenandoah. For sixty years he had been the terror of all who heard his name, when he listened to the gospel message from Mr. Kirkland, and immediately became a little child, in meekness and every Christian grace. He lived more than a hundred years; and when, a little while before he died, a friend called and asked concerning his health, he said, "I am an aged hemlock; the winds of a hundred winters have whistled through my branches. I am dead at the top, (referring to his blindness). Why I yet live, the Great Good Spirit only knows. When I am dead, bury me by the side of my good minister and friend, that I may go up with him at the great resurrection."

Kusick was a Tuscarora Chief, and where shall we look for a nobler instance of friendship than his towards Lafayette, or for Christian principle more firm and true than he evinced concerning his pension.

In the war of the Revolution he was under Lafayette's command. Many years after peace was concluded, as he was passing through Washington, he accidentally heard the name of his old commander spoken in the office where he stopped for business. The moment his ear caught the sound, with eyes lighted and full of earnestness, he asked:

"*Is he yet alive?*"

"Yes," was the reply, "he is alive, and looking well and hearty."

With deep emphasis he said, "I am glad to hear it."

"Then you knew Lafayette, Kusick?"

"Oh yes," he answered, "I knew him well; and many a time in the battles, I threw myself between him and the bullets, *for I loved him!*"

On being asked if he had a commission, he said "Yes, General Washington gave him one, and he was lieutenant."

This suggested to his friends that he was entitled to a pension, and on looking over the records, the truth of what he said was confirmed, and he received one for several years.

Afterwards, Congress passed a law making it necessary that each recipient should swear that he could not live without the pension. When the old chief was called upon to do this, he said, " Now here is my little log cabin, and it's my own; here's my patch where I can raise corn, and beans, and pumpkins; and there is Lake Oneida, where I can catch fish; with these I can make out to live without the pension, and to say I could not, would be to *lie to the Great Spirit.*" This was the honor of an Indian Chief; how many among those of our own people who receive pensions would have done likewise for conscience' sake? Kusick could speak the English language very well, but when he made an audible prayer or said grace at table, he used his native Tuscorara, " because," said he, " when I speak English I am often at a loss for a word; when therefore I speak to the Great Spirit, I do not like to be perplexed, or have my mind distracted to look after a word. When I use my own language, it is like my breath; I am composed." In this is exemplified that he fully understood the reverence which was due to the Great Ruler.

Instances might be multiplied a hundred fold, to prove that the religion of Christ can soften and renew the heart of the fiercest warrior of the wilderness, as well as the heart of the child of civilization. The records of missions numbers forty thousand Indian converts; and, if only half these have become genuine followers of the cross of Christ, the patient and faithful missionary has not labored in vain.

There is a little remnant still left among us; and if

these are permitted to perish, it will not be the fault of our fathers, and the dark age in which they lived. We know their wants and their capacities, and have abundant means for all the good we please to accomplish.

Of the Iroquois there are three thousand; of Indians within our jurisdiction, three hundred thousand. They should be citizens of our republic; their oaths should be respected in our courts of justice; and their representatives should be in our national councils; then we should see hope dawn in their bosoms, and ambition revive their energies.

One who had the means of making the estimate, and no motive for stating it incorrectly, says we have become possessed of all these fair domains at the paltry price of *two cents and three quarters an acre!* By robbery we have grown rich.

It was suggested in Congress, not long since, that "a person be employed to collect and arrange the treaties, and other authentic documents, tending to illustrate the history of the relinquishment of land titles by native Indian tribes, and to prepare such means of illustration as may be necessary for a full knowledge of the acquirement of the States of the title to their lands." To which it was answered: "Let us do no such thing. Let us rather gather up and destroy—commit to the flames all that records the progress of our acquisitions. Leave only to tradition, or forget entirely, the infamy which we acquired with the titles we enjoy—for who can look unmoved upon the parchment that tolls how many miles square were bought with a few strings of paltry beads—how the council fires that had burned for ages were put out, and the bands that gathered round them for ages were scattered—their birthrights, their wigwams, and their hunting grounds bartered away for a score of worthless rifles, or a bundle of useless trinkets,—how we first debased, and then defrauded, the children of the forest out of all their hills and valleys, their lakes and rivers, over which are scattered the millions whose representatives are asked to perpetuate the records of wrongs inflicted by their ancestors. Doubtless there was necessity for the wrong—for the extermination of one race, for the increase of another. But there exists no necessity that we should make a parade of the means by which that extermination was effected. *They* may be forgiven; we may, at least, forget them." \*

It is too late to blot out these dark records; but it is not yet too late to prove that we

"Are wiser than our '*Fathers*' were,
And better know the Lord."

It is confidently predicted that we are on the verge of another Indian war, more terrible than our country ever experienced; and yet with our rich, powerful, and consolidated government, it is perfectly possible to prevent this war. The Indian of the West is the same as the Indian of the East; and it is a thousand times better to soften his heart by kindness than to pierce it by a bullet.

A traveller describes the following Sabbath morning scene, far beyond the confines of civilization, among the Chippewas, Menomonies, and Winnebagoes, where only the trader and the missionary had been.

"The dawn of this Sabbath morning was peculiarly beautiful; 'rosy fingers' did seem 'to unbar the gates of light.' Violet and purple with a wide and widening circle of 'orient pearl,' all met my eye with their charming and chastening influences—and then there was such silence!

\* *Daily Times*, February 12th, 1855.

Not a leaf rustled, and the waves broke in softer murmur on the shore. Yet, all this silence was broken in upon this morning—for, just between the time when the eastern sky was made mellow with the sun's light, and the light began to tip the tops of tree and mountain, and all was so quiet, my ears were greeted by sweet sounds of music! They came from a lodge of Christian Indians, which was hard by in the woods. They had risen with the day 'to worship God!' They sang in three parts, base, tenor, and treble, and with a time so true, and with voices so sweet, as to add harmony even to nature itself. Notes of thrush and nightingale sound sweeter when poured forth amidst the grove; so sounded those of these forest warblers in the midst of the green foliage and in the stillness of the woods. I attended their worship, and was present with them again in the evening; and as I listened to their songs of praise, and their prayers, I felt humbled and ashamed of my country, in view of the wrongs it had inflicted, *and still continues to inflict*, upon these desolate and destitute children of the forest. There were flowers and gems there, which needed only to be cultivated and polished, to insure from the one the emission of as sweet odors as ever regaled the circles of the civilized; and from the other, a brilliance as dazzling as ever sparkled in the diadem of queenly beauty. And yet they were, and are, neglected, trodden down, and treated as outcasts!"

But no missionary society has the means of accomplishing the work of carrying the gospel and education, to such a multitude of roving people, over such a wide extent of country. This is the duty of the government, and if wisely planned, would not be so difficult of execution. It would not cost so much as a war, and would save us from the retribution which must certainly come upon those who make cruelty and treachery the purchase money with which to gain territory, and enrich it with the blood of the innocent and helpless.

Extinction may be the doom of the Indian, but it does not require a prophet's authority to enable us to say, " Woe unto those by whom this offence cometh."

# APPENDIX.

## THE LANGUAGE OF THE IROQUOIS.

If the Indian should be entirely banished from our borders, the memory of him cannot die. For, as I have elsewhere quoted,

"Their names are on our waters,
We cannot wash them out."

The dialects of the Six Nations bore a strong resemblance to each other, though there were still differences which marked them as distinct. Those who understood one were able to converse in each of the others, and in council the representatives of each nation had no difficulty in interpreting what was said by all. The Mohawk and Oneida strongly resembled each other, and the Seneca and Cayuga were the same. The Onondaga "was considered by the Iroquois as the most finished and majestic," while to our ears it is the most harsh, and the Oneida the most musical.

They used nineteen letters, having no labials or liquids, except occasionally is heard among the Mohawks the sound of L and among the Tuscaroras the sound of F. The Senecas and Cayugas talk all day without shutting their lips, and there are no oaths in their language. Before an Indian can be profane he must learn French or English, and his language is so constructed too, that evasion is almost impossible. Metaphors are in constant requisition in Indian speeches and conversation. If one comes in when the weather is very cold, he says, "It is a nose-cutting morning." If he wishes to reflect upon a proposition before deciding, he says, "I will put the matter under my pillow, and let you know." He says of an emaciated person, "He has dry bones." A steamboat is called "The ship impelled by fire." A horse is a "*log carrier*," a cow a "*cud chewer*," and a goat a "scented animal."

In ancient times when the hunters encamped in the woods, they kept warm by covering themselves with boughs of hemlock, and now if an Indian is about to repair his cabin, he says, "I will surround it with hemlock boughs," meaning I will make it warm and comfortable. When a chief has made a speech at the opening of a Council, he finishes with saying, "the doors are now open, you can proceed." The messenger of the Six Nations to the Senecas was called "the man who carries the fire or smoke," meaning that he had charge of the Council-fire and kept it bright.

The Iroquois call themselves the *real people;* and in speeches or conversation, if allusion is made to white people, they say invariably "our younger brethren." The President of the United States is called "the city-eater," and Washington, "the residence of the city-eater."

The Iroquois had the masculine, and feminine, and neuter genders. The masculine and feminine were denoted, sometimes by giving the same animal different names, in the way we say buck and doe, and sometimes by prefixing words which signify male and female. All inanimate objects were placed in the neuter gender. They had not the indefinite article *a* or *an*, but used *the*, and the usual varieties of adjective and adverb. They abounded in interjections, but had no participles. As a substitute for the infinitive mood they used the word *that.* Instead of saying, "Direct *He-mo* to come and give us rain," they said, "Direct that *He-mo* come and give us rain."

They could count by one, two, three, nearly to a hundred, and used the numerals, firstly, secondly, thirdly, &c.

The following are specimens of names, with the Lord's prayer and a hymn in Seneca.

| | |
|---|---|
| O-hee-yu, | *The beautiful river.* |
| Os-we-go, | *Flowing out.* |
| On-yit-Lah, | *Bird of the strong wing.* |
| Ga-no-so-te | *A house.* |
| O-on-do-te | *A tree.* |
| O-ya | *Fruit.* |
| Je-da-do | *A bird.* |
| O-ya-han | *Apples split open.* |
| Ga-no-geh | *Oil on the water.* |
| Ga-osé-ha | *Baby frame.* |

## THE LORD'S PRAYER.

Gwä-nee' gä-o-yü'-geh che-de-oh'; sü-sa-no-do'-geh-teek; gä-o' ne-dwa na' sa-nunk-tä; na-huk' ne-yü-weh' na yo-an'-jü-geh ha'-ne-sü-ne-go'-dä ha ne-de-o'-dä na' gä-o-yü'-geh. Dun-dä-gwü-e'-wä-sä-gwus na' ong-wi-wä-na-ark-seh' na' da-yä-ke'-wü-sä-gwü'-seh na' onk-ke-wü-na'-ä-ge. Dä-ge-o'-na-geh'-wen-nis'-heh-da na' ong-wü-quä'. Sä-nuk' na-huh' heh'-squä-ü ha' gä-yeh na' wü-ate-keh' na-gwä' na' dä-gwü-yü-duh'-nuh-onk ha' gä-yeh na' wä-ate-keh'; na' sch-eh' na ese' sü-wä na' o-nuk-ta' kuh' na' gä-hus-ta-seh' kuk' na' da-gä-ä-sü-uh'. Na-huh'-ne-yü-weh.*

\* If an attempt should be made to give a literal translation of each word, or phrase, it would render transposition necessary, and change the formation of the words in some respects, as the following will exhibit.

Gwä-nee', che-de-oh' gä-o'-yä-geh, gä-sa-nuh', ese' sa-nuk-ta'
Our Father, which art in heaven, hallowed be thy name, thy kingdom
gä-oh' ese' sne'-go-eh ne-ya-weh' yo an-ja'-geh ha' ne-de-o'-deh
come, thy will be done on earth as it is
gä-o'-yä-geh. Dun-dä-gwä-e'-wä-sä-gwus ong-wä-yeh'-his-heh'
in heaven. Forgive us our debts
da-yä-ke'-a-wä-sä-gwus-seh' ho-yeh'his. Dä-ge-oh' ne' na-geh'
as we forgive our debtors. Give us this
wen-nis'-heh-deh e' na-hä-da-wen-nis'-heh-geh o-ä'-qwa. Hä-squä'-ah
day our daily bread. Lead
e' sä-no' ha' wä-ate-keh', na-gwä' dä-gwä-yä-dan'-nake ne'
us not into temptation, but deliver from us
wä-ate-keh', na-seh'-eh nees' o-nuk'-tä na-kuh' na gä-hus'tes-heh,
evil, for thine is the kingdom, and the power,
na-kuh' da-gä-ä-sä-oh'.
and the glory.

Na-huh'-se-yä-weh.

APPENDIX. 301

(*Specimen of Indian Hymn.*)

GAA NAH 8. L. M.

O gwe nyoo' găh', a ga deăh'seek
Heh syah daa deh, lis' ne Jesus;
Tăh'ăh ; tăh ăh deh o gwe nyooh',
Neh huh' noo'wak ni gooh'da aak.

Iis, săh ăh, ji sa'yah daa gwăh',
Na gat hwa is băh; aa'gă noh,
Gih shăh', deh sa'yah da geh băh,
A yò dăs'theh oh, naeh, ne neh.

Deh oi'wa yăs doh na'ga deăh,
Iis ne găh sa dyă nohk'dah oh
He yoan jadeh, kuh, he goh heh;
Iis, kuh, des găh'nya doh dyòt gont.

Deɪ oi wah'gĕh na ga deăh seek ;
Tăh ăh, waeh, Nais, heh sa deăh oh,
Oi wa neă'gwat ni ya'wah oh,
Sgie'yah sech heh, de ga yah sont.

Da gyah'da geh'hă aak', dih' sho,
Ne' dyòt gont neh ă ges' nyet haak',
He ni sah'sanno'nă ă gwat,
Kuh' he ni sa da ni dăă oh.

The number of Senecas at the last census was 2,449.

The three Reservations which now remain to the Indian in Western New York, are called Tonawanda, Cattaraugus, Alleghany, containing in all about sixty-six thousand acres. No white family is allowed to settle upon these lands, and the law forbids the trusting of an Indian or the selling him intoxicating drinks.

There are at present 14 Schools, 16 Teachers, 480 Scholars, one Boarding School with 50 scholars, 8 Missionaries, 47 Church members.

## NO. II.

During the winter of 1855 a bill was passed by the Legislature of New York, incorporating an Orphan Asylum, and appropriating two thousand dollars ($2000) for a building, and ten dollars a year for each child received and retained under the care of the managers. This is one of the most important benefits conferred upon the Indians. By it a home will be provided for the destitute little ones of this scattered people. And by beginning early, an opportunity will be afforded of securing to them a proper course of moral and physical training, and more surely than by any other way preserve them from destruction.

The experiment was first tried by taking a few into the family of a benevolent lady residing on the Reservation, which, proving successful, an earnest appeal for aid was made to the State.

The institution is incorporated under the name of the "Thomas Asylum for orphan and destitute Indian Children," as a tribute of acknowledgment to the individual whose name it bears, for his long and earnest efforts to assist and benefit the Seneca nation.

It is located upon the Cattaraugus Reservation, but is intended to receive children from all the Reservations in the State of New York. As the appropriation of ten dollars a year for the support and education of each child, is quite insufficient for the purpose, it is hoped that if the attempt to preserve from destruction this noble race should promise success, that the State of New York—the only State on the Atlantic borders of this Confederation, in which an organized body of the once numerous aborigines of our country has been permitted to remain—will hereafter further extend towards this institution its fostering care and aid.

## NO. III.

The following documents from the INDIAN STATE DEPARTMENT, will show the advance which has been made in the science of government, and the art of diplomacy:

The nation has recently undergone quite a revolution, and the people have substituted a popular Representative Government, for the government of the Chiefs, which has heretofore existed. At a Convention, held at Cattaraugus on the 4th of December, 1848, the delegates, in a very formal manner, abrogated the old government, and proclaimed the new order of things, very much after the manner of the founders of our government. Their Declaration is not quite as long as the Mecklenburgh meeting, while its style is not unlike Mr. Jefferson's. The Constitution, defining the duties and powers of the officers of government, is quite detailed. The Supreme Judiciary is composed of three judges, who are designated Peace-Makers. The legislative powers of the nation are vested in a Council of eighteen, chosen by the universal suffrages of the nation; but no treaty is to be binding, until it is ratified by three fourths of all the voters, and *three fourths of all the mothers in the nation!* This may be considered an advance, even beyond the legislative theory of the French Assembly. One provision of this Constitution exhibits a degree of national frugality, well worthy of imitation by those gentlemen in our own Congress, who spend so much of the "dear people's" money in talking about their rights and interests. The Seneca Constitution declares that the compensation of members of the Council, shall be one dollar each per day, while in session; "*but no member shall receive more than twenty-six dollars during any one year.*" With such a provision, they will need no one-hour rule, and there will be no danger of their Council becoming "*en permanence.*"

Among the acts of the Convention, was the re-naming an estimable citizen of Baltimore—Philip E. Thomas; a gentleman whom the Senecas recognize as an old and true friend. In acknowledgment of the many kindnesses which they had received at his hands, they had on a former occasion made Mr. Thomas a Chief, giving him the name of Sagaoh (Benevolent). But now it became necessary to give him a new title, and he was accordingly named *Hai-wa-noh*, which signifies the Ambassador. The minutes of the Convention state that this ceremony was performed amidst "*great sensation, and applause of approbation!*"

DECLARATION OF THE SENECA NATION OF INDIANS—*Changing their form of Government, and adopting a Constitutional Charter:*

We, the people of the Seneca Nation of Indians, by virtue of the right inherent in every people, trusting in the justice and necessity of our undertaking, and humbly invoking the blessing of the God of Nations upon our efforts to improve our civil condition, and to secure to our nation the administration of equitable, wholesome laws, do hereby abolish, abrogate and annul our form of government by Chiefs, because it has failed to answer the purposes for which all governments should be created.

It affords no security in the enjoyment of property.

It provides no laws regulating the institution of marriage, but tolerates polygamy.

It makes no provision for the poor, but leaves the destitute to perish.

It leaves the people dependent on foreign aid for the means of education.

It has no judiciary, nor executive departments.

It is an irresponsible, self-created aristocracy.

Its powers are absolute and unlimited in assigning away the people's rights; but indefinite and not exercised in making municipal regulations for their benefit or protection.

We cannot enumerate the evils growing out of a system so defective, nor calculate its overpowering weight on the progress of improvement.

But to remedy these defects, we proclaim and establish the

following Constitution, or Charter, and implore the Government of the United States, and the State of New York, to aid in providing us with laws, under which progress shall be possible.

Sec. 1. Our Government shall have a Legislative, Executive, and Judiciary Departments.

Sec. 2. The legislative power shall be vested in a Council of eighteen members, who shall be termed the Councillors of the Seneca Nation, and who shall be elected annually on the first Tuesday in May in each year; and who shall be apportioned to each Reservation, according to its population—two thirds of whom assembled in regular session, and duly organized, shall constitute a quorum, and be competent for the transaction of business; but to all bills for the appropriation of public moneys, the assent of two thirds of the members elected shall be necessary, in order that the bill should become a law.

Sec. 3. The executive power shall be vested in a President, whose duty it shall be to preside at all meetings of the Council—having only a casting vote therein—and to see that all laws are duly executed; and to communicate to the Council, at every session, a statement of the condition of the national business, and to recommend for the action of the Council such matters as he may deem expedient. In the absence of the President, the Council may choose a presiding officer pro tempore.

Sec. 4. The judiciary power shall be vested in three Peace-Makers on each Reservation; and two of whom shall have power to hold courts, subject to an appeal to the Council, and to such courts of the State of New York as the Legislature thereof shall permit. The jurisdiction, forms of process, and proceeding in the Peace-Makers' courts, shall be the same as the courts of the justices of the peace of the State of New York, except in the proof of wills, and the settlement of deceased persons' estates—in which cases the Peace-Makers shall have such power as shall be conferred by law.

Sec. 5. All causes over which the Peace-Makers have not jurisdiction, may be heard before the Council, or such courts of the State of New York as the Legislature thereof shall permit.

SEC. 6. The power of making treaties shall be vested in the Council; but no treaty shall be binding upon the nation until the same shall be submitted to the people, and be approved by three fourths of all the legal voters, and also by three fourths of all the mothers in the nation.

SEC. 7. There shall be a clerk and treasurer, and superintendent of schools, and overseers of the poor, and assessors, and overseers of highways, whose duties shall be regulated by law.

SEC. 8. Every officer who shall be authorized to receive public money, shall be required to give such security as the President and the attorney for the Seneca nation shall approve.

SEC. 9. There shall be a marshal, and two deputies, on each Reservation (Cattaraugus and Allegany), who shall execute all processes issued by the courts, and do such other duties as shall be prescribed by law.

SEC. 10. All officers named in this Constitution, or Charter, shall be chosen at the same time, in the same manner, and for the same time, as members of the Council, and vacancies occurring in any office shall be filled in the manner to be prescribed by law; and every male Indian of the age of twenty-one years and upwards, either residing on one of the Reservations (the Cattaraugus, Allegany, or Oil Spring), or owning, possessing, and occupying any lands upon either of said Reservations, and which lands may have been taxed for highways, or other purposes, shall be entitled to vote at all elections.

SEC. 11. Any legal voter shall be eligible to any office named in this Constitution or Charter; and all officers elect shall be inducted into office, and if necessary shall be impeached by the use of such forms and regulations as shall be prescribed by law.

SEC. 12. The compensation of members of the Council shall be one dollar per day while in session; but no member shall receive more than twenty-six dollars in any one year. The compensation of all the officers shall be prescribed by law.

SEC. 13. The Council shall meet annually on the first Tuesday in June, and extra sessions may be convened by the President at any time he shall think proper.

SEC. 14. The Council shall have power to make any laws not inconsistent with the Constitution of the United States, or of the State of New York.

SEC. 15. All offences which shall be punishable by the laws of the United States, or of the State of New York, shall be tried and punished in the Peace-Makers' Court, or before the Council, as shall be prescribed by law.

SEC. 16. The right of any member of the ancient confederacy of the Iroquois to the occupancy of our lands, and other privileges, shall be respected as heretofore; and the Council shall pass laws for the admission of any Indian of other tribes or nations to citizenship and adoption into the Seneca nation of Indians by his or her application, for his, or herself, or family.

SEC. 17. This Charter may be altered or amended by a Council of the people, convened for that purpose, on three months' previous notice, by a vote of two thirds of the legal voters present at such convention.

SEC. 18. The saw-mills on the different Reservations, now in operation, are hereby declared to be national property, and the funds accruing therefrom shall be by the Council appropriated to national purposes. But nothing in this Charter shall be construed as prohibiting the erection of mills and other works for manufacturing or other purposes, by any private individual, upon his own premises, provided that in so doing he do not trespass upon the rights of any other individual; and all such erections by individuals shall be respected as strictly private property.

SEC. 19. The laws passed by the Legislature of the State of New York for the protection and improvement of the Seneca nation of Indians, and also all laws and regulations heretofore adopted by the Chiefs, in legal council assembled, shall continue in full force and effect as heretofore, except so far as they are inconsistent with the provisions of this Constitution or Charter.

I hereby certify that the above copy has been examined

and compared with the original, now on file in the Archives of the Seneca nation of Indians, by me, and is a correct transcript of the same and of the whole of said Declaration, Constitution, and Charter.

WILLIAM JEMERSON,
Clerk of the Seneca nation of Indians,
Cattaraugus Reservation, Erie County.

NEW YORK, *December* 5, 1848.

## RESOLUTIONS,
*Adopted by the Convention of the Seneca Nation of Indians, December 4th, 1848.*

*Resolved,*—That this Convention feel grateful for the religious and scientific instruction which benevolent societies and individuals have bestowed upon us, as well as for the introduction of proper means among us for our improvement; and particularly do we desire to express our gratitude to the Society of Friends; they were the first to introduce the means for our culture and improvement, and laid the foundation of our education and civilization, by which means we have become wiser and enlightened, and been enabled to see and understand our rights; they also befriended and aided us when friendless, and without means to sustain ourselves in time of peril—always zealous and unremitting in their labors for our welfare. Also to the American Board of Commissioners for Foreign Missions, in sending us missionaries and teachers to enlighten our minds, and direct us to the true light, and teach us the plan of salvation: and also the State of New York, for their benevolent efforts in enacting laws for our protection and improvement, as well as for the large and generous appropriations made by them for the erection of school-houses, and the payment of school teachers among our people, and we desire that these kind offices may be continued.

*Resolved,*—That inasmuch as we have abolished our former Government; that by so doing all appointments have now become annulled; therefore

*Resolved,*—That the Seneca nation of Indians in this General Convention assembled, do hereby express their thanks to their friend and brother Sagaoh (Philip E. Thomas), of the city of Baltimore and State of Maryland, for the faithful discharge of his duties as representative of our nation (under our late Government) to the United States Government at Washington, and having undiminished confidence in his integrity and ability, we do hereby constitute and appoint him our ambassador, under our new form of Government, to represent us, and to have charge of all the interests and affairs of the Seneca nation of Indians to the United States Government at Washington.

*Resolved,*—That as it is customary among our people, that whenever any important event occurs in the history of our nation, either by the natural transition from childhood to manhood, from Warrior to Chieftain, or from Chieftain to Sachem; therefore we declare, that in consequence of this change in our Government of his re-appointment under the new, and with the consent of the relatives of our friend Sagaoh, that the name Sagaoh shall cease to be his name, by which he was called and known among us, and that hereafter his name shall be Hai-wa-noh (Ambassador, Representative or Charge d'Affaires) because he is to represent our nation and people, by which appellation he is henceforth to be known among us, and that the ceremony of christening him be immediately performed. Whereupon the ceremony of changing the former Indian name and christening Philip E. Thomas of Baltimore, was performed according to our customs and usages, by Sa-dye-na-wa (John Hudson), and declared that the said Thomas may hereafter be known by the name of Hai-wa-noh. (Great sensation and applause of approbation).

*Resolved,*—That the clerk and President are hereby authorized and empowered to prepare the credentials of Hai-wa-noh (Philip E. Thomas), our Ambassador, whom we have hereby constituted and appointed; and forward the same to him as soon as practicable, together with the Declaration, and Constitutional Charter, and request him immediately to repair to the seat of the United States Government, and present them to the proper authorities, and also to notify him of the change of his name, and his appointment as an officer of the Government of the Seneca nation of Indians.

*Resolved*,—That copies of the Declaration, Constitutional Charter, and resolutions of this convention, be forwarded by the clerk to the joint committee of the Society of Friends on Indian concerns; and to the Governors of the States of New York and Massachusetts, with the request that the same be put on file in the proper offices; and that our Representative be requested to present copies of the same to the Congress of the United States, now covened at Washington, and to the Secretary at War, with the request that the same be put on file in their respective departments.

*Resolved*,—That we have unabated and undiminished confidence in the abilities and qualifications of the United States interpreter (Peter Wilson) for this agency, having always discharged his duty faithfully, and that inasmuch as the late chiefs under our former Government have petitioned for his removal, without just and reasonable cause, we hereby request our representative to protest and remonstrate against his removal.

*Resolved*,—That the clerk be hereby instructed to prepare and forward copies of the doings and proceedings of this Convention, to the publishers of the Buffalo Commercial Advertiser, and the New York Tribune, with the request that the same be printed in their respective papers.

I do hereby certify that the above copy has been examined and compared with the original now on file in the archives of the Seneca nation of Indians, by me, and is a correct copy of the same, and of the whole of said resolutions passed by the General Convention.

WILLIAM JEMERSON,
Clerk of the Seneca nation of Indians.

Cattaraugus Reservation,
Erie County, N. Y.
December 5, 1848.

SIR:—You are hereby nominated, constituted, and appointed an Ambassador, Envoy Extraordinay, and Minister Plenipotentiary to the seat of Government of the United States of America, by the Constitutional Convention and Government of the Seneca nation of Indians, residing in the State of New York, to represent them in their names and behalf, with full powers and privileges of said office to take charge of the interests and affairs of your Government and nation: and whatever you may do in our names and behalf will be binding upon us, and of the same effect as if we had been present and consenting thereto; and you are hereby authorized and empowered to proceed with the business of your nation as they shall from time to time direct, and as you may deem just and proper.

You are also hereby authorized and requested to proceed immediately to the seat of the United States Government, and present this, your credentials, to the proper authorities.

You are also informed that your official duties commence with the date of this commission and appointment as an officer of the Seneca nation of Indians.

By order of the Convention and Government of the Seneca nation of Indians.

S. W. McLANE, *President.*
WILLIAM JEMERSON, *Clerk.*
Cattaraugus Reservation, Erie County, N. Y.,
December 5th, 1848.
To *HAI-WA-NOH*, (*Philip E. Thomas*,)
*Ambassador, &c., &c.,*
*Baltimore, Maryland.*

---

## NO. IV.

The following extracts from the proceedings of the yearly meetings of the Friends of Baltimore, in the year 1850, will give some idea of the present condition of the women, and the understanding they have of governmental as well as domestic affairs:

"Thus we see the Seneca nation with a government 'calculated,' to use their own language, 'to answer the purpose for which all governments should be created.' We find their women mostly withdrawn from the field, and occupying their proper station in their families,—their children suitably cared for at home, and at school, having the benefit of literary and scientific learning. We have, for several years past, had among them an Institution for the instruction of their daughters in the duties of housewifery, and other appropriate domestic employments. They are provided with good dwelling-houses and barns—are the undisputed owners of a fertile, productive soil, of ample extent for all their purposes, yielding more than the nation can consume; and in addition to these advantages, they are in receipt of annuities more than sufficient to defray all the expenses of their government.

"When the present joint committees first visited the Reservations, in the years 1839 and 1840, a very large portion of the Indians lived in wigwams, or poor log huts—covered with bark, boards, or other materials, hardly sufficient to shield them from the weather. Many of them had earth floors, on which they slept in buffalo skins and blankets. They set no table, had no regular meals—used no plates, nor knives and forks. An iron pot was generally found placed over the fire, into which they put beans and hominy, and a piece of some sort of meat—either pork or venison. When any one of the family was hungry, he helped himself to what he wanted, putting it in a small wooden vessel, and feeding himself with a wooden or iron spoon. The interior of the dwellings generally presented to the eye a spectacle by no means calculated to warm the imagination in favor of Indian life. The truth is, that woman had been driven from her proper sphere, and no domestic happiness could enter the dwelling in her absence.

"The Manual-labor School was established as one of the means of restoring woman to the station evidently designed for her, in the benevolent order of her Creator, an order which cannot be broken with impunity. This school was held in the dwelling erected for the use of Friends at Cattaraugus. The average number of pupils was about twenty-eight, genererally under *twenty years of age.* They were boarded in the family, at the expense of the committee, and were taught to card and spin wool, knit stockings, cut out and make garments, &c. A part of their number was daily admitted into the family of the Superintendent, where they were taught to wash and iron clothes, &c., make bread, do plain cooking, and every other branch of good housewifery, pertaining to a country life. In this department all were admitted by turns, generally four at a time, and continued until the necessary proficiency was attained. As such left the school, others took their places, by which arrangement, a large number of young women became qualified to take charge of families, and extend to succeeding generations the comforts and blessings of domestic life.

### MEMORIAL OF THE SENECA WOMEN TO P. E. THOMAS.

*[Original sent to the Indian Bureau.]*

CATTARAUGUS RESERVATION, Oct. 18, 1848.

To our Respected Friend, Philip E. Thomas:

The women of Cattaraugus Reservation wish to address to you a few words, in this time of our trouble, and we do so the more cheerfully, because the Friends are always laboring to promote the welfare of the females among the Indians, and to improve their condition. We would also request you to secure the influence of the Society of Friends, so that our words may be strengthened, and become sufficiently powerful to be heard by the Secretary of War, that we women have an equal right to our annuities, with the men, and with the chiefs. We are all on the same footing as to the amount we are entitled to receive—chiefs and warriors, men, women and children. We were glad when we heard that the Secretary had instructed our new Agent, to pay the annuities for this year to the heads of families. We see no other way by which our rights can be secured to us, and justice done alike to all. We hope you will urge the Secretary to confirm his former instructions, for we were greatly perplexed and troubled, when the Agent was induced to delay the payment, on the ground that the chiefs insisted on the observance of the old custom in regard to it. *We ask for our just rights and nothing more;* but we repeat it, that *we do not feel* that our rights will be safe, if these instructions to the Agent shall be reversed. We regret that the Agent should have thought it necessary to delay a strict compliance with his instructions, but we do not yet feel disheartened, for we have confidence that the Secretary will manifest a due regard to our rights. Only we beg leave to repeat our request, that you will bring all the weight of your influence, and that of your Society, to bear upon this question, that he may be willing to confirm his former decision, and give every Indian woman, and child, no less than others, the apportionment which of right belongs to each.

And we would desire to add, that we have already suffered greatly from the proceedings of the chiefs, through whose instrumentality our poverty has been increasing upon us, and we wish to entreat that we may never again, hereafter, be exposed to be deprived by them of our rights, but that we and our children, from time to time, may be permitted to receive the full and proper share which rightfully belongs to us. We are fully sensible that it is a hard case to have a difficulty with the chiefs, but we feel that we have been wronged by them, and our children have suffered already, and for a long time past, through their avarice and pride, and we believe the things they have said in justification of themselves are not true. It is by our pain and sorrow that children are brought into the world, and we are, therefore, interested in whatever concerns the welfare of our children. We have examined this subject, and we are satisfied that the party who are laboring to bring about an equal division of the whole of our annuities, are the party really striving for the best interests of our children.

We have taken the same view of the matter which was taken by the old men long since dead, who first entered into these arrangements. They decided that every individual man, woman, and child, had an equal right to our moneys, and to our lands—in short, to all our national property; that it was so from the beginning, and that it always should be so. We have taken the liberty to express our views, because we believe this to be the real truth, and we would earnestly desire the President and Secretary of War to secure to us now, and to our posterity in all time to come, the fulfilment of the original stipulations, that *as long as wood should grow, or water run, or a Seneca live to behold the light of the sun, these annuities should be faithfully paid and righteously distributed.*

With great respect, your friends,

Their<br>
Betsey + Snow.<br>
Julia + Ann Snow.<br>
Jane + Scott.<br>
Ganna + Hon.<br>
Polly + Johnson.<br>
Martha + Phillips.<br>
marks.

On behalf of the Seneca women.

Done in the presence of
Joseph S. Walton,
Asher Wright.

## Memorial of the Seneca Women to the President.

To his Excellency General Zachary Taylor, President of the United States of America:

The undersigned, mothers, heads of families, wives, and grown up daughters of the Seneca nation of Indians, residing in Western New York, respectfully represent to our Father the President, that we have heard with extreme regret that an educated young man from among our sons and brothers is at Washington, importuning the President to undo the good which has been done for our people by his predecessors, and to destroy the effect, as far as the Senecas are concerned, of the wise regulation, that a portion of all the Indian annuities should be distributed just at seedtime, every spring, in order to facilitate and encourage agriculture. We wish our sons to be industrious—to be in the field, stirring the soil betimes, procuring a bountiful harvest as the fruits of God's blessing upon their own honest exertions: not leaving it for the women to raise corn, as did their hunting, fishing, and fighting forefathers. The days of hunting and fishing, and we trust, also, of Indian fighting, are gone by for ever, and it pains us exceedingly that an educated son of ours, and one, too, who, if he would consult the well-being of his people, might be so smart and useful, should now be trying, either of his own will, or under the direction of those whom, if they had sought the public good, we should have rejoiced to call our chiefs, to thwart the wishes of this people, check the pursuits of agriculture, and bring embarrassing and perplexing want upon the destitute, who have been relying upon the stability of the counsels of the United States Government for the relief of their necessities. We have many and to us weighty reasons why our Father, the President, should not heed the petition of our son, whom we did not send to speak for us to the President; but lest it should be thought that Indian women have tongues that never tire, we only add that it is the earnest prayer of the undersigned, in their own behalf, and in behalf of a large majority of the mothers, wives, and daughters of the Seneca nation, that the recognition of the new Government may be permitted to stand; and that we may be paid our annuities according to the rule adopted in 1847, for the payment of all the tribes receiving annuities from the government, i. e., during the current month; and your memorialists, as in duty bound, will ever pray.

    Signed,     Gua-na-ea, and
              Nineteen other females.

*April 4, 1849.*

### REPLY OF PHILIP E. THOMAS TO THESE WOMEN.

BALTIMORE, 4 mo., 8th, 1849.

MY RESPECTED SISTERS:—Your address to the President of the United States has reached me, and has received my careful attention. I am glad to inform you that all you ask in regard to the manner of paying your annuities, and the acknowledgment of your new Government, has been decided as you wish. The annuities hereafter will be paid by the United States Agent to the heads of families—to the women as to the men, and none will again be paid to the chiefs except their own respective portions.

By the acknowledgment of your new Constitution, the Government of the United States recognizes that excellent article in it, which provides that no sale of Land can hereafter be made without the consent of three fourths of all the mothers in the nation. This wise provision assures to you the security of your homes; for I have too much confidence in my Indian Sisters to believe they will ever be prevailed on to take the land from their children, and send them away to perish in the wilderness.

It gave me pleasure to read your address to the President. It proved to me that you were beginning to understand your rights, and were disposed to exercise them. I hope you will remember the good advice the committee gave you in the year 1845, and as some of you may not have heard it then, I now send you a copy of it under care of my brother Joseph S. Walton.

Bear this advice in your minds; it is good counsel, and endeavor to practise it.

Whenever you may desire to make any communication to me, you are at liberty to do it.—You will find me your faithful friend and brother,

P. E. THOMAS.

# A LIST OF NEW WORKS
## IN GENERAL LITERATURE,
PUBLISHED BY
### D. APPLETON & COMPANY,
346 & 348 Broadway.

*⁎* *Complete Catalogues, containing full descriptions, to be had on application to the Publishers.*

### Agriculture and Rural Affairs.

| | |
|---|---|
| Boussingault's Rural Economy, | 1 25 |
| The Poultry Book, illustrated, | 5 00 |
| Waring's Elements of Agriculture, | 75 |

### Arts, Manufactures, and Architecture.

| | |
|---|---|
| Appleton's Dictionary of Mechanics. 2 vols. | 12 00 |
| " Mechanics' Magazine. 3 vols. each, | 3 50 |
| Allen's Philosophy of Mechanics, | 3 50 |
| Arnot's Gothic Architecture, | 4 00 |
| Bassnett's Theory of Storms, | 1 00 |
| Bourne on the Steam Engine, | 75 |
| Byrne on Logarithms, | 1 00 |
| Chapman on the American Rifle, | 1 25 |
| Coming's Preservation of Health, | 75 |
| Cullum on Military Bridges, | 2 00 |
| Downing's Country Houses, | 4 00 |
| Field's City Architecture, | 2 00 |
| Griffith's Marine Architecture, | 10 00 |
| Gillespie's Treatise on Surveying, | |
| Haupt's Theory of Bridge Construction, | 3 00 |
| Henck's Field-Book for R. Road Engineers, | 1 75 |
| Hoblyn's Dictionary of Scientific Terms, | 1 50 |
| Hull's Manual of Electro-Physiology, | 1 25 |
| Jeffers' Practice of Naval Gunnery, | 2 50 |
| Knapen's Mechanics' Assistant, | 1 00 |
| Lafever's Modern Architecture, | 4 0 |
| Lyell's Manual of Geology, | 1 75 |
| " Principles of Geology, | 2 25 |
| Reynold's Treatise on Handrailing, | 2 00 |
| Templeton's Mechanic's Companion, | 1 00 |
| Ure's Dict'ry of Arts, Manufactures, &c. 2 vols. | 5 00 |
| Youmans' Class Book of Chemistry, | 75 |
| " Atlas of Chemistry. cloth, | 2 00 |
| " Alcohol, | 60 |

### Biography.

| | |
|---|---|
| Arnold's Life and Correspondence, | 2 00 |
| Capt. Canot, or Twenty Years of a Slaver, | 1 25 |
| Cousin's De Longueville, | 1 00 |
| Cromwell's Memoirs, | 2 00 |
| Evelyn's Life of Godolphin, | 50 |
| Garland's Life of Randolph, | 1 50 |
| Gilfillan's Gallery of Portraits. 2d Series, | 1 00 |
| Herman Cortez's Life, | 38 |
| Hull's Civil and Military Life, | 2 00 |
| Life and Adventures of Daniel Boone, | 38 |
| Life of Henry Hudson, | 38 |
| Life of Capt. John Smith, | 38 |
| Moore's Life of George Castriot, | 1 00 |
| Napoleon's Memoirs. By Duchess D'Abrantes, | 4 00 |
| Napoleon. By Laurent L'Ardèche, | 3 00 |
| Pinkney (W.) Life. By his Nephew, | 2 00 |
| Party Leaders: Lives of Jefferson, &c. | 1 00 |
| Southey's Life of Oliver Cromwell, | 38 |
| Wynne's Lives of Eminent Men, | 1 00 |
| Webster's Life and Memorials. 2 vols. | 1 00 |

### Books of General Utility.

| | |
|---|---|
| Appletons' Southern and Western Guide, | 1 00 |
| " Northern and Eastern Guide, | 1 25 |

| | |
|---|---|
| Appletons' Complete U. S. Guide, | 2 00 |
| " Map of N. Y. City, | 25 |
| American Practical Cook Book, | |
| A Treatise on Artificial Fish-Breeding, | 75 |
| Chemistry of Common Life. 2 vols. 12mo. | |
| Cooley's Book of Useful Knowledge, | 1 25 |
| Cust's Invalid's Own Book, | 50 |
| Delisser's Interest Tables, | 4 00 |
| The English Cyclopaedia, per vol. | 2 50 |
| Miles on the Horse's Foot, | 25 |
| The Nursery Basket. A Book for Young Mothers, | 38 |
| Pell's Guide for the Young, | 38 |
| Reid's New English Dictionary, | 1 00 |
| Stewart's Stable Economy, | 1 00 |
| Spalding's Hist. of English Literature, | 1 00 |
| Soyer's Modern Cookery, | 1 00 |
| The Successful Merchant, | 1 00 |
| Thomson on Food of Animals, | 60 |

### Commerce and Mercantile Affairs.

| | |
|---|---|
| Anderson's Mercantile Correspondence, | 1 00 |
| Delisser's Interest Tables, | 4 00 |
| Merchants' Reference Book, | 4 00 |
| Oates' (Geo.) Interest Tables at 6 Per Cent. per Annum. 8vo. | 2 00 |
| " " Do. do. Abridged edition, | 1 25 |
| " " 7 Per Cent. Interest Tables, | 2 00 |
| " " Abridged, | 1 25 |
| Smith's Mercantile Law, | 4 00 |

### Geography and Atlases.

| | |
|---|---|
| Appleton's Modern Atlas. 34 Maps, | 3 50 |
| " Complete Atlas. 61 Maps, | 9 00 |
| Atlas of the Middle Ages. By Koeppen, | 4 50 |
| Black's General Atlas. 71 Maps, | 12 00 |
| Cornell's Primary Geography, | 50 |
| " Intermediate Geography, | |
| " High School Geography, | |

### History.

| | |
|---|---|
| Arnold's History of Rome, | 3 00 |
| " Later Commonwealth, | 2 50 |
| " Lectures on Modern History, | 2 00 |
| Dew's Ancient and Modern History, | 2 00 |
| Koeppen's History of the Middle Ages. 2 vols. | 4 50 |
| " The same, folio, with Maps, | 4 50 |
| Kohlrausch's History of Germany, | 1 50 |
| Mahon's (Lord) History of England, 2 vo's. | 4 00 |
| Michelet's History of France, 2 vols. | 3 50 |
| " History of the Roman Republic, | 1 00 |
| Rowan's History of the French Revolution, | 63 |
| Sprague's History of the Florida War, | 2 50 |
| Taylor's Manual of Ancient History, | 1 25 |
| " Manual of Modern History, | 1 50 |
| " Manual of History. 1 vol. complete, | 2 50 |
| Thiers' French Revolution. 4 vols. Illustrated, | 5 00 |

### Illustrated Works for Presents.

| | |
|---|---|
| Bryant's Poems. 16 Illustrations. 8vo. cloth, | 3 50 |
| " " " cloth, gilt, | 4 50 |
| " " " mor. antique, | 6 00 |

# D. Appleton & Company's List of New Works.

| | |
|---|---:|
| Gems of British Art. 30 Engravings. 1 vol. 4to. morocco, | 18 00 |
| Gray's Elegy. Illustrated. 8vo. | 1 50 |
| Goldsmith's Deserted Village, | 1 50 |
| The Homes of American Authors. With Illustrations, cloth, | 4 00 |
| "    "    "    cloth, gilt, | 5 00 |
| "    "    "    mor. antiq. | 7 00 |
| The Holy Gospels. With 40 Designs by Overbeck. 1 vol. folio. Antique mor. | 20 00 |
| The Land of Bondage. By J. M. Wainwright, D. D. Morocco, | 6 00 |
| The Queens of England. By Agnes Strickland. With 79 Portraits. Antique mor. | 10 00 |
| The Ornaments of Memory. With 18 Illustrations. 4to. cloth, gilt, | 6 00 |
| "    "    Morocco, | 10 00 |
| Royal Gems from the Galleries of Europe. 40 Engravings, | 25 00 |
| The Republican Court; or, American Society in the Days of Washington. 21 Portraits. Antique mor. | 12 00 |
| The Vernon Gallery. 61 Engrav'gs. 4to. Ant. | 25 00 |
| The Women of the Bible. With 19 Engravings. Mor. antique, | 10 00 |
| Wilkie Gallery. Containing 60 Splendid Engravings. 4to. Antique mor. | 25 00 |
| A Winter Wreath of Summer Flowers. By S. G. Goodrich. Illustrated. Cloth, gilt, | 3 00 |

## Juvenile Books.

| | |
|---|---:|
| A Poetry Book for Children, | 75 |
| Aunt Fanny's Christmas Stories, | 50 |
| American Historical Tales, | 75 |

### UNCLE AMEREL'S STORY BOOKS.

| | |
|---|---:|
| The Little Gift Book. 18mo. cloth, | 25 |
| The Child's Story Book. Illust. 18mo. cloth, | 25 |
| Summer Holidays. 18mo. cloth, | 25 |
| Winter Holidays. Illustrated. 18mo. cloth, | 25 |
| George's Adventures in the Country. Illustrated. 18mo. cloth, | 25 |
| Christmas Stories. Illustrated. 18mo. cloth, | 25 |
| Book of Trades, | 50 |
| Boys at Home By the Author of Edgar Clifton, | 75 |
| Child's Cheerful Companion, | 50 |
| Child's Picture and Verse Book. 100 Engs. | 50 |

### COUSIN ALICE'S WORKS.

| | |
|---|---:|
| All's Not Gold that Glitters, | 75 |
| Contentment Better than Wealth, | 63 |
| Nothing Venture, Nothing Have, | 63 |
| No such Word as Fail, | 63 |
| Patient Waiting No Loss, | 63 |
| Dashwood Priory. By the Author of Edgar Clifton, | 75 |
| Edgar Clifton; or Right and Wrong, | 75 |
| Fireside Fairies By Susan Pindar, | 63 |
| Good in Every Thing. By Mrs. Barwell, | 50 |
| Leisure Moments Improved, | 75 |
| Life of Punchinello, | 75 |

### LIBRARY FOR MY YOUNG COUNTRYMEN.

| | |
|---|---:|
| Adventures of Capt. John Smith. By the Author of Uncle Philip, | 38 |
| Adventures of Daniel Boone. By do. | 38 |
| Dawnings of Genius. By Anne Pratt, | 38 |
| Life and Adventures of Henry Hudson. By the Author of Uncle Philip, | 38 |
| Life and Adventures of Hernan Cortez. By do. | 38 |
| Philip Randolph. A Tale of Virginia. By Mary Gertrude, | 38 |
| Rowan's History of the French Revolution. 2 vols. | 75 |
| Southey's Life of Oliver Cromwell, | 38 |

| | |
|---|---:|
| Louis' School Days. By E. J. May, | 75 |
| Louise; or, The Beauty of Integrity, | 25 |
| Maryatt's Settlers in Canada, | 63 |
| "    Masterman Ready, | 63 |
| "    Scenes in Africa, | 63 |
| Midsummer Fays By Susan Pindar, | 63 |

### MISS M'INTOSH'S WORKS.

| | |
|---|---:|
| Aunt Kitty's Tales, 12mo. | 75 |
| Blind Alice; A Tale for Good Children, | 38 |
| Ellen Leslie; or, The Reward of Self-Control, | 38 |
| Florence Arnott; or, Is She Generous? | 38 |
| Grace and Clara; or, Be Just as well as Generous, | 38 |
| Jessie Graham; or, Friends Dear, but Truth Dearer, | 38 |
| Emily Herbert; or, The Happy Home, | 37 |
| Rose and Lillie Stanhope, | 37 |
| Mamma's Story Book, | 75 |
| Pebbles from the Sea-Shore, | 37 |
| Puss in Boots. Illustrated. By Otto Specter, | 25 |

### PETER PARLEY'S WORKS.

| | |
|---|---:|
| Faggots for the Fireside, | 1 12 |
| Parley's Present for all Seasons, | 1 00 |
| Wanderers by Sea and Land, | 1 12 |
| Winter Wreath of Summer Flowers, | 3 00 |

### TALES FOR THE PEOPLE AND THEIR CHILDREN.

| | |
|---|---:|
| Alice Franklin. By Mary Howitt, | 38 |
| Crofton Boys (The). By Harriet Martineau, | 38 |
| Dangers of Dining Out. By Mrs. Ellis, | 38 |
| Domestic Tales. By Hannah More. 2 vols. | 75 |
| Early Friendship. By Mrs. Copley, | 38 |
| Farmer's Daughter (The). By Mrs. Cameron, | 38 |
| First Impressions. By Mrs. Ellis, | 38 |
| Hope On, Hope Ever! By Mary Howitt, | 38 |
| Little Coin, Much Care. By do. | 38 |
| Looking-Glass for the Mind. Many plates, | 38 |
| Love and Money. By Mary Howitt, | 38 |
| Minister's Family. By Mrs. Ellis, | 38 |
| My Own Story. By Mary Howitt, | 38 |
| My Uncle, the Clockmaker. By do. | 38 |
| No Sense Like Common Sense. By do. | 38 |
| Peasant and the Prince. By H. Martineau, | 38 |
| Poplar Grove. By Mrs. Copley, | 38 |
| Somerville Hall. By Mrs. Ellis, | 38 |
| Sowing and Reaping. By Mary Howitt, | 38 |
| Story of a Genius, | 38 |
| Strive and Thrive. By do. | 38 |
| The Two Apprentices. By do. | 38 |
| Tired of Housekeeping. By T. S. Arthur, | 38 |
| Twin Sisters (The). By Mrs. Sandham, | 38 |
| Which is the Wiser? By Mary Howitt, | 38 |
| Who Shall be Greatest? By do. | 38 |
| Work and Wages. By do. | 38 |

### SECOND SERIES.

| | |
|---|---:|
| Chances and Changes. By Charles Burdett, | 38 |
| Goldmaker's Village. By H. Zschokke, | 38 |
| Never Too Late. By Charles Burdett, | 38 |
| Ocean Work, Ancient and Modern. By J. H. Wright, | 38 |
| Picture Pleasure Book, 1st Series, | 1 25 |
| "    "    2d Series, | 1 25 |
| Robinson Crusoe. 300 Plates, | 1 50 |
| Susan Pindar's Story Book, | 75 |
| Sunshine of Greystone, | 75 |
| Travels of Bob the Squirrel, | 37 |
| Wonderful Story Book, | 50 |
| Willy's First Present, | 75 |
| Week's Delight; or, Games and Stories for the Parlor, | 75 |
| William Tell, the Hero of Switzerland, | 50 |
| Young Student. By Madame Guizot, | 75 |

## D. Appleton & Company's List of New Works.

### Miscellaneous and General Literature.

| | |
|---|---:|
| An Attic Philosopher in Paris, | 25 |
| Appletons' Library Manual, | 1 25 |
| Agnell's Book of Chess, | 1 25 |
| Arnold's Miscellaneous Works, | 2 10 |
| Arthur, The Successful Merchant, | |
| A Book for Summer Time in the Country, | 50 |
| Baldwin's Flush Times in Alabama, | 1 25 |
| Calhoun (J. C.), Works of. 4 vols. publ., each, | 2 00 |
| Clark's (W. G.) Knick Knacks, | 1 25 |
| Cornwall's Music as it Was, and as it Is, | 63 |
| Essays from the London Times. 1st & 2d Series, each, | 50 |
| Ewbanks' World in a Workshop, | 75 |
| Ellis' Women of England, | 50 |
| " Hearts and Homes, | 1 50 |
| " Prevention Better than Cure, | 75 |
| Foster's Essays on Christian Morals, | 50 |
| Goldsmith's Vicar of Wakefield, | 75 |
| Grant's Memoirs of an American Lady, | 75 |
| Gaieties and Gravities. By Horace Smith, | 50 |
| Guizot's History of Civilization, | 1 00 |
| Hearth-Stone. By Rev. S. Osgood, | 1 00 |
| Hobson. My Uncle and I, | 75 |
| Ingoldsby Legends, | 50 |
| Isham's Mud Cabin, | 1 00 |
| Johnson's Meaning of Words, | 1 00 |
| Kavanagh's Women of Christianity, | 75 |
| Leger's Animal Magnetism, | 1 00 |
| Life's Discipline. A Tale of Hungary, | 63 |
| Letters from Rome, A. D. 138, | 1 90 |
| Margaret Maitland, | 75 |
| Maiden and Married Life of Mary Powell, | 50 |
| Morton Montague; or a Young Christian's Choice, | 75 |
| Macaulay's Miscellanies. 5 vols. | 5 00 |
| Maxims of Washington. By J. F. Schroeder, | 1 00 |
| Mile Stones in our Life Journey, | 1 00 |

**MINIATURE CLASSICAL LIBRARY.**

| | |
|---|---:|
| Poetic Lacon; or, Aphorisms from the Poets, | 38 |
| Bond's Golden Maxims, | 31 |
| Clarke's Scripture Promises. Complete, | 38 |
| Elizabeth; or, The Exiles of Siberia, | 31 |
| Goldsmith's Vicar of Wakefield, | 38 |
| " Essays, | 38 |
| Gems from American Poets, | 38 |
| Hannah More's Private Devotions, | 31 |
| " " Practical Piety. 2 vols. | 75 |
| Hemans' Domestic Affections, | 31 |
| Hoffman's Lays of the Hudson, &c. | 38 |
| Johnson's History of Rasselas, | 31 |
| Manual of Matrimony, | 31 |
| Moore's Lalla Rookh, | 38 |
| " Melodies. Complete, | 38 |
| Paul and Virginia, | 31 |
| Pollok's Course of Time, | 38 |
| Pure Gold from the Rivers of Wisdom, | 38 |
| Thomson's Seasons, | 38 |
| Token of the Heart. Do. of Affection. Do. of Remembrance. Do. of Friendship. Do. of Love. Each, | 31 |
| Useful Letter-Writer, | 38 |
| Wilson's Sacra Privata, | 31 |
| Young's Night Thoughts, | 38 |
| Little Pedlington and the Pedlingtonians, | 50 |
| Pneumatics. Tales and Poems, | 1 25 |
| Papers from the Quarterly Review, | 50 |
| Republic of the United States. Its Duties, &c. | 1 00 |
| Preservation of Health and Prevention of Disease, | 75 |
| School for Politics. By Chas. Gayarre, | 75 |
| Select Italian Comedies. Translated, | 75 |
| Shakespeare's Scholar. By R. G. White, | 2 50 |
| Spectator (The). New ed. 6 vols. cloth, | 9 00 |
| Swett's Treatise on Diseases of the Chest, | 3 00 |
| Stories from Blackwood, | 50 |

**THACKERAY'S WORKS.**

| | |
|---|---:|
| The Book of Snobs, | 50 |
| Mr. Browne's Letters, | 50 |
| The Confessions of Fitzboodle, | 50 |
| The Fat Contributor, | 50 |
| Jeames' Diary. A Legend of the Rhine, | 50 |
| The Luck of Barry Lyndon, | 1 00 |
| Men's Wives, | 50 |
| The Paris Sketch Book. 2 vols. | 1 00 |
| The Shabby Genteel Story, | 50 |
| The Yellowplush Papers. 1 vol. 18mo. | 50 |
| Thackeray's Works. 6 vols. bound in cloth, | 6 00 |
| Trescott's Diplomacy of the Revolution, | 75 |
| Tuckerman's Artist Life, | 75 |
| Up Country Letters, | 75 |
| Ward's Letters from Three Continents, | 1 00 |
| " English Items, | 1 00 |
| Warner's Rudimental Lessons in Music, | 50 |
| Woman's Worth, | 38 |

### Philosophical Works.

| | |
|---|---:|
| Cousin's Course of Modern Philosophy, | 2 00 |
| " Philosophy of the Beautiful, | 62 |
| " on the True, Beautiful, and Good, | 1 50 |
| Comte's Positive Philosophy. 2 vols. | 4 00 |
| Hamilton's Philosophy. 1 vol. 8vo. | 1 50 |

### Poetry and the Drama.

| | |
|---|---:|
| Amelia's Poems. 1 vol. 12mo. | 1 25 |
| Brownell's Poems. 12mo. | 75 |
| Bryant's Poems. 1 vol. 8vo, Illustrated, | 3 50 |
| " " Antique mor. | 6 00 |
| " " 2 vols. 12mo. cloth, | 2 00 |
| " " 1 vol. 18mo. | 63 |
| Byron's Poetical Works. 1 vol. cloth, | 3 00 |
| " " Antique mor. | 6 00 |
| Burns' Poetical Works. Cloth, | 1 00 |
| Butler's Hudibras. Cloth, | 1 00 |
| Campbell's Poetical Works. Cloth, | 1 00 |
| Coleridge's Poetical Works. Cloth, | 1 25 |
| Cowper's Poetical Works, | 1 00 |
| Chaucer's Canterbury Tales, | 1 00 |
| Dante's Poems. Cloth, | 1 00 |
| Dryden's Poetical Works. Cloth, | 1 00 |
| Fay (J. S.), Ulric; or, The Voices, | 75 |
| Goethe's Iphigenia in Tauris. Translated, | 75 |
| Gillillan's Edition of the British Poets. 12 vols. published. Price per vol. cloth, | 1 00 |
| Do. do. Calf, per vol. | 2 50 |
| Griffith's (Mattie) Poems, | 75 |
| Hemans' Poetical Works. 2 vols. 16mo. | 2 10 |
| Herbert's Poetical Works. 16mo. cloth, | 1 00 |
| Keats' Poetical Works. Cloth, 12mo. | 1 25 |
| Kirke White's Poetical Works. Cloth, | 1 00 |
| Lord's Poems. 1 vol. 12mo. | 75 |
| " Christ in Hades. 12mo. | 75 |
| Milton's Paradise Lost. 18mo. | 38 |
| " Complete Poetical Works, | 1 00 |
| Moore's Poetical Works. 8vo. Illustrated, | 3 00 |
| " " Mor. extra, | 6 00 |
| Montgomery's Sacred Poems. 1 vol. 12mo. | 75 |
| Pope's Poetical Works. 1 vol. 16mo. | 1 00 |
| Southey's Poetical Works. 1 vol. | 3 00 |
| Spenser's Faerie Queene. 1 vol. cloth, | 1 00 |
| Scott's Poetical Works. 1 vol. | 1 00 |
| " Lady of the Lake. 16mo. | 38 |
| " Marmion, | 37 |
| " Lay of the Last Minstrel, | 25 |
| Shakespeare's Dramatic Works, | 2 00 |
| Tasso's Jerusalem Delivered. 1 vol. 16mo. | 1 00 |
| Wordsworth (W.). The Prelude, | 1 00 |

### Religious Works.

| | |
|---|---:|
| Arnold's Rugby School Sermons, | 50 |
| Anthon's Catechism on the Homilies, | 06 |
| " Early Catechism for Children, | 06 |
| Burnet's History of the Reformation. 3 vols. | 2 50 |
| " Thirty-Nine Articles, | 2 00 |

## D. Appleton & Company's List of New Works.

| | |
|---|---|
| Bradley's Family and Parish Sermons, | 2 00 |
| Cotter's Mass and Rubrics, | 25 |
| Coit's Puritanism, | 1 00 |
| Evans' Rectory of Valehead, | 50 |
| Grayson's True Theory of Christianity, | 1 00 |
| Gresley on Preaching, | 25 |
| Griffin's Gospel its Own Advocate, | 1 00 |
| Hecker's Book of the Soul, | 50 |
| Hooker's Complete Works. 2 vols. | 4 00 |
| James' Happiness, | 25 |
| James on the Nature of Evil, | 1 00 |
| Jarvis' Reply to Milner, | 75 |
| Kingsley's Sacred Choir, | 75 |
| Keble's Christian Year, | 37 |
| Layman's Letters to a Bishop, | 25 |
| Logan's Sermons and Expository Lectures, | 1 13 |
| Lyra Apostolica, | 50 |
| Marshall's Notes on Episcopacy, | 1 00 |
| Newman's Sermons and Subjects of the Day, | 1 00 |
| " Essay on Christian Doctrine, | 75 |
| Ogilby on Lay Baptism, | 50 |
| Pearson on the Creed, | 2 00 |
| Pulpit Cyclopædia and Ministers' Companion, | 2 50 |
| Sewell's Reading Preparatory to Confirmation, | 75 |
| Southard's Mystery of Godliness, | 75 |
| Sketches and Skeletons of Sermons, | 2 50 |
| Spencer's Christian Instructed, | 1 00 |
| Sherlock's Practical Christian, | 75 |
| Sutton's Disce Vivere—Learn to Live, | 75 |
| Swartz's Letters to my Godchild, | 38 |
| Trench's Notes on the Parables, | 1 75 |
| " Notes on the Miracles. | 1 75 |
| Taylor's Holy Living and Dying, | 1 00 |
| " Episcopacy Asserted and Maintained, | 75 |
| Tyng's Family Commentary, | 2 00 |
| Walker's Sermons on Practical Subjects, | 2 00 |
| Watson on Confirmation, | 06 |
| Wilberforce's Manual for Communicants, | 38 |
| Wilson's Lectures on Colossians, | 75 |
| Wyatt's Christian Altar, | 38 |

### Voyages and Travels.

| | |
|---|---|
| Africa and the American Flag, | 1 25 |
| Appletons' Southern and Western Guide, | 1 00 |
| " Northern and Eastern Guide, | 1 25 |
| " Complete U. S. Guide Book, | 2 00 |
| " N. Y. City Map, | 25 |
| Bartlett's New Mexico, &c. 2 vols. Illustrated, | 5 00 |
| Burnet's N. Western Territory, | 2 00 |
| Bryant's What I Saw in California, | 1 25 |
| Coggeshall's Voyages. 2 vols. | 2 50 |
| Dix's Winter in Madeira, | 1 00 |
| Huc's Travels in Tartary and Thibet. 2 vols. | 1 00 |
| Layard's Nineveh. 1 vol. 8vo. | 1 25 |
| Notes of a Theological Student. 12mo. | 1 00 |
| Oliphant's Journey to Katmundu, | 50 |
| Parkyns' Abyssinia. 2 vols. | 2 50 |
| Russia as it Is. By Gurowski, | 1 00 |
| " By Count de Custine, | 1 25 |
| Squier's Nicaragua. 2 vols. | 5 00 |
| Tappan's Step from the New World to the Old, | 1 75 |
| Wanderings and Fortunes of Germ. Emigrants, | 75 |
| Williams' Isthmus of Tehuantepec. 2 vols. 8vo. | 3 50 |

### Works of Fiction.

#### GRACE AGUILAR'S WORKS.

| | |
|---|---|
| The Days of Bruce. 2 vols. 12mo. | 1 50 |
| Home Scenes and Heart Studies. 12mo. | 75 |
| The Mother's Recompense. 12mo. | 75 |
| Woman's Friendship. 12mo. | 75 |
| Women of Israel. 2 vols. 12mo. | 1 50 |
| | |
| Basil. A Story of Modern Life. 12mo. | 75 |
| Brace's Fawn of the Pale Faces. 12mo. | 75 |
| Busy Moments of an Idle Woman, | 75 |
| Chestnut Wood. A Tale. 2 vols. | 1 75 |
| Don Quixote. Translated. Illustrated, | 1 25 |
| Drury (A. H.) Light and Shade, | 75 |
| Dupuy (A. E.). The Conspirator, | 75 |
| Ellen Parry; or, Trials of the Heart, | 63 |

### MRS. ELLIS' WORKS.

| | |
|---|---|
| Hearts and Homes; or, Social Distinctions, | 1 50 |
| Prevention Better than Cure, | 75 |
| Women of England, | 50 |
| | |
| Emmanuel Philibert. By Dumas, | 1 25 |
| Farmingdale. By Caroline Thomas, | 1 00 |
| Fullerton (Lady G.). Ellen Middleton, | 75 |
| " " Grantley Manor. 1 vol. 12mo. | 75 |
| " " Lady Bird. 1 vol. 12mo. | 75 |
| The Foresters. By Alex. Dumas, | 75 |
| Gore (Mrs.). The Dean's Daughter. 1 vol. 12mo. | 75 |
| Goldsmith's Vicar of Wakefield. 12mo. | 75 |
| Gil Blas. With 600 Engravings. Cloth, gt. edg. | 2 50 |
| Harry Muir. A Tale of Scottish Life, | 75 |
| Hearts Unveiled; or, I Knew You Would Like Him, | 75 |
| Heartsease; or, My Brother's Wife. 2 vols. | 1 5— |
| Heir of Redclyffe. 2 vols. cloth, | 1 50 |
| Hirloise; or, The Unrevealed Secret. 12mo. | 75 |
| Hobson. My Uncle and I. 12mo. | 75 |
| Holmes' Tempest and Sunshine. 12mo. | 1 00 |
| Home is Home. A Domestic Story, | 75 |
| Howitt (Mary). The Heir of West Wayland, | 50 |
| Io. A Tale of the Ancient Fane. 12mo. | 75 |
| The Iron Cousin. By Mary Cowden Clarke, | 1 25 |
| James (G. P. R.). Adrian; or, Clouds of the Mind, | 75 |
| John; or, Is a Cousin in the Hand Worth Two in the Bush, | 25 |

### JULIA KAVANAGH'S WORKS.

| | |
|---|---|
| Nathalie. A Tale. 12mo. | 1 00 |
| Madeline. 12mo. | 75 |
| Daisy Burns. 12mo. | 1 00 |
| | |
| Life's Discipline. A Tale of Hungary, | 63 |
| Lone Dove (The). A Legend, | 75 |
| Linny Lockwood. By Catherine Crowe, | 50 |

### MISS McINTOSH'S WORKS.

| | |
|---|---|
| Two Lives; or, To Seem and To Be. 12mo. | 75 |
| Aunt Kitty's Tales. 12mo. | 75 |
| Charms and Counter-Charms. 12mo. | 1 00 |
| Evenings at Donaldson Manor, | 75 |
| The Lofty and the Lowly. 2 vols. | 1 50 |
| | |
| Margaret's Home. By Cousin Alice, | |
| Marie Louise; or, The Opposite Neighbors, | 50 |
| Maiden Aunt (The). A Story, | 75 |
| Manzoni. The Betrothed Lovers. 2 vols. | 1 50 |
| Margaret Cecil; or, I Can Because I Ought, | 75 |
| Morton Montague; or, The Christian's Choice, | 75 |
| Norman Leslie. By G. C. H. | 75 |
| Prismatics. Tales and Poems. By Hayward, | 1 25 |
| Roe (A. S.). James Montjoy. 12mo. | 75 |
| " To Love and to Be Loved. 12mo. | 75 |
| " Time and Tide. 12mo. | 75 |
| Reuben Medlicott; or, The Coming Man, | 75 |
| Rose Douglass. By S. R. W. | 75 |

### MISS SEWELL'S WORKS.

| | |
|---|---|
| Amy Herbert. A Tale. 12mo. | 75 |
| Experience of Life. 12mo. | 75 |
| Gertrude. A Tale. 12mo. | 75 |
| Katherine Ashton. 2 vols. 12mo. | 1 50 |
| Laneton Parsonage. A Tale. 3 vols. 12mo. | 2 25 |
| Margaret Percival. 2 vols. | 1 50 |
| Walter Lorimer, and Other Tales. 12mo. | 75 |
| A Journal Kept for Children of a Village School, | 1 00 |
| | |
| Sunbeams and Shadows. Cloth, | 75 |
| Thorpe's Hive of the Bee Hunter, | 1 00 |
| Thackeray's Works. 6 vols. 12mo. | 6 00 |
| The Virginia Comedians. 2 vols. 12mo. | 1 50 |
| Use of Sunshine. By S. M. 12mo. | 75 |
| Wight's Romance of Abelard & Heloise. 12mo. | 75 |

D. APPLETON & CO.'S PUBLICATIONS.

**The most Authentic and Entertaining Life of Napoleon.**

# Memoirs of Napoleon,
## HIS COURT AND FAMILY.
### BY THE DUCHESS D'ABRANTES, (Madame Junot.)

Two Volumes, 8vo. 1134 pages. Price $4.

**List of Steel Engravings contained in this Illustrated Edition.**

| | | |
|---|---|---|
| NAPOLEON. | LUCIEN BONAPARTE, | JEROME BONAPARTE, |
| JOSEPHINE. | MARSHAL JUNOT, | LOUIS BONAPARTE, |
| MARIA LOUISA, | CHARLES BONAPARTE, | CARDINAL FESCH, |
| DUKE OF REICHSTADT, | PAULINE BONAPARTE, | LOUISA, QUEEN OF PRUSSIA, |
| MADAME LAETITIA BONAPARTE, | ELIZA BONAPARTE, | JOSEPH BONAPARTE. |
| CHARLES BONAPARTE, | | |

Probably no writer has had the same opportunities for becoming acquainted with NAPOLEON THE GREAT as the Duchess D'Abrantes. Her mother rocked him in his cradle, and when he quitted Brienne and came to Paris, she guided and protected his younger days. Scarcely a day passed without his visiting her house during the period which preceded his departure for Italy as COMMANDER-IN-CHIEF. Abundant occasion was therefore had for watching the development of the great genius who afterwards became the master of the greater part of Europe.

MARSHAL JUNOT, who became allied to the author of this work by marriage, was the intimate friend of Napoleon, and figured in most of the BRILLIANT ENGAGEMENTS which rendered him the greatest military captain of the age. No interruption took place in the intimacy which she enjoyed, so that in all these scenes, embracing a period of nearly THIRTY YEARS, the Duchess became familiar with all the secret springs of NAPOLEON'S ACTIONS,

either through her husband or by her own personal knowledge and observation at the Court of Napoleon.

JOSEPHINE, whose life and character so peculiarly attract the attention of all readers, occupies a great part of the first volume. The character and the deeds of THE EMPERORS AND KINGS, THE GREAT MEN OF THE DAY, THE MARSHALS OF THE EMPIRE, THE DISTINGUISHED LADIES OF THE COURT, are described with minuteness, which personal observation only admits of. The work is written in that FAMILIAR GOSSIPING STYLE, and so interspersed with anecdotes that the reader never wearies. She has put every thing in her book—great events and small. BATTLES AND BALLS, COURT INTRIGUES AND BOUDOIR GOSSIP, TREATIES AND FLIRTATIONS, making two of the most charming volumes of memoirs, which will interest the reader in spite of himself.

---

*Opinions of the Press.*

"These anecdotes of Napoleon are the best yet given to the world, because the most intimate and familiar."—*London Literary Gazette.*

"We consider the performance now before us as more authentic and amusing than any other of its kind."—*London Quarterly Review.*

"Every thing relating to Napoleon is eagerly sought for and read in this country as well as in Europe, and this work, with its extraordinary attractions, will not fail to command a wide circulation. Madame Junot possessed qualifications for writing a semi-domestic history of the great Corsican which no other person, male or female, could command."—*Life Illustrated.*

D. APPLETON & CO.'S PUBLICATIONS.

A Work abounding in Exciting Scenes and Remarkable Incidents.

# Capt. Canot;

OR,

## TWENTY YEARS OF AN AFRICAN SLAVER:

BEING AN ACCOUNT OF HIS CAREER AND ADVENTURES ON THE COAST, IN THE INTERIOR, ON SHIPBOARD, AND IN THE WEST INDIES.

*Written out and Edited from the Captain's Journals, Memoranda, and Conversations.*

## BY BRANTZ MAYER.

One Volume, 12mo. With eight Illustrations. Price $1 25.

*Criticisms of the Press.*

"The author is a literary gentleman of Baltimore, no Abolitionist, and we believe the work to be a truthful account of the life of a man who saw much more than falls to the lot of most men."—*Commonwealth.*

"A remarkable volume is this; because of its undoubted truth: it having been derived by Mayer from personal conversations with Canot, and from journals which the slaver furnished of his own life."—*Worcester Palladium.*

"Capt. Canot, the hero of the narrative, is, to our own knowledge, a veritable personage, and resides in Baltimore. There is no doubt that the main incidents connected with his extraordinary career are in every respect true."—*Arthur's Home Gazette.*

"Under one aspect, as the biography of a remarkable man who passed through a singularly strange and eventful experience, it is as interesting as any sea story that we have ever read."—*Boston Evening Traveller.*

"Capt. Canot has certainly passed through a life of difficulty, danger, and wild, daring adventure, which has much the air of romance, and still he, or rather his editor, tells the tale with so much straightforwardness, that we cannot doubt its truthfulness."—*New York Sunday Despatch.*

"The work could not have been better done if the principal actor had combined the descriptive talent of De Foe with the astuteness of Fouche and the dexterity of Gil Blas, which traits are ascribed to the worthy whose acquaintance we shall soon make by his admiring editor."—*N. Y. Tribune.*

"The general style of the work is attractive, and the narrative spirited and bold—well suited to the daring and hazardous course of life led by the adventurer. This book is illustrated by several excellent engravings."—*Baltimore American.*

"The biography of an African slaver as taken from his own lips, and giving his adventures in this traffic for twenty years. With great natural keenness of perception and complete communicativeness, he has literally unmasked his real life, and tells both what he was and *what he saw*, the latter being the *Photograph* of the Negro in Africa, which has been so long wanted. A nephew of Mr. Mayer has illustrated the volume with eight admirable drawings. We should think no book of the present day would be received with so keen an interest."—*Home Journal.*

"Capt. Canot has passed most of his life since 1819 on the ocean, and his catalogue of adventures at sea and on land, rival in grotesqueness and apparent improbability the marvels of Robinson Crusoe."—*Evening Post.*

"If stirring incidents, hair-breadth escapes, and variety of adventure, can make a book interesting, this must possess abundant attractions."—*Newark Daily Advertiser.*

"This is a true record of the life of one who had spent the greater part of his days in dealing in human flesh. We commend this book to all lovers of adventure."—*Boston Christian Recorder.*

"We would advise every one who is a lover of 'books that are books'—every one who admires Le Sage and De Foe, and has lingered long over the charming pages of Gil Blas and Robinson Crusoe—every one, pro-slavery or anti-slavery, to purchase this book."—*Buffalo Courier.*

*D. APPLETON & CO.'S PUBLICATIONS.*

**Rev. Samuel Osgood's Two Popular Books.**

## I.
# Mile Stones in our Life Journey.

SECOND EDITION.

One Volume, 12mo. Cloth. Price $1.

*Opinions of the Press.*

"In so small a compass, we rarely meet with more Catholic sympathies, and with a clearer or more practical view of the privileges enjoyed by, and the duties enjoined, upon us all, at any stage of our mortal pilgrimage."—*Church Journal.*

"Some passages remind us forcibly of Addison and Goldsmith."—*Independent.*

"This little volume is one of those books which are read by all classes at all stages of life, with an interest which loses nothing by change or circumstances."—*Pennsylvanian.*

"He writes kindly; strongly and readably; nor is their any thing in this volume of a narrow, bigoted, or sectarian character."—*Life Illustrated.*

"His counsels are faithful and wholesome, his reflection touching, and the whole is clothed in a style graceful and free."—*Hartford Relig. Herald.*

"This is a volume of beautiful and cogent essays, virtuous in motive, simple in expression, pertinent and admirable in logic, and glorious in conclusion and climax."—*Buffalo Express.*

"It is written with exquisite taste, is full of beautiful thought most felicitously expressed, and is pervaded by a genial and benevolent spirit."—*Dr. Sprague.*

"Almost every page has a tincture of elegant scholarship, and bears witness to an extensive reading of good authors."—*Bryant.*

## II.
# The Hearth-Stone;
### THOUGHTS UPON HOME LIFE IN OUR CITIES.

BY SAMUEL OSGOOD,

AUTHOR OF "STUDIES IN CHRISTIAN BIOGRAPHY," "GOD WITH MEN," ETC.

FOURTH EDITION.

One Volume, 12mo. Cloth. Price $1.

*Criticisms of the Press.*

"This is a volume of elegant and impressive essays on the domestic relations and religious duties of the household. Mr. Osgood writes on these interesting themes in the most charming and animated style, winning the reader's judgment rather than coercing it to the author's conclusions. The predominant sentiments in the book are purity, sincerity, and love. A more delightful volume has rarely been published, and we trust it will have a wide circulation, for its influence must be salutary upon both old and young."—*Commercial Advertiser.*

"The 'Hearth-Stone' is the symbol of all those delightful truths which Mr. Osgood here connects with it. In a free and graceful style, varying from deep solemnity to the most genial and lively tone, as befits his range of subjects, he gives attention to wise thoughts on holy things, and homely truths. His volume will find many warm hearts to which it will address itself."—*Christian Examiner.*

D. APPLETON & CO.'S PUBLICATIONS.

## A Great National Work.

# Party Leaders.

### SKETCHES OF

### JEFFERSON, HAMILTON, RANDOLPH, JACKSON, AND CLAY:

*Including Notices of many other Distinguished American Statesmen.*

### BY J. G. BALDWIN,

(Now of San Francisco, California.) Author of "Flush Times of Alabama and Mississippi."

One Volume, 12mo. Cloth. Price $1.

---

OPINIONS OF EMINENT MEN.

*From Ex-President* FILLMORE.

I have read "Party Leaders" with great satisfaction and delight, and return you a thousand thanks for the pleasure and instruction I have derived from the perusal.

*From Honorable* EDWARD EVERETT.

What little I have as yet been able to read of it, has impressed me very favorably in reference to the ability and impartiality with which it is drawn up. I am prepared to read it with interest and advantage, in consequence of the pleasure I derived from "The Flush Times in Alabama."

*From Honorable* J. P. KENNEDY.

I was greatly delighted with the fine, discriminating, acute insight with which the characters presented in the work are drawn, and with the eloquent style of the sketches. I but repeat the common opinion of the best judges, which I hear every where expressed, when I commend these qualities of the book.

"The Flush Times of Alabama" had whetted my desire to see this second production of Mr. Baldwin's pen, and I can hardly express to you the agreeable surprise I enjoyed in finding a work of such surpassing merit in a tone and manner so entirely different from the first—demonstrating that double gift in the author which enables him to excel in two such opposite departments of literature.

*From Hon.* R. M. T. HUNTER, *U. S. Senator from Virginia.*

I have read "Party Leaders" with great pleasure. It is written with ability, and with freshness, and grace of style, * * * The chapters on Randolph are capital.

*From Hon.* JAMES M. MASON, *U. S. Senator from Virginia.*

I have heard "Party Leaders" highly commended by those competent to judge, but confess I was not prepared for the intellectual and literary feast its rich pages have yielded.

As a literary work, I shall be much disappointed if it does not place its author at once in the first rank of American literature, and even in old England. I shall look for its place next to, if not by the side of, the kindred works of McIntosh and Macaulay.

*From a Distinguished Statesman.*

It is a noble production, full of profound thought, discriminating judgment, just criticism, and elevated sentiments, all expressed in the most captivating and eloquent style. It is a book just according to my fancy, and, I think, one of the most captivating in our language.

D. APPLETON & CO.'S PUBLICATIONS.

## A Practical Book on the Breeding of Fish.

A COMPLETE TREATISE ON

# Artificial Fifh-Breeding:

INCLUDING THE REPORTS ON THE SUBJECT MADE TO THE FRENCH ACADEMY AND THE FRENCH GOVERNMENT, AND PARTICULARS OF THE DISCOVERY AS PURSUED IN ENGLAND.

TRANSLATED AND EDITED BY

WM. H. FRY.

ILLUSTRATED WITH ENGRAVINGS.

One Volume. 12mo. Cloth. Price 75 cents.

*Opinions of the Press.*

"A very genial and entertaining, though practical and scientific book. No one who loves the existence in our rivers, brooks, or lakes, of trout and salmon, should be without it."—*Broome Republic.*

"In this little volume, the whole process of fish-culture is described so plainly and with so much minuteness that any person will have no difficulty in informing himself sufficiently well to engage in the business; provided he has the necessary facilities and leisure, with a good running stream or pond, and the proper attention, a great brood of fishes may be hatched from the eggs, and raised up for the market or the table; and such delicacies are trout and salmon, that it is evident that the business of producing them for sale may be made profitable."—*Worcester Palladium.*

"This discovery is treated as a matter of great public benefit in France and England, where it is practised under the direction and patronage of Government, and is beginning to work its results in stocking rivers and lakes, with the finest species of fish, where few or none have before existed for many years."—*Ohio Cultivator.*

"Every farmer who has a stream flowing through his land, or miller who wishes to turn his ponds to some account, should make himself acquainted with the details of the book."—*Newark Daily Advertiser.*

"A GREAT, A GLORIOUS BOOK."—Cour. & Enq.

D. APPLETON & CO., 346 & 348 BROADWAY,

HAVE JUST PUBLISHED

# THE VIRGINIA COMEDIANS;

OR,

## Old Days in the Old Dominion.

FROM THE MSS. OF

### C. EFFINGHAM, Esq.

Two vols. 12mo. paper, $1; cloth, $1 50.

A volume which has been pronounced the best novel of the day.

*Peruse the criticisms of the following papers.*

"It is not only unlike the monstrous mass of efforts which have preceded it—and therefore, attractive in the light of comparison, and for its perfect newness—but it is freighted with such an ardor of style, fervor of imagination, beauty of description, both as regards characters and scenes, and a plenitude of genial spirit, that its reader is sure to be its lover.

"The story, which commences about the middle of the last century, is located in Virginia, its *personæ in dramatis* being composed of many choice spirits who figured, or were supposed to figure, at that period. We have not seen its equal for many a day, and heartily apply to it the old verse,

'May this book continue in motion,
And its leaves every day be unfurled.'"
*Buffalo Courier.*

"The period of the story is about the middle of the last century; the place Williamsburg, Virginia, and its vicinity; the characters Virginia gentlemen of that day and generation, among whom comes *Beatrice Hallam*, the leading actress of a company of comedians of that ilk, and one of the most striking, truthful, and lovable characters in modern fiction. The interest of the book never flags. The characters are such that we cannot be indifferent to them, and the author absorbs us in their actions and their fate."
—*Courier & Enquirer.*

"The tone of the book is intensely national. It has come on us completely by surprise, for we had no conception of its character, until we were half through the first volume, and we must confess that we were at the outset extremely unprepared for such a display of literary power."—*N. Y. Express.*

*D. Appleton & Company's Publications.*

"Chestnut Wood will light up many a hearth with pleasure."

# CHESTNUT WOOD:
## An American Tale.
### BY LIELE LINDEN.

Two volumes, 12mo. Paper covers, $1 25; cloth, $1 75.

### PLOT OF THE STORY.

Chestnut Wood is a country-seat, near Sleepy Hollow, owned and occupied by Mr. Atherton, a man of stern but not unkind disposition. The better feelings of his heart are brought into action, by the circumstances of his young grand-daughter, Sybil, the heroine of the tale, who is thrown, by the death of her mother at a farm-house in the vicinity, where she has been rescued from exposure on the road, upon his protection. The father of Sybil, as may be inferred from the fate of her mother, is a worthless scoundrel, who endeavors, with the help of associates as worthless as himself, to get possession of the child. They succeed in carrying her off, and concealing her in New York, where they employ her as an unconcious agent in the circulation of counterfeit money. She escapes from the wardship of an old misshapen hag, Moll, and is brought back to her home at Chestnut Wood; where, however, she is still subject to occasional manifestations from the same source.

### Opinions of the Press.

"One of the pleasantest characters in the book is Jerry Goldsmith, a Yankee Caleb Quotem, ready to turn his hand to any thing, and more profuse in promise than performance."—*Churchman.*

"One who has read it from *preface* to *finis*, pronounces it delightful; and hence our praise. She says there are spots that those who have tears can cry over, but never so sad that the tears need scald much."—*N. Y. Daily Times.*

"We commend to men, women, and even children, a perusal of 'Chestnut Wood.'"—*Lawrence Sentinel.*

"This work will be read. It has all the elements of a successful book, viz: originality, interest, power, and strong characterization."—*Berks County Press.*

"It will please from its truthfulness to nature, and from the effect it will leave on the mind of the reader."—*Hartford Courant.*

"Its plot is well developed, is ingenious, but not too intricate, and is managed throughout with the skill of a master."—*Palladium.*

"The characters are very well and forcibly drawn, particularly the 'cute Yankee, Jerry Goldsmith.'"—*Mobile Adv.*

*D. Appleton & Company's Publications.*

"A WORK WHICH BEARS THE IMPRESS OF GENIUS."

## KATHARINE ASHTON.

By the author of "Amy Herbert," "Gertrude," &c.

2 vols. 12mo. Paper covers, $1; cloth, $1 50.

### Opinions of the Press.

We know not where we will find purer morals, or more valuable "life-philosophy, than in the pages of Miss Sewell.—*Savannah Georgian.*

The style and character of Miss Sewell's writings are too well known to the reading public to need commendation. The present volume will only add to her reputation as an authoress.—*Albany Transcript.*

This novel is admirably calculated to inculcate refined moral and religious sentiments.—*Boston Herald.*

The interest of the story is well sustained throughout, and it is altogether one of the pleasantest books of the season.—*Syracuse Standard.*

Those who have read the former works of this writer, will welcome the appearance of this; it is equal to the best of her preceding novels.—*Savannah Republican.*

Noble, beautiful, selfish, hard, and ugly characters appear in it, and each is so drawn as to be felt and estimated as it deserves.—*Commonwealth.*

A re-publication of a good English novel. It teaches self-control, charity, and a true estimation of life, by the interesting history of a young girl.—*Hartford Courant.*

Katharine Ashton will enhance the reputation already attained, the story and the moral being equally commendable.—*Buffalo Courier.*

Like all its predecessors, Katharine Ashton bears the Impress of genius, consecrated to the noblest purposes, and should find a welcome in every family circle.—*Banner of the Cross.*

No one can be injured by books like this; a great many must be benefited. Few authors have sent so many faultless writings to the press as she has done.—*Worcester Palladium.*

The *self-denial* of the Christian life, in its application to common scenes and circumstances, is happily illustrated in the example of Katharine Ashton, in which there is much to admire and imitate.—*Southern Churchman.*

Her present work is an interesting tale of English country life, is written with her usual ability, and is quite free from any offensive parade of her own theological tenets.—*Boston Traveller.*

The field in which Miss Sewell labors, seems to be exhaustless, and to yield always a beautiful and a valuable harvest.—*Troy Daily Budget.*

### D. APPLETON & COMPANY

*Have recently published the following interesting works by the same author.*

THE EXPERIENCE OF LIFE. 1 vol. 12mo. Paper, 50 cents; cloth, 75 cents.
THE EARL'S DAUGHTER. 1 vol. 12mo. Paper, 50 cents; cloth, 75 cents.
GERTRUDE: a Tale. 1 vol. 12mo. Paper, 50 cts; cloth, 75 cts.
AMY HERBERT: A Tale. 1 vol. 12mo. Paper, 50 cents; cloth 75 cents.
LANETON PARSONAGE. 3 vols. 12mo. Paper, $1 50, cloth. $2 25.
MARGARET PERCIVAL. 2 vols. Paper, $1; cloth, $1 50.
READING FOR A MONTH. 12mo. cloth, 75 cents.
A JOURNAL KEPT DURING A SUMMER TOUR. 1 vol cloth. $1 00.
WALTER LORIMER AND OTHER TALES. Cloth, 75 cents
THE CHILD'S FIRST HISTORY OF ROME. 50 cents.
THE CHILD'S FIRST HISTORY OF GREECE. 68 cents.

**New Copyright Works, Adapted for Popular Reading.**

JUST PUBLISHED.
BY D. APPLETON & CO.

I.

## PERSONAL NARRATIVE OF EXPLORATIONS AND INCIDENTS IN TEXAS, NEW MEXICO, CALIFORNIA, SONORA, AND CHIHUAHUA, CONNECTED WITH THE MEXICAN BOUNDARY COMMISSION, DURING THE YEARS 1850 '51, '52, and '53.

BY JOHN RUSSELL BARTLETT,

*United States Commissioner during that period.*

In 2 vols. 8vo, of nearly 600 pages each, printed with large type and on extra fine paper, to be illustrated with nearly 100 wood-cuts, sixteen tinted lithographs and a beautiful map, engraved on steel, of the extensive regions traversed. Price, $5.

II.

## AFRICA AND THE AMERICAN FLAG.

BY ANDREW H. FOOTE,

*Lieutenant Commanding the U. S. Brig Porpoise, on the Coast of Africa, 1851–'53.*

With tinted lithographic illustrations. One volume 12mo.

III.

## CAPT. CANOT; OR, TWENTY YEARS OF A SLAVER'S LIFE.

EDITED BY BRANTZ MAYER.

With numerous illustrations. One vol. 12mo, cloth.

IV.

## RUSSIA AS IT IS.

BY THE COUNT DE GUROWSKI.

One vol. 12mo, cloth.

V.

## TEMPEST AND SUNSHINE; OR, LIFE IN KENTUCKY.

BY MRS. MARY J. HOLMES.

One vol. 12mo, paper cover or cloth.

VI.

## FARMINGDALE.

A TALE BY CAROLINE THOMAS.

One vol. 12mo, paper cover or cloth.

*\*\** Excels in interest, and is quite equal in its delineation of character to "The Wide, Wide World."

VII.

## THE HIVE OF THE BEE HUNTER.

BY T. B. THORPE.

With several illustrations. One vol. 12mo, cloth.

## A Choice New England Tale.

# FARMINGDALE,

### A TALE.

## BY CAROLINE THOMAS.

**Two volumes, 12mo., paper covers, 75 cents, or 2 volumes in 1, cloth, $1.**

"It is a story of New England life, skilfully told, full of tender interest, healthy in its sentiments and remarkably graphic in its sketches of character. 'Aunt Betsy' is drawn to the life."—*Home Gazette.*

"Farmingdale is the best novel of the season."—*Eve. Post.*

"It will compare favorably with the 'Lamplighter,' by Miss Cummings, and the 'Wide, Wide World,' by Miss Warner, and in interest it is quite equal to either."—*Boston Transcript.*

"'Farmingdale,' the work to which we allude, in every page and paragraph, is redolent of its native sky. It is a tale of New England domestic life, in its incidents and manners so true to nature and so free from exaggeration, and in its impulses and motives throughout so throbbing with the real American heart, that we shall not be surprised to hear of as many New England villages claiming to be the scene of its story, as were the cities of Greece that claimed to be the birth-place of Homer."—*Philadelphia Courier.*

"The story abounds in scenes of absorbing interest. The narration is every where delightfully clear and straightforward, flowing forth towards its conclusion, like a gentle and limpid stream, between graceful hillsides and verdant meadows."—*Home Journal.*

"This is a story of country life, written by a hand whose guiding power was a living soul. The pictures of life are speaking and effective. The story is interestingly told and its high moral aim well sustained."—*Syracuse Chronicle.*

"'Farmingdale,' while it has many points in common with some recent works of fiction, is yet highly original. The author has had the boldness to attempt a novel, the main interest of which does not hinge either upon love or matrimony, nor upon complicated and entangled machinery, but upon a simple and apparently artless narrative of a friendless girl."—*Philadelphia Eve. Mail.*

"The author studiously avoids all forced and unnatural incidents, and the equally fashionable affectation of extravagant language. Her style and diction are remarkable for their purity and ease. In the conception and delineation of character she has shown herself possessed of the true creative power."—*Com. Adv.*

"A simple yet beautiful story, told in a simple and beautiful manner. The object is to show the devoted affection of a sister to a young brother, and the sacrifices which she made for him from childhood. There is a touching simplicity in the character of this interesting female that will please all readers, and benefit many of her sex."—*Hartford Courant.*

"The tale is prettily written, and breathes throughout an excellent moral tone."—*Boston Daily Journal.*

"We have read this book; it is lively, spirited, and in some parts pathetic. Its sketches of life seem to us at once graceful and vivid."—*Albany Argus.*

"The book is well written, in a simple, unpretending style, and the dialogue is natural and easy. It is destined to great popularity among all classes of readers. Parents who object placing 'love tales' in the hands of their children, may purchase this volume without fear. The oldest and the youngest will become interested in its fascinating pages, and close it with the impression that it is a good book, and deserving of the greatest popularity.'
*Worcester Palladium.*

D. APPLETON & COMPANY, 346 & 348 BROADWAY
HAVE JUST PUBLISHED

# LIFE IN ABYSSINIA,

Being the Personal Narrative of an Englishman, a long resident in the Country.

BY MANSFIELD PARKYNS, ESQ.

With Illustrations. 2 vols. 12mo. Price, $2 50. Cloth.

### LITERARY CRITICISMS.

"Of one thing we are convinced, and that is, that few that take up "Life in Abyssinia," will lay it down without reading it through, and without exclaiming when they come to the end "what an amusing book this is, and what an agreeable savage is Mansfield Parkyns."—*Blackwood's Magazine.*

"Since the appearance of "Typee and Omoo," we have seen no more agreeable volumes of travel than those of Mr. Parkyns."—*Eve. Post.*

"Mr. Mansfield Parkyns is no tourist, but a genuine traveller. In acquaintance with Eastern languages and manners he is a Buckhardt; his liking for Natural History and assiduity as a collector, reminds us of Waterton; while in his passion for the chase, and occasional introduction of elephants, giraffes, and lions, he bears an obvious likeness to Campbell or Gordon Cumming."—*Dublin Magazine.*

"Remarkably entertaining and interesting volumes, brimfull of adventures and life. We have read them with perfect gusto, and cordially join "Blackwood's recommendation."—*Boston Atlas.*

"A story of three years in Abyssinian life, by one so keen in observation and fond of adventure as Mr. Parkyns could not but promise a great attraction; and no one who opens this book will lay it down in disappointment. He sketches the incidents of his travels with great distinctness and vividness and portrays character, wherever he meets it, capitally."—*N. Y. Courier.*

"The author appears to have become thoroughly naturalized among the singular people with whom it was his lot to dwell, and tells the story of his adventures with a liveliness and freedom from reserve that are extremely captivating."—*Jour. of Com.*

"Dullness certainly has no share in Mr. Parkyns' composition—it is a capital book."—*U. S. Gazette.*

"This is no ordinary production."—*Albany Argus.*

"Attractive as a romance while they have the merit of usefulness."—*Boston Cour.*

"The most interesting book of travel issued from the press in many years."—*Phila. Courier.*

"In every respect the volumes are truly attractive."—*American Courier.*

"We have been highly amused, and, we must say, instructed, in the perusal of Mr. Parkyn's adventures."—*Buffalo Democrat.*

"We do not hesitate to commend the book to our readers—it will amply repay their attention."—*Hartford Times.*

"The work fulfils all the author promises."—*Christian Register.*

"To all who are in any kind of trouble from hot weather, bad temper, unpaid bills, and the like annoyances, we would recommend this book."—*Providence Journal.*

"The style is pleasant and many of the incidents are piquant and startling."—*Rochester American.*

"These are two delightful volumes of travel, fresh, racy and glowing with life."—*Com. Advertiser.*

D. APPLETON & CO.'S PUBLICATIONS.

## MRS. COWDEN CLARKE'S NEW ENGLISH NOVEL.

# The Iron Cousin, or Mutual Influence.

### BY MARY COWDEN CLARKE,

Author of "THE GIRLHOOD OF SHAKSPEARE'S HEROINES" the COMPLETE CONCORDANCE TO SHAKSPEARE," &c.

One handsomely printed volume, large 12mo. over 500 pages. Price $1.25 – cloth

"Mrs. Clarke has given us one of the most delightful novels we have read for many a day, and one which is destined, we doubt not, to be much longer lived than the majority of books of its class. Its chief beauties are a certain freshness in the style in which the incidents are presented to us—a healthful tone pervading it—a completeness in most of the characters—and a truthful power in the descriptions."—*London Times.*

"We have found the volume deeply interesting—its characters are well drawn, while its tone and sentiments are well calculated to exert a purifying and ennobling influence upon all who read it."—*Savannah Republican.*

"The scene of the book is village life amongst the upper class, with village episodes, which seem to have been sketched from the life—there is a primitive simplicity and greatness of heart about some of the characters which keep up the sympathy and interest to the end."—*London Globe.*

"The reader cannot fail of being both charmed and instructed by the book, and of hoping that a pen so able will not lie idle."—*Pennsylvanian.*

"We fearlessly recommend it as a work of more than ordinary merit."—*Binghampton Daily Republic.*

"The great moral lesson indicated by the title-page of this book runs, as a golden thread, through every part of it, while the reader is constantly kept in contact with the workings of an inventive and brilliant mind."—*Albany Argus.*

"We have read this fascinating story with a good deal of interest. Human nature is well and faithfully portrayed, and we see the counterpart of our story in character and disposition, in every village and district. The book cannot fail of popular reception."—*Albany and Rochester Courier.*

"A work of deep and powerful influence."—*Herald.*

"Mrs. Cowden Clarke, with the delicacy and artistic taste of refined womanhood, has in this work shown great versatility of talent."

"The story is too deeply interesting to allow the reader to lay it down till he has read it to the end."

"The work is skilful in plan, graphic in style, diversified in incident and true to nature."

"The tale is charmingly imagined. The incidents never exceed probability but seem perfectly natural. In the style there is much quaintness, in the sentiment much tenderness."

"It is a spirited, charming story, full of adventure, friendship and love, with characters nicely drawn and carefully discriminated. The clear style and spirit with which the story is presented and the characters developed, will attract a large constituency to the perusal."

"Mrs. Cowden Clarke's story has one of the highest qualities of fiction—it is no flickering shadow, but seems of real growth. It is full of lively truth, and shows nice perception of the early elements of character with which we become acquainted in its wholeness, and in the ripeness of years. The incident is well woven; the color is blood-warm; and there is the presence of a sweet grace and gentle power."

## THE GREAT KENTUCKY NOVEL.

### D. APPLETON & COMPANY

HAVE JUST PUBLISHED

# Tempest and Sunſhine; or, Life in Kentucky.

### BY MRS. MARY J. HOLMES.

One Volume, 12mo   Paper covers, 75 cents; cloth, $1.

· These are the most striking and original sketches of American character in the South-western States which have ever been published. The character of Tempest is drawn with all that spirit and energy which characterize the high toned female spirit of the South, while Sunshine possesses the loveliness and gentleness of the sweetest of her sex. The Planter is sketched to the life, and in his strongly marked, passionate, and generous nature, the reader will recognize one of the truest sons of the south-west.

### OPINIONS OF THE PRESS.

"The book is well written, and its fame will be more than ephemeral."—*Buffalo Express.*

"The story is interesting and finely developed."—*Daily Times.*

"A lively romance of western life—the style of the writer is smart, intelligent, and winning, and her story is told with spirit and skill."—*U. S. Gazette.*

"An excellent work, and its sale must be extensive."—*Stamford Advocate.*

"The whole is relieved by a generous introduction of incident as well as by an amplitude of love and mystery."—*Express.*

"A delightful, well written book, portraying western life to the letter. The book abounds in an easy humor, with touching sentences of tenderness and pathos scattered through it, and from first to last keeps up a humane interest that very many authors strive in vain to achieve. 'Tempest' and 'Sunshine,' two sisters, are an exemplification of the good that to some comes by nature, and to others is found only through trials, temptation, and tribulation. Mr. Middleton, the father of 'Tempest and 'Sunshine,' is the very soul and spirit of 'Old Kaintuck,' abridged into one man. The book is worth reading. There is a healthy tone of morality pervading it that will make it a suitable work to be placed in the hands of our daughters and sisters."—*New York Day Book.*

## Dumas's last and best Book.

**D. APPLETON & COMPANY,**

HAVE JUST READY THE FIFTH THOUSAND OF

## THE FORESTERS.

BY ALEX. DUMAS.

TRANSLATED FROM THE AUTHOR'S ORIGINAL MSS.

1 neat vol. 12mo. in paper, 50 cents; cloth, 75 cents.

CONTENTS.—To my Daughter.—The New House on the Road to Soissons—Mathieu Goguelue.—A Bird of Evil Omen.—Catherine Blun.—The Parisian.—Jealousy.—Father and Mother.—The Return.—Mademoiselle Euphrosine Raisin.—Love's Young Dream.—The Abbé Gregoire.—Father and Son.—The Village Fête.—A Snake in the Grass.—Temptation and Crime.—The Ranger's Home.—Apprehension.—The Book of the Innocent.—Mathieu's Trial.

### Notices of the Press.

"A lively story of love, jealousy, and intrigue."—*N. Y. Com. Advertiser.*

"Another proof of Dumas's unrivalled talent."—*Middletown Sentinel.*

"The tale is a simple one, but exciting and interesting. The scene is laid in Villers-Cotterets in France. The reputation of the author is so firmly established, that in our saying that the translation is a faithful one, our readers who are novel readers will have heard sufficient."—*Phila. Register.*

"A capital story. The reader will find the interest increase to the end."—*Phila. Gas.*

"The present volume fully sustains the high reputation of its author; it shows a very high order of genius. The translation is such perfectly good English, that we easily forget that we are not reading the work in the language in which it was originally written."—*Albany Argus.*

"A short, but stirring romance."—*Boston Atlas.*

"This work of Dumas's is an interesting one. The plot is well laid, and the incidents hurry on, one after another, so rapidly that the interest is kept up to the close."—*Hartford Courant.*

"It is a capital story, and an unmistakable Dumas's work. To say this, is to bestow upon it sufficient praise."—*Troy Times.*

"This new story of Dumas will afford a delightful resource for a leisure hour."—*The Bizarre.*

"This very entertaining novel is indubitably one of Dumas's best efforts: it cannot fail to become widely popular."—*N. Y. Courier.*

"A pleasing, romantic love story, written with the author's usual vigor."—*Newark Adv.*

"A quiet domestic tale that must charm all readers."—*Syracuse Daily.*

"This is a lively story of love, jealousy and intrigue, in a French village."—*Phila. Daily Times.*

"The fame of the author will alone secure a wide circulation for this book. He is one of the best novel writers living. 'The Foresters' fully sustains his great reputation."—*Troy Daily Times.*

"This exceedingly entertaining novel is from the pen of one of the most eminent and celebrated of Modern French novelists—Alexander Dumas."—*Binghampton Republican.*

"This production of the celebrated author, is written in the same masterly style for which all his works are noted."—*Hartford Times.*

"The Foresters, as a work by itself, is one of many charms. That the book will be eagerly sought after, there can be no doubt. That every reader will admire it is none the less certain."—*Buffalo Morning Express.*

"It will be found an interesting story."—*Arthur's Home Gazette.*

"The plot is extremely pleasing, and the book must meet with a ready and extensive sale."—*Syracuse Daily.*

www.ingramcontent.com/pod-product-compliance
Lightning Source LLC
Chambersburg PA
CBHW031849220426
43663CB00006B/551